CONTEXTUALIZING
THE FAITH

A HOLISTIC APPROACH

A. SCOTT MOREAU

B
Baker Academic
a division of Baker Publishing Group
Grand Rapids, Michigan

Published by Baker Academic
a division of Baker Publishing Group
PO Box 6287, Grand Rapids, MI 49516-6287
www.bakeracademic.com

Printed in the United States of America

Library of Congress Cataloging-in-Publication Data
Names: Moreau, A. Scott, 1955– author.
Title: Contextualizing the faith : a holistic approach / A. Scott Moreau.
Description: Grand Rapids, MI : Baker Publishing Group, [2018] | Includes bibliographical
    references and index.
Identifiers: LCCN 2018003791 | ISBN 9781540960009 (pbk. : alk. paper)
Subjects: LCSH: Christianity and culture. | Missions.
Classification: LCC BR115.C8 M66725 2018 | DDC 261—dc23
LC record available at https://lccn.loc.gov/2018003791

18 19 20 21 22 23 24   7 6 5 4 3 2 1

"Drawing upon three decades of global ministry and teaching about contextualization, Scott Moreau offers us a rich, creative, and responsible treatment of the relation between the gospel and particular contexts. *Contextualizing the Faith* is a wise and reliable guide to issues that are as urgent as they are complex."

—**Harold Netland**, Trinity Evangelical Divinity School

"Moreau pushes the boundaries of contextualization beyond systematic theology in significant ways that will impact Christian witness. Engaging the critical need for a full-orbed approach to contextualization, including storytelling, the performing arts, and life rituals, he offers a grounded approach to making Christ known."

—**Roberta R. King**, Fuller Theological Seminary

"Approaching contextualization holistically (broader than evangelism and theology and in light of all that the church is and does) is a messy but much-needed task. Thankfully, Moreau lets us in on three decades of thought and practice to offer clarity on this critical topic. This book ought to be read in the classroom and the mission field."

—**Edward L. Smither**, Columbia International University

"Nearly fifty years ago, the word 'contextualization' first appeared on missiology's radar. This concept has been debated ever since, and no definition has been universally accepted by scholars and practitioners. Moreau's approach is not to propose a new definition or to deconstruct the concept, but to help us understand the goal of contextualization—that is, Jesus Christ as the incarnate God. Christ is real and can be experienced daily in all areas and aspects of life. This book is for teachers and students of missions, denominational and mission agency executives, strategists, field-workers, pastors, and parishioners."

—**Sadiri Joy Tira**, Catalyst for Diasporas, Lausanne Movement

"In this highly readable and engaging text, Moreau reminds us that contextualization, despite the controversies that surround it, has always been part and parcel of Christian theology and life, and is therefore here to stay. So we should better understand it and discover tools to help us better practice it. Moreau answers the question of how people understand, conceptualize, and live out their faith in light of the values of their society and context. His approach is indeed holistic, going well beyond just contextualizing theology and worship, as he considers seven different dimensions of contextualization. With a judicious amount of theories, illustrations, case studies, biblical examples, questions for reflection, and implications for contextualization, *Contextualizing the Faith* is comprehensive without being encyclopedic. Missiologists and missionaries have been waiting a long time for a book like this, and Moreau has filled that gap exceedingly well, giving us a book with a global perspective that will likely become a classic text in this crucial area of understanding and living out our faith as followers of Jesus."

—**Darrell Whiteman**, missiological anthropologist, Global
Development Inc., Gig Harbor, Washington

"For decades, Scott Moreau has been a voice for accessible missiology, producing literature that can withstand the test of academia but remain comprehensible to missionaries in training, church leaders looking to expand their outreach, or even business leaders desiring to share their faith with colleagues. *Contextualizing the Faith* is Scott's magnum opus, combining his years of cross-cultural experience with his teaching. This is a must-read for anyone seeking to effectively communicate the good news of the gospel across cultures. It goes far beyond adapting biblical doctrine to other contexts because it identifies how all the issues of society—family, the marketplace, and more—play a part in understanding cultures, so that we might be understood in our communication."

—**Paul Borthwick**, senior consultant, Development Associates International

"*Contextualizing the Faith* is a gift to the global church. Moreau broadens the landscape of contextualization, helping us to see the whole human ecosystem wherein culture and Scripture meet. Rich in illustrations, challenging in case studies, thoughtful in questions, sound in scholarship, profoundly practical, and robustly anchored in the Word, this book sings with reasoned thinking, insights for understanding, and grounds for wise decision making, all sure to produce vigorous discussion. This may well be a classic for present and future generations. May it light our path and show us the way ahead."

—**Duane H. Elmer**, Trinity Evangelical Divinity School

CONTENTS

133298

PREFACE

I first encountered "contextualization" while in seminary in the early 1980s. In church and mission settings the term was in its infancy. Even so, battle lines had been drawn. As the term had been adopted in World Council of Churches circles from 1972 onward and framed in terms of social justice, evangelical missiologists were wary of it and its use by those more theologically liberal than they were. Well-used terms such as "adaptation" and "indigenization" were safe and useful (they remain so today), but at the same time limited. Over the several decades since then, evangelical missiologists have accepted "contextualization" into the lexicon, albeit with a different focus and orientation than Shoki Coe (1972) intended when he first used the term in his essay "Contextualizing Theology."

I've been thinking about, using, modifying, defining, and exploring the term ever since I encountered it in seminary. This book is the result of ten years of ministry practice; thirty years of teaching courses on contextualization; writing and editing numerous articles, chapters, and a book mapping evangelical approaches; talking about it with students and colleagues; and gleaning from conferences and seminars. Through all these contributions I have tried to convey the significance of the idea that contextualization is squarely at the intersection of culture, gospel, and gospel bearer (whether autochthonous or expatriate).

In the early years, my focus, like that of most of my colleagues, was on contextualizing theology. Like them, I wanted to guard against warping or even jettisoning biblical truths. I also recognized that whenever we try to organize and convey biblical truths to others who differ from us, we engage in contextualization. At the same time, I also questioned my own organization's approach to evangelism in its use of a tool known as "The Four Spiritual Laws." Originally developed for use among American college students, this linear, outlined approach to presenting the gospel had a great appeal to me as an American student majoring in engineering in my university years. It is a bare-bones listing of the fundamental facts of the gospel—with illustrations used to highlight or explain those facts. I liked the content, the order, and the call for response.

In 1978 I arrived for what became a decade of work in Africa. There I was brought face-to-face with an audience that was *not* American and *not* studying engineering, and I became far more interested in a well-told story than a linear recitation of "facts." I struggled with this while teaching science in a local Swazi high school but did not have the tools or conceptual framework to know how to move forward.

It was when I went to seminary in the United States that I was introduced to the word and the entire discipline of missiology. Prior to seminary, I did not even know it existed! After seminary, I returned to Africa to teach in a seminary that had recently been established by Cru in Nairobi (then called the Nairobi International School of Theology).

Thankfully, for me, Cru staff working in East Africa were experimenting with new ways to communicate the Four Spiritual Laws through a picture book with an accompanying script. The people pictured in the booklet were dressed traditionally (a different book was planned for each major people group). The accompanying story (available in English and the language of the people portrayed) was about a man who had been estranged from his son and followed an outline that essentially explained the same logical, linear gospel found in the Four Spiritual Laws—but in story format. This was an early version of what we call "storying" the gospel today, though we did not call it that at the time.

I did not think of this as contextualization: it was simply an adaptation of an existing tool to communicate the same message in a different setting. As my teaching service in Africa continued, however, I came to realize that this attempt to take a tool developed in one cultural setting and adapt it for use in another is indeed one approach to contextualization. Granted, it dealt with a very specific evangelistic method rather than a theology, but it served at the intersection of culture and gospel.

As I taught courses on theology and a capstone course on theological systems in Kenya, I became frustrated that contextualization was confined to theology, with an invisible boundary drawn around it to keep it from leaking into other areas of church life and ministry. I was drawn to the idea that contextualization is much, much broader than theology and evangelistic methodology. But to imagine that contextualization is dealing with an amorphous universal "everything the church is and does" made it messy and complicated and literally impossible to get a handle on. Frankly, at the time I was thankful that my teaching assignments focused exclusively on contextualizing theology.

As difficult as that was, it was much easier to handle than trying to grapple with ministry, church life, and the like—all as components of what the church is and does, and all requiring contextualization.

In 1991, I sensed God's call to return to the United States to take up a position at Wheaton College. No more systematic theology classes for me: Wheaton has an entire department dedicated to handling that, and all the Bible and theology faculty are far better trained in theology than I am with my missiology degree. In my second summer at Wheaton I offered an elective summer course on "Third World Theology" and was scolded by a theology professor, who informed me that Wheaton had an entire department for theological courses! As I reflect on that comment now, I suspect he was teasing, but it did not feel that way at the time.

A few years later I inherited a course then titled "Contextualization of Theology" (cataloged in my own department) and began to teach it as I had in Kenya, as a theological course. But by then I knew that contextualization could not be bounded exclusively in theological discussion: it must carry across the life of the church. However, as a teacher I struggled to organize this organic, formless mess into something coherent that made sense to me and my students. I expressed my frustrations to Larry Poston, a colleague who was team teaching the course with me. Larry is a religious scholar, and he pointed me to Ninian Smart's (1996) dimensional approach to religions.

Smart's approach gave me what I had been missing: an approach that could deal with the whole of church life and yet was organized in a way that it could be taken in smaller chunks. Ever since, I've continually adapted and utilized Smart's dimensional approach to teach contextualization. This book is the product of more than three decades of thinking, teaching, writing, and talking about contextualization. I invite you to walk with me through seven dimensions of contextualization that frame a holistic and healthy approach to planting, growing, discipling, developing, and nurturing a local gathering of believers into a healthy church that is both *in* their culture and thus seen by nonfollowers of Christ as "normal" in many respects, and also *out of* their culture and thus seen by nonfollowers of Christ as "strange" because believers lead lives centered on the principles of the kingdom of God rather than the "kingdom of their culture."

Outline of the Book

In an earlier work (Moreau 2012b), I outlined the major underlying presuppositions, orientations, and battlegrounds that have characterized evangelical discussions on contextualization. Drawing from an extensive search of the literature, I then mapped 249 examples of contextualization into categories based on the role of the initiator (facilitator, guide, herald, pathfinder, prophet, and restorer). In that book, and in several chapters and articles over the past decade (Moreau 2005, 2006a, 2006b, 2007, 2008, and 2012a), I presented my own approach as simply one of the examples for modeling contextualization. In this book, I expand on the model I teach and use as follows.

Chapter 1: Setting the Stage: What Is Contextualization?

This chapter provides a bird's-eye view of "contextualization"—what it is, the breadth of contextualization, and its dipolar nature. I then introduce the dimensional approach I use in the book by offering a more extended definition of each dimension than found below.

Chapter 2: The Social Dimension: Introduction, Association, and Kinship

The social dimension is so large that I split the material over four chapters. There are five systems of the social dimension. In chapter 2, I introduce the dimension and examine the systems of association and kinship. In every human society people associate: they form groups (including some, excluding others). Further, all people are born into webs of kinship relations, and through such things as marriage and going to work, they expand those webs. These networks impact such things as church growth and organization and play a critical role in contextualizing the Christian faith.

Chapter 3: The Social Dimension as Exchange: Economics

In every society people have or produce multiple types of capital ranging from physical goods to services to social statuses. Likewise, in every society people exchange those types of capital. The production and sustaining as well as the exchange of these types of capital constitute the exchange system of the social dimension. These capitals and their exchange form a deeply contextual system that functions in churches just as it does in the larger societies in which those churches operate.

Chapter 4: The Social Dimension as Learning: Education

God created people to learn: we learn through socialization, through apprenticeships, and through formal educational institutions. These channels of learning are all contextual and found inside of churches just as they are outside of churches. Understanding how people and societies idealize learning and the learning process helps us frame growth as followers of Christ in a contextual fashion.

Chapter 5: The Social Dimension as Organizational: Politics

God also created us as social creatures, and in all societies people organize the multitude of groups, associations, and organizations that exist. In this chapter I address how they do that and what it means for contextualization. "Organizational" spans a broad array from leadership to politics to organizational dynamics. As with the other social systems, the organizational patterns found in churches parallel those found in the societies in which the churches are embedded. We examine some of the ways local cultural values impact contextualizing churches, from leadership styles to the operation of Christian churches and other institutions.

Chapter 6: The Mythic Dimension

God created us as storytellers, which is not surprising since God himself is a storyteller, as evidenced by the vast majority of the Bible being narrative rather than didactic (teaching). Evangelical Christians may bristle at the use of the word "myth" in relation to the Bible, but I use the term in the academic sense of stories that guide our thinking and living rather than in the popular sense of "a story that is not true." In this chapter I explain how I intend the term to be understood and then walk through the multiple ways we "story" our faith from the biblical narrative to orality to contemporary Bollywood.

Chapter 7: The Ethical Dimension

Ethics deals with the "shoulds" and "oughts" of life. All humans grow up in an environment in which they learn to discern their family's and society's perspectives on what is right (obligations) and what is wrong (taboos): what is the right thing to do, what is the wrong thing to avoid.

Scripture also provides a deeply ethical narrative, and we explore the intersection of Scripture and society in this dimension—and how the net result can range from ethically rigorous faith that is deeply rooted in a local cultural frame of reference to outright syncretism.

Chapter 8: The Artistic and Technological Dimension

God has made us as creative people; I see that as part of being an image-bearer of a creative God. In every society, people use art and human-made technology (as McLuhan framed it; e.g., churches, pulpits, pews, offices, class-rooms, nurseries, vestments, gravestones, and so on are media that become the message). In this chapter I explore Christian understandings of art, material, and technology as extensions of who we are that in turn shape who we become—and how faith and artistic, material, and technical expressions interpenetrate one another in contextual ways.

Chapter 9: The Ritual Dimension

Scripture clearly portrays humans as deeply ritualistic people: we see rituals in heaven as well as on earth. Many evangelicals eschew ritual even as they engage in it. This chapter will lay out a basic understanding of ritual and how it plays a critical role in contextualizing our faith.

Chapter 10: The Experience Dimension: The Supernatural

Around the world today scholars are noting and studying the phenomenon of Pentecostalism and the framing of faith in light of supernatural experience. In this chapter I outline global experiences as well as frames of reference for understanding this as an important dimension ignored by many Western Christians and missionaries—to the detriment of local expressions of faith in settings everywhere on the planet.

Chapter 11: The Doctrinal Dimension

The final dimension is the one most frequently explored as the only element of contextualization: theology. I'll explain multiple approaches to "theologiz-ing" and then in synopsis form examine contextual realities that help us better understand global expressions of theology and theological development, with a focus on selected topics as they are framed in Africa—with appropriate caveats, of course.

Chapter 12: The Future of Contextualization

What have we learned? This question frames the concluding chapter, which includes a quick recap of the dimensions and observations on the future of contextualization.

A Word on "Majority World"

Many terms have been proposed and used to capture the countries of the world that have not been in the orbit called "the West." In ecumenical circles in the early to mid-nineteenth century, the terms "older" and "younger" churches were used to indicate a relationship that was too often framed in colonial terms. In secular circles, "third world" was coined, but that term has dropped from use in the academy. Many academics today use "Global South" even though that part of the world is certainly not all south of the equator. My personal frustration with Global South is that the expression of something "going south" is a metaphor of things going wrong. While it is true that the world is flat (see the good explanation in Jacobsen 2015, 9–11), that does not help us distinguish the commonalities found in many Asian, African, Latin American, and Pacific Island settings. As has been my practice, I choose to use "majority world" because it remains a more neutral designation, it does not have an implied status or hierarchy, and it reflects the simple fact that this is where the vast majority of the world actually lives.

A Word about "Religions"

Throughout this book, I refer to adherents of religions such as Buddhism, Christianity, Islam, and Hinduism. Among contemporary missionaries and practitioners, each of these terms is still used as a marker to identify a system sharing common beliefs and practices and to distinguish them from other systems. Phrases such as "Buddhists believe . . ." and "Hindus practice . . ." are common. However, they are commonly accurate only in a local sense; they may well describe adherents in one location or following one school within the religion, but they do not represent all adherents. In fact, Buddhism, Hinduism, and Islam—as well as Christianity—are neither uniform nor unified.

Of special note in this regard is that "Hinduism" is even more challenging as a term than, for example, "Buddhism" or "Islam." Like them, it serves as an umbrella term. Unlike them, however, the Supreme Court of India has defined Hinduism as both a *civilization* and a conglomerate of religions (Richard 2004, 311). To the extent that "Hinduism" refers to a civilization and an aggregate of religions, the questions that the contextualizer brings to India must go beyond the normal "religious" questions and include those normally addressed to a society. In some respects, this parallels Confucianism in China (as an ethical system or way of life) and Shinto in Japan (as a system of social ritual and obligations).

As if that were not enough of a challenge, scholars over the past few decades have shifted such that they now question even the use of "religion" as a viable category. Religious scholar Kevin Schilbrack analyzes this shift in his article, appropriately titled "Religions: Are There Any?" He details three components in the critique of the contemporary use of "religion": "that 'religion' is a social construction, that the term distorts one's perceptions of the reality it seeks to name, and that it is ideologically poisonous" (2010, 1112). Despite the critique, Schilbrack and others continue using the term, albeit with caveats, if for no other reason than that an adequate substitute does not exist.

From a Christian vantage point, H. L. Richard, long-term scholar of India, adds that the term "religion" is not found in the Bible, nor is the modern construct. He argues, "The Bible thus gives an expectation that people everywhere will have some notion of God, but does not provide teaching on religions as such, particularly not modern notions of religion" (Richard 2015, 299). In short, there is no biblical data on which to base a biblical definition of the contemporary term.

Richard poses that the idea of "changing a religion" has become problematic in missiology. He is not arguing against conversion but against the idea that a "religion" has sharply defined boundaries that must be crossed in the conversion process. For example, Westerners have generally believed that a person self-identifies as a member of only one religion. We see this in census practices of forcing respondents to choose only one religion with which they identify. However, people across the world often have more than one religious identity and use the identity that best serves them in each circumstance of life. For example, Jan Van Bragt notes, "Putting it very crudely, it is said that Shinto is the religion for the living, and Buddhism is the religion for the dead. The Japanese feel themselves to be Shintoists in the cycle of the four seasons, at the times of planting and harvesting of the rice, at the New Year, at the festival of the tutelary deity of the village, and when a child is born. They feel themselves to be Buddhists at the times of funerals and services for the dead" (Van Bragt 2002, 10).

Aware of the dangers of reductionism, I choose to refer to "Buddhists," "Christians," "Hindus," and "Muslims" throughout the book—but do so with the understanding that these overarching terms stand not only for complex systems but also as umbrella terms for *multiple* complex systems that share some common threads of belief and practice, as do terms such as Aboriginal Religions, African Traditional Religions, Afro-Caribbean Religions, Native American Religions, Tribal Religions, and the like. Historically, terms most commonly used as a kind of supercategory for all of these systems were "animism" (Van Rheenen 1991) and "primal religions" (J. Taylor 1963; H. Turner 1977).

Acknowledgments

As with every book, while the author is the lead, many people play important roles in turning an idea into a reality. They helped me avoid some mistakes; I alone am responsible for those that remain. I offer special thinks to Andrea Rodriguez and Lauren Clausen, who proofread the manuscript and offered numerous helpful suggestions and questions that strengthened and sharpened the discussion. I also thank Jim Kinney of Baker, who patiently waited for me as I dithered in being able to commit myself to the task of putting the book together. Finally, I thank God, who makes all things possible: he has put me in a position to be able to write with a job at Wheaton College (an institution that values and promotes writing) and the resources needed to successfully engage the task. To God be the glory!

1
SETTING THE STAGE
WHAT IS CONTEXTUALIZATION?

The word "contextualization" is a mouthful! For many, it's intimidating—and it sounds like one of those academic terms that don't apply to the real world. Over the past several decades of learning, arguing, teaching, and more learning about the term, I've discovered just how down-to-earth the term really is. As adopted in 1972 for mission and church contexts, it's fairly new, especially in the universe of theological terms; it is still in its infancy, so to speak. And yet in the world of missions and missiology, no term has simultaneously generated more excitement and controversy over the brief life span of its use.

Contextualization

Whether used as a term of approbation or celebration, "contextualization" is a term (and an underlying idea) that has an emotional resonance with many Christians around our world. It resides at the intersection of God's unchanging Word and the ever-changing settings in which people live out their faith as followers of Christ (Conn 1984). By "unchanging Word," I'm referring not only to Scripture itself, but also to Jesus Christ as the Word of God and to the gospel he established and communicated through his incarnation, life, death, and resurrection.

The Breadth of Contextualization

Contextualization happens everywhere the church exists. And by church, I'm referring to the people of God rather than to buildings. Contextualization refers to how those people live out their faith in light of the values of their societies. It is not limited to theology, architecture, church polity, ritual, training, art, or spiritual experience: it includes them all and more. Whether we meet in cushioned pews in a climate-controlled European Gothic cathedral, or take the Lord's Supper of potato bread and palm wine, or actively seek supernatural signs and wonders, or sculpt expressions of our faith from tragedy to triumph, or enter sweat lodges to face our sin and find purification, or go to early morning prayer meetings or late-night concerts, we are all in the process of expressing or engaging our faith in highly contextual ways.

One problem with this is the idea that if contextualization is indeed everything Christians do, then the word becomes meaningless. But contextualization does not focus purely on what we do; it also examines why we do it the way we do. At the intersection of faith and culture, it forces us to step back (as impossible as that is) from ourselves and ask questions about why we practice our faith the way we do. From the simple to the profound, at the heart is the fact that as human beings our faith is *always* enfleshed because, despite our spiritual nature, we are enfleshed beings (we have physical bodies).

John paints a wonderful picture in Revelation 7:9–10 of followers of Christ "from every nation, tribe, people and language," standing before the throne of God. John says that they cry out, "Salvation belongs to our God, who sits on the throne, and to the Lamb." This wonderful picture is a simultaneous blend of uniformity (white robes, all holding palm branches) and diversity (nations, tribes, peoples, languages). Have you ever wondered what language they use? At least from John's depiction, it's Greek! As I envision this massive worship experience, I imagine everyone speaking their first or heart language, but all of us understanding one another. This massive gathering of worshipers does not homogenize them: they retain their ancestral and linguistic frames of reference. But they are clearly unified in worship of God and Christ. I see this as a marvelous image characterizing contextualization.

The Dipolar Nature of Contextualization

Contextualization, in the framework of this image, can in one sense be thought of as having two "poles" that are in continual dialogue (drawing from Feinberg 1982). In the Revelation 7 image, one pole is the commonality: the white robes, the palm branches, and the declaration. The other pole is the individuality: nation, tribe, people, language. I'm using them as metaphors for the dipolar nature of contextualization. These two poles—one universal and one local, one transcendent and one immanent, one eternal and one limited in time and place—are in continual dialogue with each other. However, they do not share equal weight. The universal or normative pole transcends human societies, while the individual pole is the locale in which the normative pole is embodied.

The Universal or Normative Pole

As I noted, the first pole is the commonality. In the image from Revelation 7 this is represented by the sameness of the clothing and the declaration. This is the "universal" or "normative" pole. In contextualization, this universal pole is the gospel itself, a commonality that is timeless and universal. Stripped of all the additions people have tacked on over the years, I compress this gospel into a very short and simple phrase: *Jesus the Christ is Lord.* It will help to unpack this phrase before we look at the other pole.

Jesus

Jesus is the historical, incarnated man who ministered, taught, suffered, died, was resurrected, and will return. He is the very Son of God—not through a biological act, but as an ontological reality that is unique in the universe. He is the actual Son; we are adopted sons and daughters.

The Christ

I use "the Christ" in the phrase because too many people in our society think of "Christ" as his family name rather than his title—he is *the* Christ, *the* Messiah, *the* Savior. "The Christ" is his title and is unique among all creation.

Is Lord

It is this one, Son of God and very God, who is Lord of the universe. His reign is not limited in time or space, and the submission of the entire created order to his reign is its ultimate destiny.

The Local Pole

The other pole is the local setting, as with the individuality in the Revelation 7 image. Whether gathered in a secret house fellowship in a restrictive nation or assembled in an ultramodern megasanctuary in South Korea, Christians are embedded in local settings. They may be embedded enclaves of other cultures (e.g., international churches in many global cities) or never leave their birth environment; either way they remain inescapably embedded. This is the pole that is always changing and dynamic. While the universal pole is eternal, this pole is temporal and ever changing. Changing the metaphor, it is the soil in which the universal pole is embedded.

Introduction to the Dimensions

If contextualization includes every way we express our faith in Christ, how do we determine what should be included? How do we organize our approach? As I noted in the preface, this question troubled me for over a decade, until a colleague introduced me to the dimensional thinking of Ninian Smart (1996), including (in Smart's order) (1) the doctrinal or philosophical, (2) the ritual, (3) the mythic or narrative, (4) the experiential and emotional, (5) the ethical and legal, (6) the social, and (7) the material dimensions.

Smart was not thinking specifically about contextualization. Rather, he was attempting to find a way to describe religions using universal categories. He did not develop or frame his approach to facilitate my agenda in relation to contextualization. However, even though his approach is a universal and etic (outsider) paradigm framed in a modernist worldview, it does provide a platform for the examination and exploration of contextualization of Christian faith in multiple non-Christian religious settings on their terms. This enables us to consider how we as Christians might contextualize our faith in settings of other religions in ways that make sense to people who practice those religions.

The danger, of course, is that of syncretism: intermingling inappropriate elements of other religions into our Christian faith (Moreau 2000a). This drives some of the criticism of contextualization, namely, that it leads to syncretism (Moreau 2012b, 123–29). However, the reality is that all expressions of the Christian faith are local, embedded in contexts. Our heritage is one of religious encounter and, in some cases, assimilation (such as the Christmas tree). Using Smart's dimensional analysis no more opens us to syncretism than any other approach might. Rather, it provides a very helpful paradigm of areas to consider for contextualizing our faith.

Over the past two decades I have modified Smart's dimensions for specific use in contextualization. Through the rest of the book I'll explain how I approach contextualization of all that the church is, does, and believes—not limited to Christian theology. What follows is a brief explanation of each of the seven dimensions, which I expand on in the chapters to come. Throughout this introduction I'll be referring to these as dimensions of "religion"—a reminder that I'm keeping the conversation broad at this point, including non-Christian religions, since each dimension is found within them as well as within our own Christian faith.

The Social Dimension

The social dimension refers to the dimension of religion that expresses the linking of people to each other, built on the cultural values of how people are to relate socially in religious contexts. It includes broad, universal social institutions as well as the sense of belonging inculcated through socially experienced religious events. For the purposes of contextualization, and following a framework used in intercultural communication, I identify five specific social institutions: association, kinship, exchange (or economics), learning (or education), and organizational (or political; see Moreau, Campbell, and Greener 2014, 88–94; Hiebert and Meneses 1995). Each of these institutions meets a need (whether religious or other) and has elements that can be identified as being of significance for the survival and growth of the institution. They are all found in every society on the planet. Each has a significant role to play in religious expression and life as well.

Association

Association refers to the reality that all religions are part of societies in which people form groups based on a broad variety of needs and social practices. In a very pragmatic sense, alumni associations typify this. However, our focus is on religious association. Since in associations people are members by some defining characteristic, we can rightly ask what religious types of associations exist and how people are included as well as how people are excluded. An alumni association, for example, only includes people who graduated from the institution of which they are alumni. Associations in religions are characterized by a variety of factors—from the broadest "I'm a Muslim" to the narrowest "I'm a member of the _____ group, which practices _____." Religious associations may be public or secret; they often have symbols or slogans as well as rituals of incorporation and intensification. They also have means of inclusion and exclusion, whether formal or informal. These include such things as assent to specified beliefs and/or practices, belonging to a particular lineage, having undergone a particular ritual or trial, and much more.

Kinship

Every faith must provide for the biological reproduction of new members and see that they are nourished and cared for during infancy and childhood.

It is typically the family (whether nuclear or extended) that provides the basic context for the performance of these activities. Often the early training and socialization of children into a faith is either initiated or takes place by concerned relatives in the family structure. Many faiths also express metaphorical family relationships (spiritual father, mother, brother, sister, child) as well as prescriptions and prohibitions on things such as marriage, inheritance, authority, residence, and the like.

Exchange

Every faith must have some way of producing and distributing various types of capital. There are many types of capital: material (goods, services, money), social (status, power, authority, knowledge), and spiritual (efficacy of prayer, connection to the divine or the supernatural, spiritual vitality). Each type of capital sustains the lives and faith of its members. The institutions and roles that are organized around the production and exchange of these types of capital—including concepts of obligation, debt, pricing, payment, and so on—constitute the exchange system of the faith. Often there is an idealized portrait of the system, which may not correspond to the actual exchanges in the lives of average adherents, and especially in the lives of those at the bottom of the social and/or spiritual capital scale.

Learning (Education)

Learning is a facet of the socialization process that is necessary for all faiths. Whether through formal educational systems (religious schools), nonformal means (apprenticeships), or informal means (socialization through youth groups, faith-based small groups, reading of religious materials, religious experiences, and so on), this component of the social dimension includes all those activities that contribute to providing members with the knowledge, values, and skills of the faith that are considered essential. They are transmitted to members to prepare them to understand and live out their faith in religiously acceptable ways.

Organizational (Political)

All faith communities must have some means of maintaining internal order as well as regulating the relations of their members with other faith communities. Internal threats to a faith's existence come from the competition for power and control over the various types of religious and other capital noted previously. Since the availability of power has limits in every community, regulation of (and conflict over) the use of those capital resources is inevitable. The legal and political system—how a faith organizes itself—is the network of institutions and social roles that exist to regulate this access to and competition for power. Religions maintain order through formal and informal laws and policies, means of governance, enforcement, leadership to regulate lives of members, and so on.

The Mythic Dimension

The mythic dimension refers to the stories of a culture that reflect its thinking about the world, itself, its laws, and its values. Myth concretizes important values for the culture and enables those values to be passed from generation to generation. Mythography, the study of myth, typically focuses on religious epics including the timeless stories of creation, redemption, and human/divine drama found in a religion's scriptures, epics, and classics.

In terms of contextualization, I use the term to include contemporary stories as well. They range from stories of heroism to martyrdom, from great success to great failure. I also include oral components including folklore and proverbs. People tell stories of great heroes of their faith, but as warnings they also use stories of people who fail in their religious faith or obligations. In the contemporary sense, Hollywood, Bollywood, Nollywood (Nigeria), the Marvel Universe, DC Comics, manga, and anime are all purveyors of myth on a global scale. When it comes to myth, as we will see in chapter 6, the question is not, Is it true? Rather, the questions are (1) Does it *draw on* or *utilize* the basic ideals of a society? (2) Does it *challenge* the basic ideals of a society? and (3) Does it *capture* the imagination?

The Ethical Dimension

The ethical dimension fundamentally refers to how people *should* behave as they relate to other people, animals, and the world. Ethics are found on the personal, group, and social (or systemic) levels. They are deeply interwoven into the cultural values and doctrine and often enshrined in heroic (or evil) acts discussed in cultural myth. They provide the behavioral maps that we negotiate as we live and interact with others. In this sense, the Ten Commandments and Golden Rule fit the ethical category rather than the doctrinal category. Both the Ten Commandments and the Golden Rule are founded on fundamental truths such as these: God is the creator of humankind, we are made in his image, and God has the right to determine proper codes of conduct for his creation. However, they are codes of living that arise from the truths rather than "truths" in and of themselves. In the Ten Commandments, the commands to love God and neighbor (and thus not lie, steal, lust, or cheat) are all *applications*. They are certainly "true" in the sense that they conform to who God is, but they are not religious truths per se. Rather, they are natural obligations based on religious truths from which they are derived. Ethics are typically stated by using words such as "should," "must," or "ought": "Thou shalt . . ." in King James English of the Ten Commandments exemplifies this.

The Artistic and Technological Dimension

By the artistic, or material, dimension I refer to the multitude of ways people symbolically capture and express ideas, values, and themes of their religion or of their personal approach to their religion. By "material" I refer to what Marshall McLuhan meant by "technology"—and his idea that we create things and they in turn re-create us (Lochhead 1994). This certainly includes things we normally think of as technology, but it also includes anything we create that enables us to extend ourselves through artistic and other types of expression. The "material" can include such mundane things as a pencil, but for this dimension the focus is on how we use that mundane pencil to create art, from sketching to writing poetry or songs or stories to even using the pencil itself as an object in an artistic creation. This dimension includes architecture, art (sculptures, paintings), objects (crosses), locations (cemeteries, holy sites), religious fashion and decoration, and so on. It also includes art as performance, from singing to sermonizing to creating music and drama.

The Ritual Dimension

By ritual I mean regularized ceremonies of religious life. This can be as mundane as bowing before a person of high status to an uncommon event such as the investiture of a global religious figure (e.g., a pope). Ritual runs the full gamut of religious experience, and every religion is loaded with ritual. While American evangelicals over the past century often disdained the formal ritual of liturgical or mainline churches, at the same time we created our own rituals that serve the same purposes as those we disdained, such as small-group Bible studies, quiet times, and weekend conferences. In this chapter we'll explore ritual along the lines that scholars of ritual have long noted: (1) rituals that enable *transition* from one state to another (e.g., baptism), (2) rituals that *intensify or strengthen* the religious beliefs or faith of a person or group of people (e.g., a worship service), and (3) rituals that offer a means to deal with a *crisis* (e.g., prayer for a sick person).

The (Supernatural) Experience Dimension

Smart characterized the experiential dimension as focusing on general religious experience, including such things as the emotions connected with those experiences. Because I'm particularly focusing on Christian contextualization, I narrow the focus to *how we experience the transcendent in our lives*. This can range from the mundane to the sublime, though generally we focus more on the latter. By "supernatural experiences" I refer not only to supernatural experiences that Christians encounter—such as dreams, visions, the various sign gifts (e.g., tongues and interpretation), and encounters with supernatural beings (angels or demons). I also include in this category supernatural experiences noted by practitioners of other religions, such as out-of-body experiences (OBE), near-death experiences, trances, possession, shamanic journeys, and so on. By including non-Christian supernatural experiences in this list, at this stage I am not distinguishing between the genuine and the contrived or fake, nor am I indicating the sources of such experiences. Instead, I'm simply recognizing that these are reported as genuine experiences and therefore I include them in this dimension. This dimension includes not only encounters with the transcendent, but also and whether we consider such encounters to play a significant role in our religious lives.

The Philosophical or Doctrinal Dimension

The final dimension is the one most commonly discussed and argued over by evangelicals. Smart referred to this as the philosophical dimension, a term better able to handle the range of perspectives that the religions of the world have on "truth." However, my focus is on contextualizing Christian faith. Thus the word "doctrine" (or perhaps "theology") better captures the central idea for Christians. This dimension includes important truths expressed in religious form. Religions often seek to answer central and abiding questions, such as, What is the truth about the world, people, and the unseen powers? Although across religions the answer ranges from "It's all illusion" to "What you see is what really is," I limit my focus to Christian contextual expressions of doctrine or truth.

Conclusion

So far I have set the stage by giving a very cursory overview of how I understand contextualization together with an equally cursory introduction to the seven dimensions of contextualization. In the rest of the book I turn to a more detailed examination of each dimension in turn, following roughly the same general outline for each dimension: (1) an introduction to the dimension (or component), (2) a discussion of how that dimension shows up in Scripture, and (3) selected examples of what contextualization of that dimension entails.

THE SOCIAL DIMENSION
INTRODUCTION, ASSOCIATION, AND KINSHIP

The overarching framework for the social dimension is *how people connect to each other*. Just as Ninian Smart analyzed religions from a dimensional perspective, social scientists analyze the social dimension of cultures by examining significant, universally found social systems. They have identified systems found in every human society, such as kinship, politics, health, transportation, and so on. Social scientists view "religion" as one of those systems.

To help us understand contextualization, rather than seeing religion as one social system alongside the other social systems, I will utilize religion as the lens through which I view the other major social systems. I limit my examination to five major systems as they are reflected in religious life and practice: (1) association, (2) kinship, (3) exchange (or economics), (4) learning (or education), and (5) organization (or politics/law).

In this chapter I focus on the first two systems: association and kinship. Bear in mind throughout that our goal is *learning how to contextualize*. Thus, for both systems, I start with a broad introduction to the system, survey examples found in Scripture of that system, and provide examples of contextualization within that system.

Association

Humans are associational creatures. Christians recognize that this originates from being made in God's image. We are relational as God is relational: he wants to connect intimately with those he created. Being in his image, we were created as creatures who need to associate with others and be in relationship with them. This is fundamental to what it means to be human.

Not surprisingly, the associational system is a challenge to unpack because it is so pervasive. In the broadest sense, it refers to people connecting with each other in any way they choose to connect. Study of association also includes the fact that by connecting with some, we end up disconnecting with others. Whenever we associate with some people while using a set of criteria (e.g., fans of a sports team), we inevitably dissociate with those who do not meet the criteria (e.g., people who are not fans of our team). The associational system, then, is simultaneously inclusive and exclusive.

Further, cultural variations on how people associate are significant. For example, and at the risk of oversimplification, those from individualist societies often associate based on personal inclinations, likes, or dislikes. On the other hand, people from collective societies are often perceived to be birthed into associations that are already connected to their extended family. They are members of associations not by virtue of personal likes or dislikes, but by virtue of social obligations they inherit through their extended families.

Association in Society

We may identify at least three significant foci for the system of association in societies: (1) institutions by which people associate, (2) how those social institutions maintain their identity, and (3) how individuals maintain their own identity through associations. We will reserve discussion on the *operation* of institutions for chapter 5.

Institutions

As you can imagine, the number of ways people might associate with each other is impossible to count. From social media to physical neighborhoods, in every society people make connections with each other and form groups based on those connections. Those groups can be informal (childhood friends) or formal (alumni associations), temporary (environmental organizations) or lifelong (family), professional (physicians) or organic (fan clubs). In individualistic societies, these groups are typically voluntary, and a person will stay connected only as long as there is personal benefit from the connection. In collective societies, a person's associations may well be more involuntary due to obligations on the part of the in-groups into which people are born.

How Institutions Maintain Institutional Identity

Institutions maintain their identity through multiple modes all operating simultaneously. They may use physical symbols ranging from business cards to body adornment (hairstyle, tattoos, and scarification). They may use symbolic language when relating to each other (familial language, titles, and honorifics). They may behave uniformly (e.g., think of sports clubs), including observing obligations (e.g., cheer on your team) and avoiding taboos (e.g., do not cheer on your team's rivals). These commitments are part of the ethical dimension (chap. 7), while enforcing them is part of the organizational system in the social dimension (chap. 5). Members may isolate themselves from nonmembers physically, socially, or spiritually. They participate with other members in shared activities (whether ritual or not and whether tied to

---

SIDEBAR 2.1
QUESTIONS ABOUT ASSOCIATION

Below are some questions to consider as you explore association in your own setting. Asking and exploring the answers to these questions will enable you to better understand local examples of association—but more importantly will help you think more clearly about church and the means Christians may use to associate with each other in light of local societal norms.

Answers to these questions could be used to compromise the gospel or the biblical definition of church. That is not my intention. Rather, the questions equip you to find biblically appropriate and culturally sound ways for Christians to associate with other Christians. They help you avoid the danger of simply establishing only the types of associations that make sense from your own cultural setting. As you ask these questions, also be asking yourself how the answers impact what type of Christian associations might make sense to local people without compromising their relationship with Christ.

1. What associations, religious or otherwise, do you see here?
2. How do adherents of each association relate to outsiders?
3. How are barriers to and options for associational affiliation supported by local religious beliefs?
4. What symbols are used to identify members of various associations? Which among these symbols might be repurposed for use by Christians? Which symbols should Christians avoid?
5. How are new associations formed (historically and in contemporary times)?
6. In what ways does the gospel condone or condemn indigenous means of associating?

a calendar or arising spontaneously). Together these serve to maintain group identity through building various types of group cohesion.

How Individuals Develop and Maintain Identity through Association

In addition to group or institutional identity, a significant factor in association is that of individual identity. The groups with which we associate play a significant role in both forming and maintaining our identity. Growing up in either a nuclear or an extended family system provides people with a sense of who they are and what roles they are to play in life. The organizations or groups they are affiliated with provide them with roles appropriate to their statuses in each. In their associations, they play out those roles. The possibility of growing into new roles, whether by age or skill set or other criteria, offers reasons for them to become more deeply embedded in the institutions. As they receive affirmation for their participation, they have a psychological basis for perceiving who they are and how they fit into their world. In sum, people identify themselves—they know and understand who they are—through the associations they have.

To assist you in considering association, sidebar 2.1 offers several questions you can ask about religious associations in your setting.

Association in Acts: An Example

In Acts 11:19–26 we find a wonderful example illustrating association. After Stephen was stoned, Paul (then called Saul) led the persecution of the church. The church scattered from Jerusalem—after which Paul encountered Christ in a vision and came to faith. As the persecuted Jewish believers scattered, they continued to share Christ—but only among fellow Jews. However, men from Cyprus and Cyrene witnessed to the Greeks in Antioch, many of whom came to faith. News of this influx of non-Jews becoming followers of Christ reached the Christian leaders in Jerusalem, so they sent Barnabas to investigate. Barnabas saw what God had done among the believers in Antioch and was convinced that their conversion was of God. He then went to Tarsus (Paul's home city) to get Paul and bring him to Antioch, where they taught together for a year. It was there that these believers were given the name "Christians," likely a derogatory name but a clear demonstration that they were being recognized as a new type of religious association.

Several associational elements stand out:

1. The first believers did not go beyond their normal religious associational group (Jews).

2. When people not of their group came to believe in Christ, the leaders decided to send a representative to check out their faith.

3. Their investigator was so excited that he traveled to find the very person who had been the primary persecutor and to bring him to them to teach this new body of believers. Thus, Barnabas provided the bridge connecting Paul with them while also connecting them with the core of the church in Jerusalem.

4. This continues the shift in the book of Acts: Paul, former persecutor of the church, turns into the apostle to the gentiles (Rom. 11:13) and takes center stage in the narrative.

5. The associational element is that gentiles, formerly disassociated from Jews, were coming to Christ and were connected to Jews in mutual faith. Today we've lost sight of just how much of a cultural and emotional earthquake this was for the Jewish believers.

Implications for Contextualization

What does all of this mean for contextualization? In each area of the following discussion I focus on the theme of identity, which is at the heart of association. What does it mean to be identified with Christ—and with others who follow him? First, let's look at two examples: Jesu bhaktas and the non-church in Japan.

Example 1: Jesu Bhaktas in Christian Ashrams in India (Hoefer 2007)

Across India there are multiple examples of Indians who have come to Christ but who are not connected with historic Christian institutions. Some of them are developing ashrams as their own institutions, which in turn maintain their institutional identity in Indian ways. One example is that of Jesu bhaktas (a *bhakta* is a devotee; a Jesu bhakta is a devotee of Jesus) who join ashrams. The idea of Christian ashrams came from Indian Christians, borrowing from the Indian tradition of an ashram as a place in an isolated setting for training. For Christians, this would be a place of spiritual training and devotion to Christ, albeit not necessarily in an isolated setting (see R. Taylor 1979, 283; see also chap. 4 in this volume).

Herbert Hoefer, a long-term missionary in India, delineates the institutional practices that Jesu bhaktas use to maintain their identity (2007, 137–38). First, concerning the Jesu bhaktas as individuals, Hoefer notes the following (the points are all from Hoefer, though I have rearranged the order):

- They have named themselves. They call themselves "Jesu bhaktas," "devotees of Jesus."
- They are public about their faith in Christ, but they keep themselves separate from the organized church.
- Many came to faith through miracles, visions, and answered prayers in Jesus's Name.
- Christian *sanyassis* (wandering holy men) have taken the traditional vows of poverty and celibacy of the Hindu guru and traveled around the land wearing the saffron robe, teaching disciples.
- They welcome pious Christian pastors into their home for prayer and instruction.
- They participate in the social dimensions of Hindu festivals, but separate themselves from the religious aspects.

The final point is fraught with challenges. To the extent that the Jesu bhaktas can separate religious from social identity, some readers may consider this parallel to American Christians participating in cultural events such as Veteran's Day. Other readers may condemn any participation in a non-Christian religious festival. It is important to bear in mind, at least as Hoefer portrays it, that their participation is from their own initiative and not from the urging of non-Indian missionaries.

When Jesu bhaktas join Christian ashrams, they are participating in institutions that also need to maintain their institutional identity. How do they do that? Drawing again from Hoefer (2007; with the points reordered), we note these practices:

- They have started "ashrams" . . . in sacred places and around charismatic figures.
- They use the traditional *bhajan* (an antiphonal response between leader and congregation) for their worship, with the traditional hand bell to keep rhythm.
- They sit on the floor with the leader seated similarly on a slightly elevated platform.
- They have no organization or central leaders, only the spiritual individuals whom they respect.
- Pilgrimage places have spontaneously developed in locations where prayers to Jesus have been found to be powerful.

- Baptisms are carried out as a family and community celebration in the home.
- They access church facilities and occasions such as roadside shrines, open sanctuaries (usually Roman Catholic), mass rallies, correspondence courses, radio/TV programs.
- They encourage the Jesu bhaktas to remain in their families and communities as a witness.
- They are proud of their cultural identity and seek to promote and protect it.
- They are not registered on church rosters as Christians in the country, but remain legally as Hindus.
- They consider "Hinduism" (which is a way of life followed by those of many different religious beliefs in India) to be their culture, not their religion, and people accept them as part of the "Hindu" community.

Hoefer's final two points will likely be the most controversial to readers. This movement as portrayed by Hoefer has arisen from within India and is not being driven by missionaries. So whether we approve of them or not, these markers are means by which they maintain their identities, both individual and institutional.

Clearly Jesu bhaktas in Christian ashrams exemplify one of the most significant challenges in contextualization, namely, what are called "insider movements." These movements have generated voluminous and heated discussion among missionaries and missiologists over the past twenty years (see below and also Moreau 2012b, 155–61, 314; also C. Kraft 2016, 3–24).

Example 2: Non-church in Japan (Howes 2007)

"Uchimura Kanzō (1861–1930) was an extremely accomplished Meiji Christian convert who emphasized a Christianity he considered in tune with traditional Japanese religiosity and free of Western influence," notes John Howes (2007, 127). To better understand the non-church movement Uchimura founded, an overview of the major events in his life is critical (derived from Howes 2007).

Born a Samurai, Uchimura came to Christ through the influence of his instructors while studying English in Hokkaido just ten years after that conversion would have brought him a death sentence in Japan. He poured himself into developing a church with fellow students and continued with the church after finishing his study program. In the process of seeking out leadership opportunities in ministry, he fell in love with a Christian and married her.

Unfortunately, the marriage did not work out, and he returned his pregnant wife (whom he accused of cheating) to her family and refused to even try to reconcile. In response, his Christian friends turned their backs on him. He then traveled to the United States to study.

After he spent a stint working with children in a mental institution, benefactors enabled him to enter Amherst College to study theology. Disappointed with the casual attitude of the American students toward the ministry, he left Amherst and returned to Japan, anticipating ministry among Japanese Christians.

He landed a job as principal at a private school that also employed missionaries as English teachers. However, disagreements with the missionaries resulted in the loss of his job, and he was forced to find a new post, this time at a Japanese government school. About this time Japanese officials were promoting a statement (called the Imperial Rescript on Education) intended for daily recitation by Japanese students. The statement was a recitation of ethical injunctions that were the foundation of Japanese society, with the anticipation that daily recitation would enable Japanese students to withstand Christianity. Elaborately printed copies with the personal signature of Emperor Meiji were distributed to the best schools in Japan, each deciding how to receive it. Uchimura's own school decided to present it at an assembly during which everyone present was to bow before the document. Conflicted, Uchimura only bobbed his head, while everyone else bowed from the waist. His refusal to give full honors to the document resulted in a nationwide uproar:

> His act infuriated conservatives throughout the country. They took it to represent the treachery of Christian influence. A careful historian over half a century later found over two thousand books and articles occasioned by Kanzō's indecision [Ozawa 1961]. It lives in postwar Japan as one of the very few occasions when Japanese individuals took a public stand based upon the demands of their consciences in opposition to nationalist policies. (Howes 2007, 131)

This one act lost Uchimura any chance to continue his career in government education, and he had already lost the option to work in private education through his prior disagreement with the missionaries. After a period of itinerant tutoring (during which his second wife died of pneumonia), he married for the third time and turned to writing. He secured an advance on anticipated royalties, which provided survival income for him while he wrote. In the following three-year span, Uchimura produced seven books and five significant articles on biblical as well as contemporary political issues. The latter drew the attention of the publisher of Japan's largest newspaper, who invited Uchimura to become its chief editor. He stayed at the helm for six years, but he and his fellow editors resigned in protest in 1903 when the newspaper's publisher supported Japanese government officials who were planning to attack Russia.

During the stint as chief editor of the newspaper, Uchimura founded three magazines. The first failed after supporters disagreed with one another. The second, called *Mukyōkai* (see below), helped Christians grow spiritually, and the third, *Seisho no kenkyū* (The Bible Study), successfully ran for almost thirty years, during which Uchimura wrote roughly half of the content. This magazine fulfilled Uchimura's dream of making the Bible at home in Japan, and it provided the income stream he needed for the rest of his life.

At the time of his resignation, Uchimura lived near the government school where he had refused to bow. The principal, a longtime friend, directed students who were interested in religious ideas to Uchimura, who interviewed them and then invited those whom he deemed had potential to gather in his home for lectures on the Bible every Sunday. Writing for his magazines and teaching Sunday Bible studies became the pattern for the rest of his life.

Fifteen years into this pattern, in 1918, as World War I continued, Uchimura's popularity skyrocketed when he announced that history was drawing to a close and Christ was coming back. People flooded to his lectures, filling the largest auditoriums in the country, an astonishing fact for Japan. One year into the process, Uchimura came to realize that he did not have the energy to sustain living as though Christ could come at any moment. He returned to his weekly Sunday Bible lectures. However, he now gave them in front of eight hundred paying people in a lecture hall across the street from the Imperial Palace. Howes (2007, 133) notes,

> Gradually those who attended the lectures began to call their group "*Mukyōkai*," the word Uchimura had used to name the smallest of the three magazines he had started. . . . The term consists of the word for church, *kyōkai* . . . with the prefix *mu* . . . that means simply "lack of." Uchimura first used the word to mean "without a church" to describe his isolation from his fellow Christians after his divorce. Then as the number of those who attended his nondenominational Bible study meetings grew, they began to refer to themselves with the term.

In part due to his study at Amherst, and in part due to missionaries in Japan advocating different denominations (which made little sense to the Japanese), Uchimura argued that the differences among denominations were less due to doctrinal differences and more due to social conditions. He reasoned that if you could talk about *national* versions of Christianity (e.g., American Christianity and German Christianity), then why not also a "Japanese Christianity" free of the secular history that led to denominations in Western countries? And why could not that "Japanese Christianity" rest directly on the individual's relation to God with the Bible as intermediary? If it did, Japanese Christianity would escape the tortured theological debate that so vexed Japanese otherwise attracted to Jesus' life and acts. While they admired Jesus, they cared little for the differences between denominations to which evangelists, mostly foreigners, exposed them. . . . Attendants at Uchimura's Bible lectures accepted such logic. (Howes 2007, 134)

One of the themes found in his writing is independence "from all early institutions, with dependence on God alone" (Howes 2007, 138). This helps us frame his approach to "church" and shows that he saw all existing churches as human institutions trapped in social systems: he advocated personal freedom from those human constraints. This guides our understanding of his 1911 portrayal of the true church: "There is a true church. It is *Mukyokai* (Nonchurch). It is not a church where a man rules over the others under the system. It is a church where people love, encourage, and help each other through the spirit. Their union and harmony are invisible. There, there is no danger at all of them becoming corrupted. This is the true Holy Catholic Church" (cited in Miura 1996, 98). His Sunday Bible studies in effect were his church—one without human organization or systemization or orchestration.

Uchimura was the most prolific Japanese Christian writer ever (over 20,000 pages of works), and his ideas were widely disseminated among the Japanese intellectual elite. In his writings he presents "churchless Christianity as Japan's contribution to world Christianity" (Howe 2007, 127). Decades later, many of these students became leaders in Japan's post–World War II government, advocating and popularizing democratic ideals among the Japanese public. As I noted in 2012: "Uchimura poses a significant contextual challenge to evangelicals. He prophetically discerned significant issues with the church—and the church's understanding of itself. Ultimately turning his back on it, he still centered his life and thought on Bible study and growing in his understanding of Jesus—but in a way that made sense to him as a Japanese lover of Jesus, not as a Westerner" (Moreau 2012b, 285).

Contextualizing Christian Institutions

What type of institutions (groups, organizations) do you see at your own church? Depending on the size of your church, in the United States this can include such things as Bible study groups, women's groups, men's groups, "golden age" (senior) groups, prayer groups, discipleship groups, Sunday school classes, leadership groups (elders, deacons, or both; the pastoral team), special project groups, short-term mission teams, dinner clubs, book clubs, church softball or bowling teams, and citywide, statewide, regional, and national church networks—the list is dizzying!

Most of these institutions are also seen in churches globally. However, the very idea of "church" is being reframed in multiple global settings. A partial list includes Christian ashrams (Ralston 1987), "churchless Christianity" (Hoefer 2001), and *satsangs* (Stevens 2007) in India; non-church churches in Japan (Nabetani 1983); "Gatherings" (of Francis Chan) in the United States (Brandon 2009); house *masjids* in Muslim settings (Goble and Munayer 1989); Christ-centered communities in Buddhist Asia (DeNeui 2015); messianic synagogues (Spielberg and Dauermann 1997); locally initiated church movements in Africa (A. Anderson 2001), Asia (Golf and Lee 2013), and the Middle East (Garrison 2014); and church multiplication movements around the world (Garrison 2004). These are all ways "church" is being contextually framed, but even this list does not include the multitude of institutions and associations found *within*, *among*, and *alongside* churches.

How does the associational system help us better contextualize? The first and most important question to consider is this: In what ways does the gospel condone or condemn indigenous associations, whether religious or not? In this question I do not specify that these are *Christian* associations. I'm thinking about the associations *as associations*: I'm not exclusively considering what they teach or believe. The focus in the question is on *how the people connect to one another and what that connection means for the members' identity*. Even though an association might be used for wrong purposes, the type of association it represents is not necessarily wrong in and of itself.

At the intersection of faith and culture, the contextualizer looks at the surrounding culture and asks whether there are associations already part and parcel of the society that can be properly utilized in establishing movements of people to Christ. The goal is not to simply and blindly reproduce the types of associations with which the Christian newcomers are familiar in their own local settings. Rather, it is to see whether indigenous associations and institutions exist in forms that can be bridges or channels for propagating, developing, and sustaining faith in Christ (and to have the discernment to recognize that some types of association are antithetical to following Christ). At the same time, we also have the global church to draw on for establishing associations that are faithful to Christ.

So in contextualization we seek to utilize local resources and means, but we also draw on global resources and means. The goal is not really to attract people to the gospel by establishing foreign-looking and foreign-feeling institutions, but to take advantage of the human capacity (and need) to associate in ways that make sense locally and that can be utilized for faith nurture and maintenance.

Churches globally range from small house fellowships to massive megachurches; Scripture does not specify one model for all local fellowships. At the time of the New Testament, believers' gatherings in synagogues and in local houses were well known and widespread. Christians formed associations then in fluid and flexible ways, not bound by denominational hierarchy (there was a hierarchy from Jerusalem through the apostles, but it was clearly not the denominationalism that we know today). In a contemporary world of megachurches with vast worship complexes, we might do well to learn from the simplicity of local congregations in New Testament times.

Contextualizing How Christian Institutions Maintain Institutional Identity

Christian institutions maintain their identity by using a variety of means: circulating stories about their history or founder (Stahl 2010; Martin 1976), commitments to particular doctrines or catechetical practices, wearing symbolic jewelry such as crosses, dressing modestly (e.g., in rural Africa the Christian women generally refrain from wearing jeans and the like) or in specific Christian style (e.g., the dress of Zionists in South Africa), using specialized vocabulary or speech patterns ("Christianese").

How does understanding the ways Christian institutions establish and sustain their identity help us in contextualization? These vary widely around the world. For example, long-term Christian communities in Muslim settings, though sharing a common language such as Arabic, have in many cases over the centuries developed specialized religious vocabulary and language use that set them apart from their Arabic-speaking Muslim neighbors. Participation in public events such as marches on the streets on Saturdays or Sundays by African Initiated Churches serves as a boundary marker for the participants, as does the specialized clothing worn by Zionists in South Africa. Easter vigils such as carrying the cross and voluntarily undergoing torture by Filipino Christians cements the identity not only of the individuals undergoing the trials, but also of those who participate by following them along in their pilgrimage. Short-term mission trips from churches around the world make concrete for participants the needs and realities of the global church, and also bond the participants together, strengthening their association with one another and with those who send them.

All of these examples are specific instances of Christian institutions maintaining their own identity. But contextualization asks, Can we draw on the way *non-Christian* institutions do this where we live? For example, religious institutions around the world utilize specialized buildings (sweat lodges for Native Americans), furniture (the stand for the Qur'an), decorations (the architecture of Balinese Hindu temples), and traditions (removing shoes before entering a religious building) as means of maintaining identity. Most of these symbolic markers are not anti-Christian in and of themselves (think of the Christmas tree, which was not Christian in origin). Does that mean they can simply be co-opted?

Appropriate caution is necessary: often we do not understand the full implications of what will result when we try to adapt a local symbol for Christian use. As noted previously, we should neither blindly reproduce the means we see in the local setting nor simply bring what we know from our home setting. But at least we should be willing to ask whether local institutional markers can be properly used by local believers as forms of institutional practices that build and maintain Christian institutional identity.

Contextualizing How Christians Develop and Maintain Identity through Association

By now it should be clear to the reader that associations play a key role in developing and maintaining a Christian's identity. Association with a group that engages in rituals, dresses distinctively, and/or meets in unique establishments forces participants to engage in activities and actions that cement their identification with both the institution and their fellow participants. (In the discussion on the ritual dimension in chap. 9, we'll explore this in greater depth.)

What associations do you have that help you maintain who you are in Christ? You have a personal *relationship* with Christ, but what about the other Christ-followers with whom you are connected? Likely you go to church; perhaps you are part of a small-group Bible study or have a group of friends who are Christians with whom you hang out.

Picture yourself in a new setting, one that is radically different from yours. What types of associations do Christ-followers make in that setting? How do they connect? How do they separate themselves from others? What are the ways they develop and maintain their own identity as people who love and follow Christ? To answer these types of questions, we will turn briefly to identity theory.

Tim Green (2013a, 2013b) and Kathryn Kraft (2012) have helpfully applied contemporary identity theory to contextualization in a way that offers a better framing for the sharp debates about insider movements. While Green and Kathryn Kraft focus their scholarship on Muslims coming to Christ but still identifying as Muslims, identity theory can also help us better understand the Jesu bhaktas discussed above.

Green, having noted that identity theory is in many respects a complex minefield, follows identity theorist Benjamin Beit-Hallahmi (1989) in identifying three layers that shape identity (Green 2013a; see fig. 2.1 herein): (1) core identity, (2) social identity, and (3) collective identity. These layers are also associated with differing academic disciplinary discussions of identity. In broad brushstrokes, core (or ego) identity is who people believe themselves to be at their "core" (psychology). Social identity refers to a person's self-identity in relation to their groups and associations (social psychology and sociology). Collective identity is the identity of a group in the eyes of the world around them (anthropology). For a concise depiction with application to the insider movement among Muslims, see Don Little's *Effective Discipling in Muslim Contexts* (2015, 183–86).

As illustrated in figure 2.1, there are multiple ways people understand their identity. Following Green, I will describe them from the top down.

People are born into a *collective identity*. It might be national (Thailand), but it might also include a religious framing (e.g., "to be Thai is to be Buddhist"). Often a person born into a Muslim family in a Muslim country may well not want to identify as "Christian" following conversion simply because "Christian" is understood as Western, sexually immoral, and greedy. They have seen Westerners in media and heard about them from their teachers and friends (just as Westerners too often pick up from their friends and media the idea that most Muslims are terrorists).

In many societies, national or regional rituals are used to embed collective identity, such as the American Pledge of Allegiance. In our depiction of the

Figure 2.1: Levels of identity

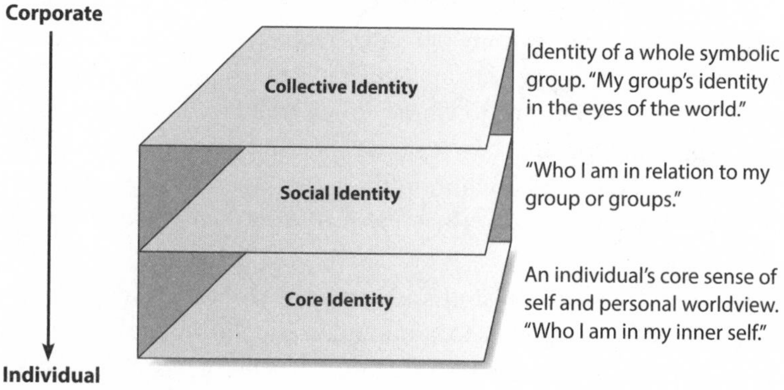

Corporate

Collective Identity — Identity of a whole symbolic group. "My group's identity in the eyes of the world."

Social Identity — "Who I am in relation to my group or groups."

Core Identity — An individual's core sense of self and personal worldview. "Who I am in my inner self."

Individual

Source: Little 2015, 183, figure 9.1

non-church movement in Japan, we noted that the Japanese framers of the statement of ethical injunctions anticipated that recitation of it by students in Japan would strengthen them in their Japanese identity and protect them from Christianity. Uchimura, as a Christian, could not submit to such a document, and his refusal created a national furor.

A person grows into a *social identity* through the process of socialization; "social identity is absorbed gradually by that person through actual relationships with 'significant others'" (Green 2013a, 46). This person's identity is linked to the identity of their household (including extended family), their neighborhoods, and the institutions they attend. In traditional Muslim societies, one is automatically assumed to be Muslim unless one specifically declares otherwise (thereby committing apostasy). The socialization traditionally provided in Muslim, Hindu, and Buddhist societies forms a cradle-to-grave protective shield for members. For all three groups, a ritual such as baptism is perceived to be a rejection of the entire system, including one's family. Is it not surprising that people from these groups take baptism more seriously than many in the West do? In today's flat, connected, and globalized world, traditional systems of security are eroding, as the global millennial generation reads, watches, and listens to things that challenge their social identity in ways their parents never experienced.

On the individual level, while our *core identity* is shaped by family, neighborhood, and nationality, people eventually come to face a choice of claiming or discarding the core identity with which they were raised. This core identity is typically assumed in many societies (you don't need to *become* a Buddhist since you were born one); yet without taking individual ownership of the identity, adherents may remain nominal adherents of their faith heritage.

Before the advent of global migration, this was not a concern, since people typically lived and died in their birth community. In today's world, however, the core identity poses a significant challenge for migrants who have moved to countries of a different dominant religion. Green observes:

> Some second generation British Muslims have chosen to locate their core identity not in the cultural Islam of their parents but in an intensified personal Islam, a standpoint which allows them to critique their parental traditions on the one hand and their British environment on the other. Others have opted to reject Islam and declare themselves as "ex-Muslims." Still others resolve their identity crises through conversion to Christ. "I had always struggled with having two identities; I didn't know what I was," one British Pakistani woman told me. "When I became a Christian, it gave me one united identity. It was astounding!" (Green 2013a, 47)

Identifying three layers of identity provides a tool to better understand such things as insider movements. For example, a question that identity theory helps us better articulate is whether a core-level commitment to Christ *necessitates* a social-level commitment to Christianity. This is crucial in settings where the church is a minority that is significantly different socially, economically, and politically from the social setting of the convert. Proponents of insider movements argue that we should not dislocate people and thus destroy the natural bridges of witness that remain intact as long as they remain part of the social identity. Opponents argue for the gospel demand that all believers be ready to pay the price for coming to Christ, and that to try to remain in their religious social circles is a betrayal of Jesus himself. There are no indications that this issue will be resolved in the near future; recent reflections about multireligious identity and the very idea of conversion from one religion to another show that missiologists continue to learn and wrestle with the underlying questions (Richard 2015).

Kinship

Kinship is a subset of association, built around marriage, biological progeny, and extended biological relationships. As a subset of association, the framing, issues, and questions we discussed in exploring the association system apply to kinship. However, kinship is so deeply embedded in societies and so significant that anthropologists have long treated it separately from association. Rather than review the associational elements we just examined, in this section I focus on the peculiarities of kinship as it relates to contextualization.

A society that does not reproduce does not continue. Kinship is the vehicle through which this reproduction is worked out in that society. Association is how people connect in general; kinship is focused on biological connections through marriage, lineage and inheritance, kinship roles, and ancestral obligations. I briefly explore each in turn.

Marriage

In societies around the world we find arranged marriages, love marriages, luck marriages, and marriages of political or other convenience (to cement alliances or to make immigration possible). In many parts of the world romantic love is not the bottom line for marriage. Instead, it's fit—and that fit is determined based on such things as family honor, obligation, opportunity, and reciprocity. Potentially these may be determined in light of religious teaching, not just social convention or political opportunity. And in many societies, marriage is not just a fit of the individuals; it's also the fit of each individual's extended kin. Marriage then becomes a joining of two extended families rather than a joining of two individuals.

When unmarried people come to faith in Christ, finding a mate in a non-Christian setting is a challenge. The case study at the end of this chapter clearly illustrates the dilemma in an Indian setting.

Additionally, there may be religious obligations and sanctions to consider, such as the traditional taboo against marrying across caste lines in Hindu settings, or allowing a Muslim man to marry a non-Muslim woman but not letting a Muslim woman marry a non-Muslim man (since the male determines the religious lineage for Muslims).

Another important kinship contextual issue is divorce. What are the rules and regulations about divorce in Buddhist settings versus Christian teaching? And how do those operate in secular settings? How do you know someone is divorced, and what stigmas are attached to divorce? Are those who are divorced able to marry again?

While every society in the world opposes incest, how each defines it differs. This plays a role in whom a person can marry. Leviticus 18:6 prohibits sexual relations with close relatives. Islam prohibits such relations between not only close relatives but also those who have taken breast milk from the same person. Hindus forbid marriage within the same *gotra* (clan).

Marriage is a crucial component of the kinship system; understanding the way people in your setting think about and practice marriage customs is an important step in contextualization.

Lineage and Inheritance

Religious beliefs can play a significant role in beliefs about lineage and inheritance. For example, traditionally for Hindus the idea of religious conversion made little sense. After all, they reasoned, you were born into your current state because of your karma (the accumulated merit or demerit gained/lost in your previous lives). Conversion to a new religion is in effect an attempt to change your karma, which you cannot do. You cannot voluntarily change caste in India: you are simply born into the caste your karma requires.

As previously noted, Muslim men have relative freedom to marry non-Muslim wives because any children they produce are automatically Muslim. Traditionally, Muslim women do not have the same option. This follows the pattern of most societies: the children are the inheritance of the father more often than of the mother.

We see a similar pattern in religious inheritance regulations. In Jewish law at the time of the Bible, the firstborn son received double the inheritance of the other sons—but the daughters were left out unless there was no son. During a normal life, it was assumed that a daughter would marry and would benefit from her husband's inheritance, so her needs were not perceived to be the same as the husband's.

Societies also differ in relation to the inheritance of social and religious roles. Do sons or daughters succeed their fathers or mothers who are religious leaders? In collective settings this can be a challenge. For example, Pastor David Yonggi Cho, former pastor of the Yoido Full Gospel Church (the largest church in the world), has been plagued with charges of privatizing church property and ensuring that his wife and children keep control. In a personal conversation with a Korean Christian in 2006, I was told that Pastor Cho had announced he would retire at a certain age. That age came and went without his retirement. My friend informed me that Pastor Cho's family would not allow him to retire because they knew that a nonfamily member taking over would threaten their positions of significant leadership in the church and church-affiliated businesses. In 2014, Pastor Cho was convicted of embezzlement in a scheme with his son (R. Moon 2014). While some have placed the blame entirely on the son for the scheme, clearly the son was not the only one involved. This is one example of kinship inheritance of roles and obligations in the church gone awry.

What contextualization concerns can we see in the case of Pastor Cho and his family? We might start by exploring the role collectivism and in-group obligations played. Further, Korean society is Confucian, and a Confucian concept of relationships not only pervades the Korean church but also may well have played a significant role in its contemporary success story (see Lee 2011). We might well ask, What role did Confucian values of the ruler-subject and/or father-son play in putting Pastor Cho's family into positions of significant influence in the church? and How do these roles continue to play out in other Korean churches? Further, what difference does it make if Confucian relational ideals and values undergird the contemporary growth of the Korean church? Is that syncretism or contextualization?

Kinship Roles

In collective cultures, kinship is a vehicle of in-groups and out-groups. This plays out in such things as nepotism. In the individualistic United States we deplore nepotism, arguing that people should be given jobs (or other opportunities) on the basis of their qualifications rather than on the basis of their relatives. However, in many parts of the world nepotism is a positive social value rather than a negative one. People who are collective may reason, "Why wouldn't I hire somebody who's of my kin? I already know and trust that person's family; I know the type of work they're going to do. Plus if I don't hire her, my family will be unhappy with me." As previously reported, Pastor Cho's family was deeply embedded in the enterprise of Yoido Full Gospel Church and greatly benefited by their relationship with Pastor Cho. And as so often seen in settings around the world, religious "dynasties" are established by a powerful figure whose children then receive significant responsibilities and opportunities in ministry because of the founder's power and authority.

Not all kinship is biological. Christians rightly refer to each other as brother and sister: we are all part of the body of Christ and spiritual relatives of one another. Paul offers dozens of "each other" obligations through his epistles, many connected to our spiritual kinship (e.g., Gal. 6:2, "Carry each other's burdens, and in this way you will fulfill the law of Christ"). In chapter 7, I return to this idea, there framing it in terms of ethical obligations given in the New Testament of Christians toward the body of Christ. Anthropologists refer to these types of nonbiological ("fictitious") kinship as ritual kinship (Ishino 1953, 695): "The true or 'biological' kinship role is one which is automatically ascribed to a person by the sheer fact of his being born into a particular network of relatives. By contrast, a ritual kin role is always one that is achieved. A person is assigned a ritual kin role because he earns the right to membership or because he is appointed to membership by others" (697).

The Japanese practice a type of ritual kinship known as *oyabun-kobun*, "in which persons usually unrelated by close kin ties enter into a compact to assume obligations of a diffuse nature similar to those ascribed to members of one's immediate family" (Ishino 1953, 696). This system "provides the framework for integrating the activities of a group of people engaged in a common activity" (697). The contextualization question one may ask is, How might the *oyabun-kobun* system parallel (or not!) the spiritual kinship of Christ-followers for Japanese?

Ancestral Obligations

The final kinship system to consider is perhaps the most challenging. It concerns the systems of obligations and the perceived ongoing relationships with departed ancestors. Africans and Asians face this far more acutely than Americans or Europeans: African ancestors are the "living dead" (Mbiti 1991) who continue to interact with the family, guiding them, disciplining them, rejoicing with them, and weeping with them. Many Asians grow up with significant memories of rituals and other obligations offered to their ances-tors and embodied in celebrations such as the Chinese tomb-sweeping day celebrated in early April. For many in the majority world, the belief that the dead continue to be interested and involved in their descendants' lives is un-assailable. Evangelicals from Asia (Ro 1985; Park and Müller 2014; Paulin 2014) and Africa (see the discussion on Christ as ancestor in chap. 11) continue to wrestle with the pervasive beliefs and practices, especially with developing appropriate contextual responses. As I have noted elsewhere, the challenge is

SIDEBAR 2.2
QUESTIONS ABOUT KINSHIP

My intention in asking the following questions is to equip you to find biblically ap-propriate and culturally sound ways for Christians to understand local approaches to kinship. They help you avoid the danger of simply understanding kinship in ways that make sense from your own cultural setting. As you ask these questions, also be asking yourself how the answers impact what type of kinship ideals for Christians might make sense to local people without compromising their relationship with Christ.

1. What kinship values and practices are found here? What types of marriage, adoption, inheritance, or other kin-focused roles and practices exist?
2. What roles can (or must) be inherited within lineage?
3. What rules are for marriage and family?
   a. What rituals or practices precede marriage?
   b. Who is eligible for marriage (e.g., age limits, incest regulations, multiple husbands or wives, "spirit" marriages)?
   c. What are lineage rights for husband and wife?
   d. What happens to a widow or widower?
   e. Are roles predefined for either spouse if the other becomes a religious leader?
4. Are there fictitious or ritual kinship relations? If so, what are they?
5. How do religious adherents relate to nonkin?
6. How are barriers to and options for kinship supported by local religious beliefs?
7. What symbols are used to identify kin relations?
   a. Which (if any) among these symbols might be repurposed for use by Christians?
   b. Which symbols should Christians avoid?
8. In what ways does the gospel condone or condemn indigenous kinship values and practices?

finding ways to enable Christian communities to obey the fifth commandment (honoring mother and father) in their cultural context without violating warnings against contact with the dead (e.g., Lev. 19:31; 20:6, 27; Deut. 18:9–14, and 1 Sam. 28:3–20). Proposed answers have ranged from simply declaring ancestral practices Christian to abolishing them altogether. The missionary's main role is not to make decisions for the local community, but to assist that community in going to the Scriptures for guidance in evaluating the cultural beliefs and practices in light of God's revelation. (Moreau 2000a)

Questions about Kinship

Sidebar 2.2 (like sidebar 2.1) offers several questions to consider in relation to kinship and lineage in your setting. Asking and exploring the answers to these questions will enable you to better understand local examples of kinship in your context—yet more importantly help you think more clearly about church and the ways Christians might use the kinship system as a vehicle of Christian discipleship.

Conclusion

Association and kinship are foundational for every society. Understanding how the associational and kinship systems operate in a society is necessary for appropriate contextualization. We all associate with some and not with others, and every church is ultimately an association of people mutually committed to Christ. It is crucial to understand the church as an association and recognize the ways associations offer identity to the church and to individual church members.

Kinship plays a foundational role in how we associate and who we perceive ourselves to be. We all value kinship even though our definitions of kin vary widely. In the case study for this chapter, I invite you to consider the element of identity in light of a collective approach so that you can better identify with a challenge you may well face in living cross-culturally.

CASE STUDY

CONVERSION OR SOCIAL CONVENTION?
PAUL G. HIEBERT

"Leela is already twenty-one, and by our customs she should have been married five or six years ago. It is not good for a woman to remain unmarried in the village. Already the people look down on Leela and suggest that she is cursed by the gods and brings bad luck. Soon the people will accuse her of prostitution. So it is urgent that we arrange a marriage for her right away. But we are now Christians, and there are no Christian young men of our caste for her to marry. We have searched widely. The only good prospect is Krishna, a young Hindu who is willing to become a Christian if we give Leela to him as his wife. Is it sin if we marry Leela to him? Is his conversion genuine if he becomes a Christian in order to marry Leela?"

Virginia Stevens looked at the anxious mother who was pouring out her heart to her. Then she looked at the young woman sitting expectantly on the mat before her. What should she say?

For years the Lutheran missionaries had worked in Andhra Pradesh on the east coast of South India. They had many converts, but most had come from the *harijan*, or untouchable castes. A few scattered individuals had become Christians from the lower clean castes, but none from the high castes.

Then a leading South Indian evangelist, a converted Brahmin from the highest caste, held meetings in the area, and five families of Reddys became Christians. The Reddys are farmers and rank high in the caste order. Because of their land holdings, they are wealthy and control much of the regional politics.

The new Christians met in a house church led by Venkat Reddy, one of the converts. He was well educated and could read the Scriptures, but he knew little about Christian doctrine and practice. So he contacted Sam and Virginia Stevens, Lutheran missionaries serving in Guntur, a hundred miles away. They visited the new church and encouraged it in its new faith. They also spent time with Venkat Reddy to help him grow in his understanding of Christianity. The church had grown spiritually and had won three other Reddy families to Christ, but one urgent problem persisted. How should the parents arrange marriages for their children?

Indian village culture requires that parents marry their children to members of their own caste. To marry outside of caste carries a great social stigma. Those involved and their families are put out of caste and shunned. Even the untouchables will have little to do with them. But there were few Reddy Christians, and many of the new converts could find no Christian Reddys to marry their children. There were many Christian young people in the old established churches, but they were all *harijans*, and it was unheard of for Reddys to marry untouchables. To do so would bring disgrace on the Christian Reddy families and cut them off totally from their non-Christian relatives. The door for further evangelism among the Reddys would then be largely closed.

Three years had passed since the Reddy congregation was formed, and the problem was becoming more acute as the young men and women grew older. One young man ran away from home and married a Christian woman he met in college. She was from an untouchable background, so they moved to the city of Madras where they could hide from the censure of their rural communities. But this had caused great pain to the young man's parents, who remained in the village.

Then a distant relative of Leela approached her parents about the possibility of Leela marrying their son. Ram and Shanta, Leela's parents at first said no, that a Christian should not marry a non-Christian. But two months later, when the relative returned and said that Krishna, the young man in question, was willing to become a Christian and be baptized if the marriage took place, they began to reconsider.

Ram was not sure. "He will become a Christian in name only," he said.

"But he will listen to us and to Leela," said Shanta. "She is a strong Christian, and can help him grow in faith. Look at her! She's well past the age of marriage. If we pass up this opportunity, she may never get married. You don't want to condemn her to that, do you?"

Ram looked at Leela, his only daughter, and said, "I know. But we have always said that our Christian God would care for us in important matters such as this. Certainly he can provide us a Christian husband."

The next time the evangelist came to the village, Ram Reddy asked him if there were any Christian Reddy men in other parts of Andhra for his daughter. He also made several trips himself to distant towns in search of a husband. But none of his efforts turned up a suitable groom.

It was then that Krishna Reddy's father approached Ram and Shanta, urging them to arrange the marriage and reminding them that his son was willing to become a Christian and be baptized before the wedding. Ram and Shanta began to wonder whether this was God's way of opening the door for their daughter's marriage. Or was this a temptation they had to resist? Was such a conversion genuine? Did God want them to marry Leela to a Christian from an "untouchable" background instead? Could they bear the shame and ostracism that this would bring upon them in the village?

Now, as Virginia heard Shanta's story, she realized that the problem affected not only these parents, but also the future of the church among the Reddys. If Christians could not find spouses for their children, many Reddys would be afraid to convert. On the other hand, what did the Scriptures mean when it said that Christians should not be unequally yoked with unbelievers? Would Krishna's conversion be genuine if he took baptism so that he could marry Leela? What would happen if such marriages became an accepted practice in the Reddy church? And how would she feel if her own daughter were denied marriage because her mother herself had become a Christian? Virginia breathed a prayer before she responded. . . .

Reprinted with permission from Hiebert and Hiebert 1987, 161–63.

THE SOCIAL DIMENSION AS EXCHANGE

ECONOMICS

In every human society people produce and exchange goods, services, and statuses. Each of these is a type of "capital" that can be created, grown, valued, exchanged, devalued, or diminished. How people understand, value, and regulate the production and exchange of these types of capital is a deeply contextual reality that happens not only in the society but also in churches. In the United States, for example, churches and other religious institutions are responsible for generating their own financial resources, and many do so through contributions from those who regularly benefit from the services that their churches provide, from the spiritual nurture of the worship service to pastoral calls on the sick and infirm. We may also question the popular stereotype of Christians pledging themselves to God's service if he will allow them to escape extenuating circumstances or provide a miracle such as healing a loved one—and how often that is an important motivation in personal decisions for Christian service (or not, when the petition remains unanswered).

While Christians may react viscerally when asked to consider prayer as a type of exchange, many treat it just that way. We use prayer as a type of social capital exchange: we offer devotion or worship and anticipate answers or blessings of some form or another. We see this in its most crass form through some of the prosperity gospel messages in which followers are urged to give money, usually to the leader, with the expectation that God will return their contributions to them tenfold. Prayer is not the only vehicle of such exchange. At many levels we can see that such activities as mentoring/coaching/discipling, community service projects, services among the poor, social action on behalf of the oppressed, and the like are all activities involving some type of capital and its exchange.

To all of this we may add that the next generation of Americans is more in tune with the realities of issues of social power and the role such power (a form of capital) plays in the structural systems of our globalized world—inappropriately advantaging a few while simultaneously and significantly disadvantaging the rest. How might this all work out in contextualization? In the rest of this chapter we'll focus on capital and exchange in general, religious capital and exchange, and the implications for contextualization.

Capital and Exchange in Society

The exchange institution refers not only to the generation, acquisition, and exchange of social capital in and of themselves; it also refers to the rules and regulations that govern those exchanges. Many who read the word "capital" think first of "money," and indeed that is certainly a type of capital. But there are many other types of capital, which for contextual analysis I have split into four categories: monetary, political, social, and spiritual. We could consider political and spiritual capital as types of social capital, but because of the role they play in contextualization, I will treat each separately in the following discussion.

Monetary Capital

Monetary capital includes both money and possessions. In addition to the US dollar, the Euro, the Korean won, and the Kenyan shilling, monetary capital also includes material things that cost or represent money. This includes such things as mobile phones, vehicles, homes, property, clothing, and jewelry. The system of exchange of monetary capital in the West has been a market-driven approach. As Eloise Meneses notes, "The gospel of capitalism is that through hard work, saving, careful accounting, and, above all else, self-reliance, anyone can become materially wealthy, so long as the system that is based on private property and free exchange is maintained" (2015, 18).

Political Capital

Political capital is related to social status and having authority to lead others. In the positive sense, it can be seen in the goodwill that political leaders enjoy making decisions on behalf of those they lead. It can also refer to the social weight of a politician's patrons or clients. The patrons may be behind the scenes or very public. Typically, however, the clients (or followers) are the visible public face of a politician's capital or social power, as seen in votes and activist campaigns. In political circles around the world, people offer and receive political favors. This is often an informal and yet potentially ironclad system of give-and-take that permeates politics.

Social Capital

Social capital refers to the level of status or respect you have based on who you are or what you have done. You are born into a level of social capital (whether low or high), and you can gain and lose it. For example, people who receive a college degree have access to jobs and opportunities that those without a degree will not have. People who have great monetary wealth often have great social capital as an accompaniment, especially when their monetary wealth spans generations and when they have used their wealth to better society in ways that make sense to them (e.g., patrons of the arts do this by donating money to artistic causes and to artists themselves). The richest people in many societies have and employ significant social capital: they may well be the patrons behind the more visible political leaders even if they themselves remain behind the scenes.

One facet of social capital is linking capital assets: the links or connections people have with others. For example, people around the world rely on linking capital when looking for jobs or other economic opportunities. Colleges and universities have alumni associations that provide linking capital for their alumni, and they ask their alumni to offer linking capital to new graduates who are just entering the job market. Like other forms of social capital, people are born into a network of linking capital but can also develop their own linking capital by such choices as religious affiliation, educational background, and employment history. Some people are natural networkers who become social "gates" for others, helping them make connections and broaden their own networks. Just as positive relations increase social capital, so too negative relations (or broken relationships) can result in a loss of social capital. Cross-cultural workers who initiate relationships with people of low social capital run the risk of being locked out of relationships with the power brokers in a society; yet Jesus calls us to the outcasts. The juxtaposition of these realities can create significant tension when members of the same team choose to pursue relationships with people in social networks on opposite ends of the social capital scale. For example, trying to develop simultaneous social relationships with both Brahmin (high caste) and Dalits (outcasts) in India is challenging at best.

Spiritual Capital

We might be tempted to equate spiritual capital with religious capital, but in contemporary Western society "spirituality" is less frequently identified specifically as religious than it was previously. A more secular approach to

SIDEBAR 3.1
QUESTIONS ABOUT CAPITAL AND EXCHANGE

Below are some questions to consider as you explore capital production and exchange in your setting. Asking and exploring the answers to these questions will enable you to better understand local examples of capital and how it is exchanged—but more importantly help you think more clearly about church and the means Christians may use to generate various types of capital and exchange it with one another and with other members in their societies in light of local societal norms.

As I noted in the previous chapter, answers to these questions could be used to compromise the gospel or the biblical definition of church. That is not my intention. Rather, the questions equip you to find biblically appropriate and culturally sound ways for Christians to understand local views of capital and its exchange with other Christians. They help you avoid the danger of simply generating and using only the types of capital that make sense from your own cultural setting. As you ask these questions, also be asking yourself how the answers impact what type of Christian capital and exchange might make sense to local people without compromising their relationship with Christ.

1. What types of capital are found here? For each type, is it seen as limited, or can they create more of it? If the latter, what are ways to increase that type of capital?
2. What are symbolic markers of capital and capital exchange? Which among these symbols might be repurposed for use by Christians? Which symbols should Christians avoid?
3. What are formal and informal regulations for capital exchange?
4. How do religious capital obligations affect economic status?
5. How is capital used inside and outside religious institutions (including the church)?
6. How does capital stratification affect religious function?
7. What ways does the gospel condone or condemn indigenous capital use and standards?

spiritual capital includes ideas and practices that benefit all humans and help them grow, develop, nurture others, and flourish. Things bringing purpose to life, benefiting others, and uplifting fellow human beings are the types of capital that fit this category. Exchange of this type of capital includes the sharing of helpful ideas and practices, the promotion of good thinking, and so on. Naftali Brawer, a Jewish rabbi, notes his approach: "We promote a spirituality that inspires greater meaning, purpose and holism in one's life. This is achieved through a commitment to ethics, diversity, social responsibility and the environment" (Brawer, n.d.).

Without making a value judgment on this approach to spiritual capital, we note that it has an increasing presence in Western secular societies, which have cast themselves adrift from traditional religious teachings and values.

Questions about Capital and Exchange

With these four types of capital in mind, as an introductory overview, sidebar 3.1 provides questions to answer when trying to understand capital and its exchange in cross-cultural settings.

Capital and Exchange in Scripture

With a general orientation toward types of capital and their exchange in mind, what examples do we see in Scripture? Bear in mind that the economies of the biblical world were not market exchange but reciprocity based (see below under "Implications for Contextualization"), so the idea that people generated and had social value that could be exchanged was natural for the biblical authors. It is not surprising that social capital and capital exchange permeate the entire story arc of the Bible. I'll point out just a few explicit examples.

Jesus acknowledges the value of our souls in relation to the entire world in Matthew 16:26: "What good will it be for someone to gain the whole world, yet forfeit their soul?" Thus our souls are so valuable that no material exchange can match their value.

We see the exchange of social capital in Paul's Corinthian correspondence: "We have spoken freely to you, Corinthians, and opened wide our hearts to you. We are not withholding our affection from you, but you are withholding yours from us. As a fair exchange—I speak as to my children—open wide your hearts also" (2 Cor. 6:11–13). In this passage Paul views affection as a type of commodity that merits recognition and regulation in its exchange. Paul appeals to fairness in asking his readers to open their hearts to him. In his later correspondence with the same church, he notes, "Now I am ready to visit you for the third time, and I will not be a burden to you, because what I want is not your possessions but you. After all, children should not have to save up for their parents, but parents for their children. So I will very gladly spend for you everything I have and expend myself as well. If I love you more, will you love me less?" (2 Cor. 12:14–15).

Here Paul intermingles different types of capital: social, relational, spiritual, and monetary. He does not want to be an economic burden to them because he does not want them to feel obliged to meet his economic needs. Paul wants them to understand that his relationship with them is not one that demands equality in the exchange of various types of capital. Rather, like a responsible parent, he gives out of the grace that God has given to him, and they receive out of the same grace granted to them through Paul.

Paul's Letter to Philemon offers a fascinating case study of the use of social capital in the days of the New Testament. Those (like me) from North America can miss so much of this epistle because we don't see it in terms of capital and the exchange of capital. The basic story line is that Onesimus is a runaway slave who has come to a relationship with Christ. He has been of great help to Paul while Paul is in prison. Having come to faith, Onesimus is apparently considering returning to his owner (Philemon). Paul not only knows Philemon but also led him to Christ. A significant goal of Paul in this short epistle is to plead for Philemon to spare Onesimus from the rightful penalty for running away: death.

Table 3.1
Types of "Capital" in Philemon 1:8–22

Economic	Social	Linking	Spiritual
Charge it to me. (v. 18)	I prefer to appeal to you on the basis of love. (v. 9)	He could take your place in helping me. (v. 13)	[He] is my very heart. (v. 12)
I will pay it back. (v. 19)	He has become useful both to you and me. (v. 11)		I am in chains for the gospel. (v. 13)
Prepare a guest room for me. (v. 22)	Any favor you do would be voluntary. (v. 14)	He is very dear to me but even dearer to you. (v. 16)	You might have him back forever—no longer as a slave, but . . . as a dear brother. (vv. 15–16)
	If you consider me a partner, welcome him. (v. 17)		You owe me your very self. (v. 19)
	I . . . [know] you will do even more than I ask. (v. 21)		I may have some benefit from you in the Lord. (v. 20)
			I hope to be restored in answer to your prayers. (v. 22)

In table 3.1 I have noted from the verses in the epistle the types of capital Paul mentions and offers in exchange. When he talks about Onesimus as "My very heart" (v. 12) and reminds Philemon, "I am in chains for the gospel" (v. 11), he is clearly using every bit of social capital he can bring to the task. Paul is not above reminding Philemon of his obligation to Paul: "You owe me your very self" (v. 19). In English we could say that he is "punching all of his tickets" or "cashing in all his coupons." Paul's choice of vocabulary and reminders throughout build a significant case and a heavy honor debt on Philemon to spare Onesimus's life. We do not know with certainty the result of Paul's appeal, but commentators posit that it was granted (e.g., O'Brien 1982, 268).

Paul used any and every type of capital he could to grant the release of Onesimus: he utilized the exchange system for the good of the gospel. How, then, might contemporary Christians utilize local approaches to capital and exchange? To that we next turn our attention.

Implications for Contextualization

To set the stage, it will help to notice that there are basically two significant philosophies of exchange in operation globally today: market-driven (capitalism) exchange and reciprocal (gift-giving) exchange (Meneses 2015). It will further help to keep in mind that reciprocal exchange differs from barter and trade: "Reciprocity is not the same as barter and trade, although goods and services of equal value are also exchanged in barter. The difference is in the relationship of the contracting parties. In balanced reciprocity, there is an ongoing social relationship between the two parties, while in barter and trade, as in the market system, the relationship ends as soon as the economic transaction ends" (Tan 2015, 96).

Even in market-driven economies such as those found in the West, both systems operate simultaneously. For example, at Christmas many Christians use market-driven capitalism to purchase gifts that they then give away to (or exchange with) their loved ones and others to whom they feel obligated (see Meneses 2015). Christians in the West have tended to assume that a market-driven approach to an exchange system best fits the Bible.

However, if forced to choose one over the other, the societies in the biblical narrative are much better understood through the lens of communal reciprocity than the lens of individualistic capitalism. Meneses explains:

> The Bible reminds us repeatedly to value our connection to God and community. Rarely does the Bible admonish us to "stand on your own two feet" or

"take care of your own business." Independence is generally viewed as a threat.
Dependence on God and interdependence with others are commended. . . .

This understanding of the relationship between individuals and groups is
far clearer in reciprocal societies than it is in capitalist ones. The value on community life found in the Bible mirrors the principles of reciprocity much more
closely than those of market-based exchange. Individualism in the West tears
friends and family asunder in the pursuit of personal success. (2015, 14–15)

If we grant Meneses's point, then contextualization of exchange systems
that adheres to biblical values will shape people toward connection with God
and community rather than away from them toward independent wealth.
Consider, for example, that most missionaries are financially dependent on
supporters at home for their income and completely independent of the communities in which they live. Our "faith support" approach to missions, then,
has the potential to alienate us from the very people we come to serve.

Contextualizing Monetary Capital

While Paul noted that "the love of money is a root of all kinds of evil"
(1 Tim. 6:10), he did not propose that we do away with it altogether. Rather, as
he explained, eagerness to become rich is a trap that Christians should avoid.
"Christians have always cooperated with human systems, whether social,
political, or economic, for the purpose of meeting people's needs. But an open
consideration of the fundamental propositions of those systems is critical to
maintaining an independent stance as Christians and to involving ourselves in
practices that are truly reflective of the kingdom of God" (Meneses 2015, 2).

Perhaps one of the biggest challenges to contextualizing Christian thinking
and practice in monetary capital is the simple fact that our Western orientation toward market-driven capitalism is assumed to be biblical and is largely
unchallenged (for challenges to our assumptions, see Bonk 2007; Cheong
and Meneses 2015). Many who serve as missionaries have never been trained
or taught to consider more deeply their own assumptions about monetary
capital, and so it largely remains an unexplored area. Cheong identifies one
component of the challenge: "For the West, the ethos of individualism has
combined with a privatizing impulse to produce a faith that is personalized
and customized. In so doing, economic aspects of Christianity such as tithing,
benevolence or aid, and funding for church projects have become relocated to
the 'private' sphere of the church, and church and Christian life have become
separated from the public and secular world" (Cheong 2015, 70).

As if this were not already sufficiently complicated, we add that even
when a market-based approach is implemented, the surface may change,

but underneath the old system remains intact, leading to behaviors deemed unethical by the missionary and yet necessary by the local. As Tan points out, "Even though governments may attempt to modernize their economies, market capitalism may merely be overlaid on top of a society that has a reciprocity- or patronage-based system underneath. Here the old system may continue to work away from the public view, even as the new system seems to be in place" (Tan 2015, 106).

Given the insights of Cheong and Tan, we may need to reconsider long-held ideals such as the "self-financing" of indigenous churches. Self-financing is one of the three components of indigenous churches (the other two are self-governing and self-propagating) promoted over the past 150 years by Christians in mission. It expresses the ideal that all the work and ministry of an indigenous church should be funded from local resources. However, the definition of self-financing has been based on Western market-driven, privatized economic terms rather than on the ideals of reciprocity. A possible result is that an indigenous church may indeed be self-financed by Western standards, but the approach it uses for becoming financially independent could be market driven in such a way that it cuts the church off from the community in which it resides.

One area in which deep contextual thinking is needed is that of financial accountability. The approach used in Western settings is clearly market driven and individualistic, based on the idea that one can be accountable without having an actual relationship. The accountability comes through adherence to standards and reporting on that adherence, possibly vetted by an external entity (such as an accounting firm). This approach is not inherently evil, but it is clearly culturally derived. Further, it should be clear by now that this will not play out well in reciprocity-based societies, where relationships are the vehicle through which accountability plays out.

At a conference at which Korean and North American mission leaders gathered to consider perspectives on accountability (the proceedings are in Bonk et al. 2011), a Korean participant helpfully noted that US accounting is based on what he called "policy-economics" while Koreans approach accountability from the vantage point of "relational economics." By policy economics, he meant that Americans have a policy manual, and they stick to it no matter the relationship of the parties involved. Thus the policy manual acts as a type of Bible that governs decisions no matter what the relationships are. He explained that Koreans, by contrast, affirm the policy manual, but they understand and implement it in light of the relationship of the parties involved.

As I understand it, this Korean mission leader was indirectly noticing that the American approach is market driven and individualistic, while the Korean approach is reciprocity based and collective. Americans working for Korean mission agencies have experienced this firsthand, as have Koreans working for American mission agencies. This is just as much a challenge for American agencies working in Korea as it is for Korean agencies working in the United States. In what ways should Americans working in Korea operate their administrative roles more like Koreans, and in what ways should Koreans working in the United States operate their administrative roles more like Americans? It is much easier to posit the questions than to answer them! In an increasingly globalized world, these questions will remain relevant for the foreseeable future.

Contextualizing Political Capital

Political capital, especially as seen in leadership, is also found in churches. On the national level, well-known Christian leaders such as Billy Graham wield significant political capital not only within the church but outside it as well. In more local contexts, this is also true for significant church leaders such as David Yonggi Cho in Korea (before he was convicted of embezzling: because of his prominence the sentence was relatively lenient) and Desmond Tutu in South Africa.

Tutu's case is particularly enlightening. After the overthrow of apartheid in South Africa, a major challenge for the new government was bringing justice over the atrocities committed. The government established the Truth and Reconciliation Commission, tasked with providing opportunities for both victims and victimizers to hear from each other and find ways to move toward resolution. As of November 2000, over 7,000 amnesty decisions had been made. While the majority (almost 5,400) refused amnesty, almost 850 were granted (TRC, n.d.). Heralded as an unprecedented approach to dealing with atrocities, and one based on Christian concepts of justice and forgiveness, Tutu was appointed to the chair role, overseeing the amnesty hearings and decisions.

This contextual approach to some of the worst examples of human brokenness on record is certainly more than just an example of the use of political capital (it incorporates the ethical, ritual, and theological dimensions). However, it does offer a clear perspective on the contextual use of political capital in the pursuit of justice, forgiveness, and reconciliation on a national level, whether or not the ultimate goal of reconciliation was actually accomplished (see Gathogo 2012).

Contextualizing Social Capital

As noted above, social capital is connected to the level of social status one has. In many of the world's societies, this is closely linked to the concept of honor and honor's counterpart, shame. Ruth Lienhard explains the difference between them: "Honor is a basic cultural value. Shame is a mechanism for punishment and keeping individuals in line" (Lienhard 2001, 133).

In many Asian settings the term "face" is commonly used, and it is always important in such societies to maintain and (when possible) increase face. Over the past thirty years, increasing attention has been given to honor and shame in the Bible (e.g., DeSilva 1995, 2000; Neyrey 1998; Malina 2001; Gosnell 2006; Georges 2010; Watson 2010; Mudge 2014), as well as in contemporary Asian (Francis 1992; Wu 2012), African (Mbuvi 2002), and Middle Eastern societies (DeVries 2007). Missiologists have analyzed the impact of honor/shame in Christian ministry (Wu 2012, 2016; Georges and Baker 2016) and have organized networks (honorshame.com) and conferences around the issue.

To the extent that honor is a form of social capital, and to the extent that this played a significant role in biblical cultures and continues to play a significant role in many societies today, it is important for us to consider the implications for contextual ministry in cross-cultural settings. As we do so, however, we must also keep in mind that the ways societies frame and account for honor (and parallel forms of social capital) vary widely. "Honor killings" are not found among Asians with Confucian orientations; ancestral veneration as an expression of filial piety is not valued in Middle Eastern settings. Given these realities, contextualized approaches to social capital and exchange will vary widely around the world.

Communicating Christ in Honor-Based Societies

In societies where honor is a form of social capital, how might Christ be better communicated? Mark Strand, after a decade of work in China, observed that introducing the biblical concept of sin is a challenge in China in part because of "the group mentality of Chinese people, where wrong is determined primarily by consequent negative social implications rather than by failure to live up to some fixed standard. Chinese people decide if something is wrong based on personal and relational consequences more than on propositional and abstract principles" (2000, 430).

From the vantage point of social capital, shame only happens when people lose face, and this only happens when social norms are violated. Communicating "sin" in this setting as an abstract standard (commonly done in the West) will likely miscommunicate. As many note, the definition of sin needs to be put into context for a Chinese audience. One way this can be accomplished is by using terms related to filial piety, with which a Chinese audience resonates (see Strand 2000, 436–38).

Glen Francis (1992), working in Taiwan, proposed an adaptation of the Four Spiritual Laws based on Chinese thinking. In table 3.2, I place his proposed set of laws side by side with the American version of the Four Spiritual Laws so that readers unfamiliar with the American version can see the differences.

Table 3.2

Four Spiritual Laws Contextualized for Taiwan

Four spiritual laws in American context (Cru, n.d.)	Four spiritual laws for Taiwanese context (Francis 1992)
Law 1: God loves you and offers a wonderful plan for your life.	Law 1: God the Father loves all the people of the world and wants them to be in his family.
Law 2: Man is sinful and separated from God. Therefore, he cannot know and experience God's love and plan for his life.	Law 2: But people are disobedient and do not remember to show filial love to God the Father, so they now have no face.
Law 3: Jesus Christ is God's only provision for man's sin. Through him you can know and experience God's love and plan for your life.	Law 3: The only way back to God the Father is to become a righteous people.
Law 4: We must individually receive Jesus Christ as Savior and Lord; then we know and experience God's love and plan for our lives.	Law 4: The only way to become a righteous person is to come to the man on the cross.

In his adapted version, Francis focuses on the familial terms framed in Confucian ideals. Though Confucian, many of these relational ideals do not contradict the Christian message. In fact, they can be used to pave the way for a better understanding of sin among the Chinese. Rather than positing an abstract "man is sinful," Francis notes in concrete terms that "people are disobedient" and do not show true filial love; they "miss the mark" of the full obligations of filial piety. To rephrase in terms of social capital, we can say that people have no face (no honor, no social capital) before God because of their inability to live up to the filial obligations they have toward him as the Father of all human beings.

Patron-Client Indigenous Leadership

A second example of social capital is framed in terms of patron-client relationships found in many parts of the world. Typically housed in discussions of social power and power distance (e.g., Moreau, Campbell, and Greener 2014, 171–74; Backues 2015), this example illustrates social capital as power. Patrons are people with significant social capital in a setting who act as protectors and providers for those who enter into client relationships with them.

Western Christians may well deride the patron-client system as abusive, power concentrating, and ultimately evil in conception. However, that might not do justice to a biblical framework. New Testament scholar Halvor Moxnes argues that the "central theme of [Luke's] Gospel is that God acts as a benefactor-patron through Jesus. Jesus is not a patron in his own right, distributing his own resources, but a broker who gives access to the benefactions of God" (1991, 258). Patron-client relationships can be abusive, but market-driven independent individualism can be isolationist. Indeed, any human economic system is amenable to evil, but that does not mean it is inherently evil. With that in mind, we turn to an example of patron-client orientation among Pentecostal churches in Ghana.

John McCauley, a professor of government and politics at the University of Maryland, presents a fascinating case of how Pentecostalism in Ghana has developed patron-client relationships of clergy with parishioners due to several developments in Ghana (2013). First, traditional African institutions were subjected to change and destabilization in the postcolonial era. The average citizen, frustrated over the lack of traditional options and with the rise of endemic corruption, became more open to change, opening the door to religious renewal and conversion. McCauley notes, "Many new Pentecostals began to prioritize harmonious living as a response to crisis. In this manner, new values and a new form of Christian worship emerged, which drew on its transnational ties to American evangelism but ultimately expressed an independent African desire for well-being and security" (2013, 8).

Second, the state expanded control over customary practices such as land control, divorce, marriage, health, and so on. Traditional control over these at the village level was lost to newly created state institutions and bureaucracies, with the result that people were distanced from their traditional patrons (normally from their own ethnic group). Ties to the traditional ethnic-based systems of protection and patronage were increasingly challenged and effectively weakened.

Third, as the traditional ethnic ties were weakened, the state itself was less and less able to meet the welfare needs of the average citizen. Despite Ghana's relative economic health, it increasingly needed foreign aid to meet basic needs. The weakening of the traditional systems together with the increasing failure of the new state resulted in a gap that needed to be filled.

Finally, and added into the mix, urbanization resulted in individuals being separated from village and family networks that traditionally supplied communal options for securing such help as loans and daily necessities, including child care. The net effect has been the lessening of the traditional patterns of ethnic patronage and an opening of the door for new patronage options. It is into this gap that Pentecostal and charismatic pastors, especially megachurch leaders, have stepped.

However, this new system is not so new in the sense that it mirrors the model of the "big man" rule found in Melanesian societies "by encouraging members to break from their past, to trust leadership, and to commit exclusively to their religious social network" (McCauley 2013, 1). This success is a function of Pentecostalism's "ability to fill voids left by the state and to provide new social networks" (1). This plays out in movies, television series, newspapers, and comics (see Riedel 2015). Typically the main character is the victim of witchcraft and/or demonic attacks that are the root cause of that person's social ills and brokenness. After unsuccessful attempts at a variety of methods for mediation (including traditional healers), it is the Pentecostal pastor who is able to restore the person to wholeness. This mythic framing plays into the patron-client social capital orientation. Charismatic pastors offer healing, and the former victim, now saved, offers allegiance to Christ through the pastor's church.

We should be aware that these pastors (and wealthy Christians in their congregations) are not doing this with contextualization in mind: they are simply following their own cultural and spiritual convictions. They urge people to separate from traditions, to marry across ethnic lines, to focus on nuclear family units, and to rely on the church to meet spiritual needs. But in so doing, they jettison parishioners from traditional ethnic support networks and replace those with church-based support networks. Exploring this new reality in Ghana (and other countries of Africa) from the vantage point of capital and exchange helps us better understand the phenomenon and enables us to better consider appropriate contextual responses.

Linking Capital

Consider the following scenario (adapted from R. Priest and J. Priest 2008). You are a pastor in a town in Latin America, and you have no connection whatsoever to the mayor. You pastor a small evangelical church in a locale where evangelicals are not valued or welcomed. One day, through a friend living in the United States who is part of your own denomination, you are contacted by a youth pastor from the United States who asks to send a team of twenty young, energetic North Americans on a short-term mission trip. They want you to host them during their stay. You learn that they intend to bring tools and money to build a children's playground in the (currently empty) park near your church as their project. No other park in your town has a playground for children to use; your town does not have the resources for such. Suddenly you find that previously closed doors are opened to you: you can get an appointment with the mayor to explain the project. You now not only have a reason to connect with the mayor; you also have a need to do so to ensure that you have permission for the project to proceed.

You are delighted to host the team, even if the park does not need the playground and even if no one will ever use it: the project offers you a form of social capital you could otherwise never access. You can link to important people in the town, and (if the church sends another team the following year), you have a reason to develop a relationship with the mayor and staff. What mayor of a town does not want a donated, equipped playground for children? Perhaps the mayor is even asking you, "When are you going to bring another group back? Are you bringing them back next summer?"

In this case, the American church offers you honor and linking capital, whether they ever even know about your change in status. As Robert Priest and Joseph Priest note, "Whether with medical mission groups of Methodists and Presbyterians or with more evangelistic teams of Southern Baptists, the collaboration serves to open doors for them—giving them access to private homes, town plazas, to government offices, to schools, jails, or hospitals that would otherwise close them out. The foreigners serve as *carnada*, or 'bait,' to be exploited by Peruvian *evangélicos* in their own evangelistic witness" (2008, 67).

This unintended consequence is one reason why local pastors prefer not to criticize short-term missions to their community. While the status change is an unintended consequence, and not a result of purposeful contextualization on the part of short-term mission teams, it clearly illustrates how contextual thinking in terms of social capital can help us better understand some of the deeper dynamics taking place.

Contextualizing Spiritual Capital

As mentioned previously, Christians from the West might have a hard time understanding Hindu sadhus as holy people with significant spiritual capital. In the West, when we think of a holy person, we might first consider well-known, public Christian figures, especially examples such as Mother Teresa, rather than the flamboyant preacher types. After reflection, however, we might also consider those who are unrecognized in any public forum but who labor on their knees and whose lives reflect a deep and intimate relationship with Jesus Christ. What can we learn about spiritual capital, and how might we contextualize our approach to it?

What do you imagine when you consider a genuinely "spiritual" person? Certainly a life of prayer, and likely an intimacy with God (that perhaps the rest of us envy). Evangelical visions of piety were developed and expressed historically through Pietism, a movement of God in Europe during the seventeenth century that blended an emphasis on the Bible (and biblical doctrine) with religious devotion and (typically) humility. Contemporary evangelical practices such as disciplined individual and corporate prayer, fasting, spiritual retreats, and daily devotions and/or Bible reading characterize this type of piety and are markers of genuinely spiritual people. The question that contextualization asks is the extent to which this historically founded and culturally derived vision of piety is cross-cultural. Two examples will help us focus the discussion.

Sadhu Sundar Singh (b. 1889) was born to a pious Indian Sikh family. Anger over his mother's untimely death when he was fourteen drove him to attack Christians. Before long, however, Singh reached a stage in which he was desperate to encounter the divine: he vowed to kill himself unless the True God revealed himself. He experienced a vision of Christ and subsequently gave his life to Christ's service. Rejected by family for his conversion, he was baptized on his sixteenth birthday and began a life of pilgrimage, wearing the apparel of a Hindu sadhu (hence his title). Most of the rest of his life was spent walking, meditating, and preaching Christ among Hindus and speaking at Christian conferences. Because of trips to the West, he became celebrated as a mystical servant of God who was deeply pious and who recounted stories of visions and miracles.

At heart Singh was indeed a mystic, a man in close communion with God, experiencing dreams and visions on a regular basis. His wandering life, with no settled pattern, fit the mold of a sadhu. His stories of visions and dreams created an aura of supernatural presence, generating a level of notoriety that he largely ignored, though he did publish several short books in which he recounted visions and answered questions about faith in a catechetical fashion (e.g., Singh 1922). As H. L. Richard notes, "He was a striking example of viewing Christian life and faith from an Eastern perspective" (2000).

A contemporary of Singh, but born on a different continent and endowed with a different calling, Liberian William Wadé Harris (1865–1929) offers a second example of a person who generated and utilized spiritual capital not typically seen in Western Christian settings. An Episcopalian catechist, he was involved in an unsuccessful revolt in 1909 and wound up in prison. There he experienced a vision from the angel Gabriel in which he was called to become a prophet. Released in 1912, he donned a white gown and turban and began itinerant preaching, accompanied by a group of female singers, traveling from Liberia through Côte d'Ivoire to Ghana.

Carrying a staff, a Bible, a calabash rattle, and a baptismal bowl (Shenk 1998, 281), he called for repentance, healed, cast out demons, and preached against fetishes (and the colonial powers). Within two years, over 120,000 were baptized, alarming French officials, who banned "Prophet Harris" (he saw himself as a black Elijah) from Côte d'Ivoire. When Methodist missionaries arrived in 1924, they found 160 congregations with over 32,000 adherents waiting.

Like Singh, Harris was a mystic richly endowed with spiritual capital—but the type of capital that causes consternation among many Western Christians. Both are recognized as men with typical human flaws but also men who were deeply connected with God and whom God used to bring many into a living relationship with himself.

Conclusion

While few today question Singh's or Harris's choices to live as traveling preachers and mystics utilizing symbolic garments and accoutrements, they do raise the question of the extent to which similar behavior might be appropriate for a cross-cultural missionary in India or Africa. Just how far may a missionary, acting as a "cultural chameleon" (Poston 2000), go before crossing boundaries of propriety? This question is one for which no single answer has been found—and which will continue to generate heat in the years to come.

CASE STUDY

MANIFESTO ON WEALTH CREATION

At a Lausanne Consultation on the Role of Wealth Creation for Holistic Transformation, members of the Lausanne Movement and BAM Global developed a
statement intended to offer biblical guidance on wealth and wealth creation. As
you read the affirmations and appeals, consider the contextual questions raised
in this chapter. In what ways might these affirmations be universal, and in what
ways might they be contextual? How might they manifest in different cultural
settings?

Affirmations

- Wealth creation is rooted in God the Creator, who created a world that
  flourishes with abundance and diversity.

- We are created in God's image, to co-create with Him and for Him, to create
  products and services for the common good.

- Wealth creation is a holy calling, and a God-given gift, which is commended in
  the Bible.

- Wealth creators should be affirmed by the Church, and equipped and
  deployed to serve in the marketplace among all peoples and nations.

- Wealth hoarding is wrong, and wealth sharing should be encouraged, but
  there is no wealth to be shared unless it has been created.

- There is a universal call to generosity, and contentment is a virtue, but
  material simplicity is a personal choice, and involuntary poverty should be
  alleviated.

- The purpose of wealth creation through business goes beyond giving
  generously, although that is to be commended; good business has intrinsic
  value as a means of material provision and can be an agent of positive
  transformation in society.

- Business has a special capacity to create financial wealth, but also has the
  potential to create different kinds of wealth for many stakeholders, including
  social, intellectual, physical and spiritual wealth.

- Wealth creation through business has proven power to lift people and nations
  out of poverty.

- Wealth creation must always be pursued with justice and a concern for the poor, and should be sensitive to each unique cultural context.

- Creation care is not optional. Stewardship of creation and business solutions to environmental challenges should be an integral part of wealth creation through business.

Appeal

We present these affirmations to the Church worldwide, and especially to leaders in business, church, government, and academia.

- We call the church to embrace wealth creation as central to our mission of holistic transformation of peoples and societies.

- We call for fresh, ongoing efforts to equip and launch wealth creators to that very end.

- We call wealth creators to perseverance, diligently using their God-given gifts to serve God and people.

Adapted from Lausanne Movement, "Wealth Creation Manifesto," April 23, 2017, http://matstunehag.com/wp-content/uploads/2017/05/Wealth-Creation-Manifesto-v-4.0-23-April-17.pdf.

THE SOCIAL DIMENSION AS LEARNING

EDUCATION

All the evidence from both biblical framing and contemporary science points to the reality that humans are designed to grow, remember, categorize information, and learn. We do so by solving problems and abstracting general solutions, and we creatively propose new thoughts and ideas. People learn in multiple ways, exhibiting differing strengths and weaknesses in their learning repertoire. As I use it in contextualization, "learning" includes *all activities that in any way, directly or indirectly, contribute to providing members of a society with the knowledge, values, and skill sets necessary to navigate that society and be perceived as responsible members of it.*

Culture plays a significant role in how society values those strengths and weaknesses. For example, the public school my children attended gave them higher grade recognition for taking honors courses than for taking "regular" courses. In our case, my children could receive six grade points for receiving an A grade in an honors class, but only four grade points for receiving an A in a regular, nonhonors class. By contrast, athletes who excelled at a varsity sport were not given higher grade points for performing well on the highest-level team; neither were musicians for being in the top orchestra or actors for taking the lead role in a school play. In other words, building on value systems inherent in American school systems, the schools my children attended rewarded certain types of excellence (intellectual) but did not similarly reward other types (kinesthetic, musical, dramatic).

Social scientists typically refer to this social system by using the term "education." I chose to stress "learning" more than "education" because many of us too readily associate "education" exclusively with formal schooling. While formal schooling is included in the larger institution of "education," it is only one part of the whole system of learning that is part of every society. "Learning" is less likely to limit our thinking when we examine this component of the social dimension. Outside the church, learning ranges from apprenticeship to enculturation to dissertation. Inside the church, learning ranges from Sunday school classes to small-group Bible studies to discipleship. To determine what learning includes for Christians, ask yourself, What are the ways through which I learn about my faith in Christ? Contextualizing learning takes this question one step further: What are the ways people in

Figure 4.1: Educational modes

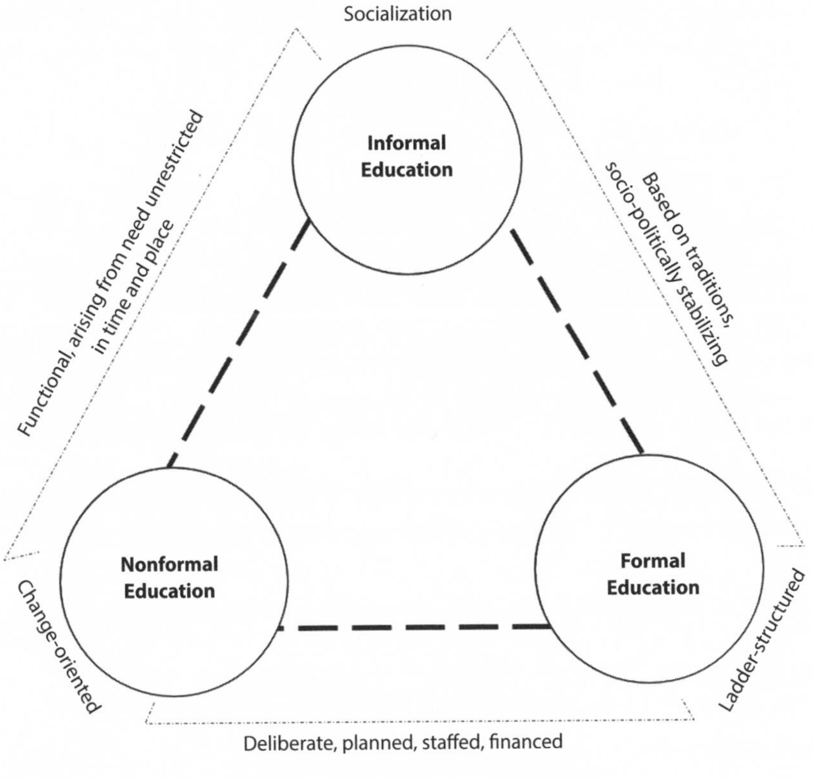

this society learn about their own religious faith? In what ways might those learning methods be harnessed for the sake of the gospel?

I frame this discussion on learning from three vantage points: (1) the general social system of learning, (2) religious learning, and (3) the implications for contextualization. With each vantage point I further divide the discussion into three modes of learning: (1) informal education or socialization, (2) nonformal education or apprenticeships, and (3) formal education (see fig. 4.1).

Each of these modes of learning is deeply contextual and framed in light of societal values and history. Each has strengths and weaknesses; for the deepest learning to take place, all three are necessary.

Of particular importance to us is how Christians learn to be followers of Christ, walking in obedience to his call on their lives, which we commonly refer to as discipleship or Christian growth. Understanding how people idealize learning and the learning processes in their own societies (and religions) helps us frame growth opportunities and patterns for followers of Christ in ways that take advantage of contextual patterns rather than fight against them (unless, of course, such patterns are patently antibiblical). Minho Song asks a question that puts a practical face on the focus of this chapter: "How does one disciple a Muslim background believer? How does one disciple a Buddhist background believer? How about those coming from the urban slums of Manila or from a Communist regime?" (Song 2006, 251).

Learning Modes

Informal

By informal learning I refer to the normal process of socialization that every person goes through growing up. From our parents and other authority figures we learn right and wrong behavior in personal and social settings, we learn from our peers how to behave when authority figures are not in sight, we learn from media ideals of behavior. As learning beings, especially throughout the course of childhood, we continually grow in our understanding of what is socially appropriate and inappropriate, and we internalize what we learn in light of our personal experiences and history, our genetic heritage, and our shared experiences with those in our community. Traditionally, many African children learned that they are interdependent on others; many Asian children learned that they are deeply connected to their extended families; American children, on the other hand, learned that they are independent individuals responsible for their own choices.

As a father of four children, I rarely thought to myself, Now I'm socializing my daughter to _____. Rather, I did what I thought was right based on my values and beliefs, and in the process I passed along at least some of those to my children without consciously thinking about what I was doing. This happens everywhere. The Japanese mother, deeply tied to her children, socializes them in Japanese norms of play and social behavior. The Russian father, perhaps less intimately connected to his children, still models what it is like to be a man and what his son should aspire to be when he grows up.

Over the past century developmental psychologists and other social scientists have tried to identify specific phases of universal childhood development (e.g., Jean Piaget, Erik Erikson, Lev Vygotsky). Too often the pioneers in these fields built their models from observations of children within their own sociocultural strata, limiting the cross-cultural viability of their studies. Others have sought to better understand the capacity for learning and thinking, most commonly measured in the West through such things as IQ tests. Such tests are now challenged and confirmed as limited to one or two dimensions of the total human cognitive skill set. However, even though Gardner's seven multiple intelligence categories (visual-spatial, bodily-kinesthetic, musical, interpersonal, intrapersonal, linguistic, and logical-mathematical) may be universal, the jury is out on how complete (or incomplete) the list is.

Nonformal

Nonformal learning refers to systems for on-the-job skills training such as conferences, workshops, training sessions, internships, shadowing, mentoring, and apprenticing. Typically more concerned with practice and less concerned with theory (unless it is necessary for practice), this learning sector focuses on skills training and development.

The nonformal learning sector in Western societies does not have the same level of social capital as the formal learning sector, but it plays a critical role in societies around the world. Nonformal learning experiences include such things as weekend training sessions (e.g., individuals learning interviewing skills to prepare for job interviews), conferences (e.g., preparing the elderly for retirement), classes for toddlers (e.g., swimming lessons), community-based programs (e.g., personal enrichment such as learning to draw or garden), and short training and night classes for specific skill development (from barbers to fashion designers).

Formal

Formal learning refers to educational institutions that are structured and hierarchical, and typically culminate in a certificate, degree, or other recognized symbol of completion. Public and private elementary, middle school, and secondary and tertiary institutions are all part of the formal educational system. Traditionally these learning institutions feature residential, face-to-face classes with a set curriculum that every student is expected to complete or appropriately master prior to completion (or graduation). At higher levels, completion culminates in some form of certification, whether a certificate, a diploma, or a degree (in countries that distinguish the latter two). Formal educational institutions are regulated, licensed, and accredited by external agencies, in most cases the educational division of the national- or regional-level government. In some cases, there is more than one accrediting body under which schools may choose to operate. The roles and functions of the accrediting institutions vary with the level of the educational system (primary, secondary, and tertiary).

SIDEBAR 4.1
QUESTIONS ABOUT LEARNING

Below are some questions to consider as you explore learning (and education) in your setting. Asking and exploring the answers to these questions will enable you to better understand local examples of learning—but more importantly help you think more clearly about church and the means Christians may use to enable other Christians to learn about their faith and train the next generation of Christ-followers in light of local societal norms.

As I noted in parallel sidebars in previous chapters, answers to these questions could be used to compromise the gospel or the biblical definition of church. That is not my intention. Rather, I want the questions to equip you to find biblically appropriate and culturally sound ways for Christians to understand local views of education and learning. They help you avoid the danger of simply generating and using only the educational or learning modes that make sense from your own cultural setting. As you ask these questions, also be asking yourself how the answers impact what type of learning approaches would make sense to local people without compromising their relationship with Christ.

1. How does the society prepare the next generation for responsible adulthood?
2. What informal (socialization) learning methods are indigenous to the setting?
3. What nonformal practices for apprenticeship or other on-the-job training are indigenous to the setting?
4. What formal educational institutions are indigenous to the setting?
5. What roles do age, class, and gender play in learning?
6. How does the use of social power affect learning processes?
7. In what ways does the gospel condone or condemn indigenous learning methods?

With the advent of online learning, some traditional brick-and-mortar institutions are moving part or even all their educational work to low- or nonresidential delivery systems (mostly online). This is especially true at the tertiary level and appears to be a trend that will continue into the foreseeable future.

As we have done in earlier chapters, in sidebar 4.1 we note several questions to be considered in any new setting as you explore the social institution of learning (or education).

Sidebar 4.1 helps you consider learning in general, but I noted earlier that understanding how people learn about their religions has the potential to point us to contextual methods of learning that we can employ in discipleship and Christian growth. Early in my Christian walk I learned about my faith by being part of a small group that worked its way through a series of short books with numerous questions that we discussed together. Will that method work in a Hindu setting? A Buddhist setting? In what ways will it appear foreign to them, and how might we harness their methods of religious learning for the sake of the gospel? First, it is critical to understand what some of those methods are, and we turn to that next.

Religious Learning Modes

The religions of the world naturally have integrated within them means of educating or training their adherents to be responsible religious practitioners. From the socialization of Zulu (South Africa) adolescents into their obligations to the ancestors, to the apprenticeship of shamans in numerous societies, the informal ashrams of Hindus, and the formal institutions of Islamic jurisprudence and Buddhist monasteries, religions offer informal, nonformal, and formal means for their adherents to learn about their faith.

Informal

As we explore in greater detail in chapter 9, across the world children and adolescents participate in religious rituals that entertain and teach them about the religious faith of their parents and community. From Chinese Lunar New Year celebrations to grave-sweeping rituals, from Zulu community divination sessions discerning the cause of misfortune to Weyewa (Indonesia) dances to the ancestors, children are incorporated into religious events such that they imbibe of the faith and practices of their communities. Hindu pujas are ritual prayers through which a particular deity is worshiped or an event (such as a life passage) is celebrated. In some respects they parallel Christian devotions and are performed in Hindu homes and temples. Families that perform daily pujas socialize their children into their religious beliefs. Muslims in Pakistan are socialized into their faith through such things as daily prayers and mosque participation; adult Muslims are socialized through such events as the hajj (pilgrimage to Mecca, required at least once in every Muslim's life). Through participation in these events they learn proper behavior and proper ritual, which demonstrate submission to Allah. Christians ministering in non-Christian settings need to consider which informal learning methods used by local religious families they might use in their discipleship practices.

Nonformal

Almost forty years after my time in Swaziland, I can still picture the *kraal* (a small collection of huts) that I drove by each time I traveled to or from the Mbabane (the capital) to the school in rural Ntonjeni, where I taught high school. The *kraal* looked like a traditional home, but I knew from cultural informants that this was actually a place where those chosen by the ancestors to become healers apprenticed to learn how to channel the spirits speaking through them to their community. There was no certification: the status of the trainer and the gradual public acceptance of the apprentice as a healer was the only certification necessary.

Across the Indian Ocean from Swaziland, in Bali (an Indonesian island), children are apprenticed in the arts Bali is so well known for—dancing, painting, sculpture, or music, and the like. In the West children also have access to such training, but it is almost always decoupled from religious framing. In Bali, by contrast, arts socialization integrally connects children to Hindu beliefs and practices. Bali is the last Hindu stronghold in a Muslim nation: one of the reasons it has retained its Hindu religious identity over the past several centuries, despite external pressure to change, is the nonformal system of embedding children into Hindu beliefs and practices through the arts into which they are socialized during childhood. Christians ministering in non-Christian settings need to consider which nonformal learning methods used by religious trainers they might adapt for use in Christian nurture and growth.

Formal

Formal religious education often exists either as integrated within the society's educational infrastructure or as a separate subset of it, with separate accreditation processes. Madrassas as schools of Islamic training at a wide variety of levels have become well known in the West because of the religious fundamentalism taught in some of them. In the West they are presented as exclusively focused on memorization of the Qur'an in Arabic, whether or not the students even know the language. However, the term covers a broad swath of educational institutions across the Middle East and South Asia, from secular training institutions to advanced schools of Islamic learning.

At one point in time Tibetan monasteries existed in the thousands, and every family had to send at least one boy for training. Traditionally the students received the only education accessible to them, and their families gained merit through their son's participation in monastic life. In the monasteries, participants learn both social and religious responsibilities. The younger boys are trained in prayer, learn to read and chant religious texts, and practice the spiritual disciplines of the monastery under the direction of older monks. Rather than written tests, applicants participate in oral debate with the high lamas, who determine whether they have passed. Those who pass the initial exams have access to further gradations of accomplishment, which in several respects parallel advanced tertiary training found in the West.

As noted in the prior two sections, Christians ministering in non-Christian settings need to consider which formal learning methods used by religious educators they might adapt for use in formal Christian training.

Learning Modes in the Bible

From the three-year training that Jesus used with the disciples to the arguments presented at the Jerusalem Council attempting to discern the connection between circumcision and salvation, to Paul's reflection that he "studied under Gamaliel and was thoroughly trained in the law of our ancestors" (Acts 22:3), there is more than ample biblical evidence that learning (and discipleship) is integral to following Christ.

Informal

One of the best biblical examples of informal learning through socialization into a life of faith comes from the Old Testament in Deuteronomy 6:6–9: "These commandments that I give you today are to be on your hearts. Impress them on your children. Talk about them when you sit at home and when you walk along the road, when you lie down and when you get up. Tie them as symbols on your hands and bind them on your foreheads. Write them on the doorframes of your houses and on your gates."

This religious socialization process involves more than just conversation or teaching within the family: religious symbols and paraphernalia are employed that make the learning more concrete and keep God's commands ever present, driving home their importance for the next generation. One challenge, of course, is that when the symbols are always present, they are easier to overlook (just as we can get used to a bad smell by living with it long enough). Finding ways to refresh or renew such symbols in the minds of children is an important part of this informal discipleship process.

In the New Testament we find an example of Paul socializing adults in Ephesus who were called "disciples" but had not even heard about the Holy Spirit (Acts 19:1–6). They had been baptized with John's baptism but did not realize that John was paving the way for Christ. Having explained this to them, Paul baptized them, and the Holy Spirit came on them in tongues and prophecies.

Nonformal

Nonformal education is seen in the Bible wherever apprenticeship or the biblical equivalent of training institutes or the like is found. In the Old Testament, Moses mentored Joshua, who served as his aide (Exod. 24:13; Num. 11:28), joining Moses when the latter met with God in the tent of meeting (Exod. 33:11). With his impending death, Moses commissioned Joshua to lead Israel after the former's departure (Num. 27:15–23). Daniel and his companions went through a nonformal three-year training period in Babylon to prepare them to serve in the king's palace (Dan. 1:3–5), during which they learned the Babylonian language and literature. Finally, there is mention of a "group [or company or school] of prophets" in 1 Samuel 19:18–24, which appears to have been a nonformal association of prophets who either were under Samuel's mentorship or lived in some type of community. We also read of groups or companies of prophets connected with Elijah and Elisha in 2 Kings 2.

In the New Testament, Paul took Timothy with him on his second missionary journey (Acts 16:1–3) and essentially apprenticed him to Christian service for several years. Likewise, Onesimus met Paul's needs while Paul was imprisoned in Rome, and the service Onesimus provided gave Paul impetus to plead for his life with Philemon (Onesimus's former master). Perhaps the closest New Testament equivalents to "training institutes" are when Paul and Barnabas taught the new believers at Antioch for a year (Acts 11:25–26) and Paul's later daily discussions with the Ephesian disciples in the lecture hall of Tyrannus for two years (Acts 19:9–10). Finally, the Jerusalem Council (Acts 15) can be seen as a nonformal learning setting in which the early church discerned how to handle gentile conversions.

Formal

Interestingly enough, models for contemporary formal education are lacking in the biblical narrative. We might consider the schools of the Pharisees and Sadducees, but those would hardly be considered success stories to emulate! As previously mentioned, Paul studied under Gamaliel (a moderate voice among the Pharisees) and was "thoroughly trained in the law of our ancestors" (Acts 22:3). While we do know that Gamaliel was one of the most highly regarded Pharisees of his day and identified with his own school (see Bruce 1988, 114–15), we do not have a depiction from the Bible itself of how that school operated and what credentialing it offered besides the honor of being able to state that one studied under Gamaliel.

Implications for Contextualization

The contextualization question is, How can we draw on religious ideas, traditions, and practices to best embed the learning required for all of Christ's disciples who want to be more like their Master? John drew on Greek philosophical categories to portray Jesus as the "Logos" of God; Paul utilized the altar to the unknown God in Corinth to point to God and used the language of power and magic in his Letter to the Ephesians (Arnold 1992). For each educational mode, I have presented at least one biblical example and now turn to contemporary examples of contextualization that highlight or build on that mode.

Informal

Relational evangelism often follows an informal model of learning. Out of a context of life and the circumstances of living in a broken world, sensitive evangelists share the good news they have found with others searching for answers to the questions they have or the pain they experience. Contextually sensitive relational evangelism holds in tension the questions of those who do not know Christ with the questions the gospel brings to the setting. One contextual example of this in Muslim settings is called the Camel Method (Greeson 2004).

While Kevin Greeson made the Camel Method known, he did not originally develop it. Rather, Muslims who had come to Christ developed it, and Greeson was invited to observe the resulting movement of churches. Before his observations, his team had experienced no results in witness among Muslims. However, utilizing the methods he found in the indigenous movement, his team reported over 8,500 Muslims baptized during a four-year span.

The three-step process is to (1) arouse curiosity, (2) identify whether the hearer is a "person of peace," and (3) bridge to the Bible to teach about Jesus. One controversial component of the Camel Method comes in the first step in that it uses a Qur'anic passage (Surah Al-Imram 3.42–55) to demonstrate how the Qur'an teaches that Jesus is more than just a prophet (CAMEL is an acronym that helps the presenter remember the key components of the passage). Critics are unwilling to use the Qur'an as a starting point since this gives credence to Qur'anic teaching, something they are unwilling to do.

My purpose in reporting the method here is twofold. First, it is framed as a learning method that is linked to normal social discourse (socialization) rather than any formal process. Second, and just as important, this method was developed by local believers rather than expatriate missionaries. It was originally indigenous to the setting and not imposed by outsiders. It thus represents a contextually driven example of utilizing informal learning to reach people for Christ.

Another example of contextualization in informal learning is orality. Starting with the insights of Bible storying, orality has arisen as a focus among many missionaries and missiologists over the past two decades (see https://orality.imb.org). Oral learning is typically informal or nonformal in nature, without stratified classes or degrees marking completion.

One important type of informal oral learning takes place through song. The contextual approach to hymnody used by *Église de Jésus-Christ sur terre par le Prophète Simon Kimbangu* (EJCSK = Church of Jesus Christ on Earth through the Prophet Simon Kimbangu) serves as an excellent example. Among the largest of the African Initiated Churches (AICs), with estimates ranging from five to ten million members, the EJCSK is not always viewed positively by evangelicals, though it is a member of the World Council of Churches.

The EJCSK traces its founding to 1921, when Simon Kimbangu, a reluctant Baptist catechist, obeyed God's prompting to heal a person he came across when returning home from the market. Following this singular event, Kimbangu ministered for three months in public, then three months in hiding from the Belgian authorities. He gave himself up for arrest and was subsequently sent to prison, where he died just over three decades later.

Indigenous Kimbanguist hymnody had played a critical role in the sustenance and growth of the EJCSK since its inception. Before Kimbangu's arrest in 1921, suspicious missionaries refused to sell hymnals to his followers. That year, a commonly told story goes, a missionary came to Kimbangu, demanding the return of books Kimbangu had borrowed. It was then that Kimbangu "was told by God that he would never look to the missionaries for anything; he would be granted all he needed for his mission of evanglisation" (Molyneux

1990, 154). The entire time Kimbangu was in prison, anything related to his work was banned by the colonial authorities. Followers met secretly, singing hymns and praying. Once the church was officially recognized in 1959 and members were allowed to practice their faith publicly without repercussion, they were able to formalize their approach.

Gordon Molyneux, who examined Kimbanguist hymnody as part of his doctoral dissertation (published as a book in 1993), noted several characteristics about the hymns incorporated into the official church corpus (565 at the time he did his work; examples are available at http://archives.kimbanguisme.net/kimbanguisme/cantiques/cantiques.htm). First, they must be recognized as revealed to the author by God rather than the work of human ingenuity. Second, they are vetted by a special branch of the EJCSK, with an office in Kinshasa, using three criteria: "First, the evaluators must be convinced that the hymn was given by God through revelation. Further, it must be pleasing to their sense of musical taste. Finally, it must be honoring to God. As an overarching consideration, the evaluators look for signs of pride or an improper sense of accomplishment in the person to whom God revealed the hymn. Impropriety in this regard can lead to the rejection of a hymn" (Moreau 2012b, 228). The ability to receive hymns by revelation is recognized as a spiritual gift; at the time of Molyneux's research (1987) there were forty-six people who were recognized as having this gift by the EJCSK (Molyneux 1990, 156).

Hymns play a significant role as an oral liturgy for Kimbanguists. They sing them in church, but also in their local community, forming choirs that engage in competitions with each other while praising God and learning from the oral framing of their faith. Compared to the Hillsong music that permeates so much of the global church today, EJCSK hymns function at a much deeper and more pervasive level, and church members (young and old) are enculturated into church life and thought through their hymnody.

Nonformal

In India, ashrams were traditionally hermitages, which were to be in rural areas, where tranquility and peace characterized life and geography. Klaudt succinctly summarizes: "A typical ashram contains a small community of people who have gathered to sustain each other during an intense spiritual quest. This quest is characterized by the relationship between the community and its guru, or spiritual leader. Meditation, asceticism, simplicity, dialogue, sharing of goods, devotion, and charity have also come to characterize the ashram" (Klaudt 1997, 25).

Examinations and conferral of rights based on a recognized level of performance are not part of the ashram orientation. However, despite being isolated from society, ashrams have a history of being deeply involved in social issues. Gandhi, for example, started his famous Salt March from the Sabarmati Ashram he founded after his arrival in India from South Africa. The Salt March was an act of nonviolent civil disobedience against the British law forbidding Indians from extracting salt for themselves and maintaining a British monopoly on salt (see O'Neill 2015). At the ashram, Gandhi practiced agricultural methods, developed a literacy program, and refined his ideology of nonviolent resistance to British rule. Today it is recognized as the home of the ideology Gandhi used to eventually gain independence for India and serves as an example of a nonformal institution that made a huge societal difference.

Christian ashrams arose in India within the same time frame as Gandhi (R. Taylor 1979, 283) at the initiative of Indian Christians rather than missionaries. They were promoted as forms of indigenization (one of the precursor terms to contextualization) and separated from traditional missions work. As early as 1920 an Indian Christian envisioned ashrams as theological institutions, but missionaries criticized his ideas (284).

Celebrated missionary E. Stanley Jones started an ashram in 1930; he later initiated Christian ashrams in six countries (W. Richardson 1964). In 1963, after three months of exploring and examining Christian ashrams in India, which he described as "thoroughly Indian and Christian" (Beaver 1965, 887), mission historian R. Pierce Beaver defined them this way: "An ashram is an ascetic community characterized by fellowship, mutual bearing of burdens, common worship, silent meditation, intercession and study, living a close family life under a rule of discipline to the glory of God, to the service of the most needy and to the communication of the gospel. It is one form of the Indian holy life baptized into the service of Jesus Christ and his church" (887).

He also noted that a guru or teacher, serving as the spiritual parent, is essential and further noted, "The great majority state that their primary purpose is evangelistic, and they make their witness chiefly through teaching, healing, maintaining orphanages, and providing various kinds of assistance to villagers—though the total life of the community is regarded as an act of witnessing" (887).

It is helpful to examine a more detailed depiction of the first major Protestant ashram. Founded in 1921 and called *Christukula* (Family of Christ), it was located southwest of Madras. Richard Taylor observes:

> The ashram was Gandhian in style. Homespun handloom cloth was worn which, in addition to being inexpensive and simple, had strong nationalist political

implications. Only vegetarian food was served. Celibacy was the rule and the membership was male, although some women school teachers did stay there and married men sometimes came for periods of time. All the work was done by the members; there were few if any servants. A long day with fixed hours for work, study and worship was kept. Because both of the founders were medical doctors, the major social service activity of the ashram was medical care. But village evangelism was a high priority with the ashram and education and agricultural development were systematically offered. Full members of the ashram were called *Sevak*, meaning "servant." There have been only four or five of these. But others come in various stages of testing their vocation, and many others come to serve for a year or more and in the process learn to be medical technicians of various kinds. Others come in holiday student camps—some under the Student Christian Movement—to learn and serve, and still others to visit for short periods.

Under its founders, *Christukula* Ashram was very effective in mission. Many in nearby villages were taught and healed. Many who came to stay for a while were deeply touched. Gandhi visited—and he did not visit many Christian institutions. The ashramites were admired and respected by their neighbours. Other ashrams were modeled on it. Some of the best bishops in several different churches testify to the personal importance of their stay there, as do some remarkable laymen—including some civil servants. This ashram's contribution to Tamil-style church architecture has been outstanding, as well as its contribution to Tamil Christian lyrics. (1979, 284–85)

Community life in the ashram is central, but service to the local community also plays a significant role. The vegetarian diet and vow of celibacy characterize Indian (Hindu) ashrams, the latter presenting a significant obstacle for those who desire to live in an ashram as a way of life. There are clear parallels with monastic orders in the Catholic Church (though with significantly less institutionalization), but far fewer parallels for Western evangelicals to draw on (though see below). Over the past century the legitimacy of Christian ashrams has occasionally been questioned, but the critiques were typically from Western Christians rather than Indians and have had little effect on the ashram movement. Ashrams clearly present a viable contextual model of community and outreach in a nonformal learning community.

A Western expression of a nonformal learning community that parallels Christian ashrams is that of the communities of New Friars that have formed over the past decade. Scott Bessenecker chronicles the rise of the New Friars, who have primarily been young, Western, suburban Christians who relinquish their privileges and choose a voluntary life of poverty, dwelling among the marginalized as marginals themselves. Bessenecker postulates:

I believe we are at the front edge of another missional, monastic-like order made up of men and women, many of whom are in their twenties and thirties, burning with a passion to serve the destitute in slum communities of the developing world—not from a position of power but from alongside them, living in the same makeshift housing, breathing the same sewage-tainted air, subject to the same government bulldozers that threaten to raze their communities. They are new friars, flying just below our radar because they have not come under any single denominational or suprachurch banner. (2006, 16)

It is the monastic-like order that characterizes the New Friars, and Bessenecker notes five historic patterns that the modern communities seek to emulate (20–22), all of which in some fashion also describe the ashram movement:

1. Incarnational: to *be* the gospel where they are rather than simply to bring the gospel
2. Devotional: organized around a set of spiritual commitments to govern their walk with Jesus
3. Communal: living together and sharing things in common ownership
4. Missional: stretching the borders of the church
5. Marginal: on the fringe of the mainstream church and among those who live on the edges of society

In addition to the commitment to downward mobility, an additional significant component of the communities that have been formed has been vows, whether of simplicity or singleness. Five groups that Bessenecker identifies (24) as pioneering this type of "evangelical monasticism" include InnerCHANGE (http://www.innerchange.org), Servant Partners (http://www.servantpartners .org), Servants to Asia's Urban Poor (http://servantsasia.org), Urban Neighbors of Hope (http://unoh.org), and Word Made Flesh (http://wordmadeflesh .org). The URLs and sophisticated websites for each organization demonstrate that while the New Friars are downwardly mobile, they also understand the need to provide opportunities for fellow twentysomethings to find and be able to support or join them—and internet connectivity is a sine qua non for this generation in a way it is not for Indian Christians and the ashrams they continue to form.

Finally, extending our previous discussion of Kimbanguist hymns as informal learning, over the past few decades ethnomusicologists have developed nonformal methods such as "New Song Fellowships" (King 2006; see also Neeley 1999) through which believers are trained and energized to employ their own musical system in composing hymns. Building on Paul Hiebert's (1985)

method of critical contextualization, King (2006) lists five essential components for the New Song workshops (the first step in developing New Song
Fellowships) as she implemented them among the Senufo of Côte d'Ivoire:

1. Bringing the God of Abraham into the Senufo culture (enabling the
   Senufo people to see that the ways God acted in Abraham's life also
   applies to them)
2. Critically dialoguing within the process (reflexively reflecting the text
   and the insights it brings to their culture)
3. Using meaningful lyric theology to confront and transform the worldview of a people (songs written that consider a particular life event or
   the event in the biblical text that addresses real-life issues)
4. Providing a platform for an emerging hermeneutical community (giving
   believers space through the workshops to evaluate their own customs
   and beliefs in light of the biblical texts)
5. Creating new rites that become integrated into the life of the people
   (encouraging workshop participants to consider ways to use ritual to
   integrate the new songs into the life of the church)

For gifted nationals these workshops serve as critical entrées into the art
of composing songs in their own musical genres that serve their churches
by giving them ownership over indigenous musical expression. While the
songs composed and sung form the informal learning mode (as noted for the
EJCSK), the *workshops* that train the musicians and artists offer the nonformal contextual learning mode.

A second type of workshop to consider is trauma-healing workshops.
People in many parts of the world, especially where governments are unstable
or regional conflicts have been ongoing for years or even decades, suffer the
trauma of war; ethnic, religious, or civil strife; crime; and the like. Clinical
psychologist Karen Carr (2006) explains trauma-healing workshops, initially
developed and deployed across West and central Africa to enable people to
face their traumas and find healing (also Hill et al. 2013). The intention is that
these two-week workshops train those who will in turn lead such workshops
in their own language for their own people. During the first week the focus
is on providing space for participants to identify their wounds and find space
for healing, working from the foundation of biblical teaching on suffering and
grief, taking pain to Jesus, forgiving perpetrators, and dealing with ongoing
conflict. Participants ask questions, share with each other, write essays or
songs of lament, and listen to those who are willing to give their stories of

brokenness and restoration, followed by group encouragement and prayer for the storyteller.

In the second week, participants are directed to commit their own list of traumas to paper and to note which ones gave them the most pain. They then pair up and share those hurts with their partner. After this, they place their notes at the foot of a cross at the front of the room. Participants next turn to the challenging task of identifying where they themselves have hurt or been the source of trauma for others: rarely are people victims without in some way becoming victimizers. Confession and experiencing Christ's forgiveness are central elements of this stage. Finally, the workshop closes with Communion.

Two years later a follow-up is held, and participants report having not only held on to their own healing but also conducting trauma-healing workshops to set their own people free. To date the trauma-healing workshops have been adapted for use in over 150 languages and societies.

As you can see from the examples, nonformal learning modes are almost infinitely flexible. Far more contextual approaches have been developed than can be explored in this brief section, but I hope you have a better perspective on nonformal learning and how God is using it to reach, heal, and strengthen the faith of countless people across the world.

Formal

It is fascinating that the mode of learning most favored in Western settings, and typically most favored by Western Christians, has such little foundation in the Bible. Given the lack of biblical foundations for the academic enterprise as we know it in the West, I have at times wondered (as one who has made my entire career in academic settings) whether the validity of requiring academic credentialing for ordination is not a mistake at a very fundamental level. I've also wondered about the entire global theological academic accreditation process built on Western models and now overseeing theological education around the world. The process of accreditation, rightly designed for students graduating from seminaries around the world to be recognized globally, is so tightly bound up with Western cultural educational models and values (see, e.g., Ferris 2000) that we risk educating people for ministry *away* from their own culture and toward a homogenized global vision of a professional Christian. I am convinced that contextual thinking can help us significantly in this regard.

Kraig Klaudt (1997, 25) says in regard to ashrams, already discussed twice in this chapter, that "a careful examination of ashram education can help us envision new possibilities for revitalizing religious education in the West."

He adds: "The ashram provides us with some new tools to help place each person's unique developmental journey at the center of educational and theological activity. The person-centered style of theological education practiced in ashrams holds great promise for helping us develop more authentic, courageous, and holistic religious leaders and should be explored by North American and European seminaries aspiring to provide a more diverse range of educational opportunities" (38).

An innovation from a different direction in formal theological training that has gained global attention over the past fifty years has been Theological Education by Extension (TEE) and Biblical Education by Extension (BEE). TEE was started in Guatemala in the early 1960s by three missionary educators who grew frustrated with the inability of national pastors to pull up roots with their families to receive training in a traditional evangelical seminary. Moving the seminary out of the city did not help, so they decided to decentralize the seminary, with the idea that "if the students could not come to the seminary, the seminary would come to them!" (J. Anderson 2000). One strength of TEE is that it is geared for established leaders rather than potential ones. A second is that the curriculum is adaptable to the educational level of the students. A third is that students receive education where they live, with immediate applicability (and feedback to the professor) so that curriculum can be continuously reviewed and enhanced, not on the basis of theory but on the basis of application. Over the years, TEE has at times been marginalized from residential seminaries, with charges of lower quality or less rigor. Clearly, however, the spread of TEE from its original home in Latin America to just about every continent in the world indicates a success story. With the advent of the internet and the possibility of online or mobile-based (cell phone) training, the final chapter of TEE has yet to be written.

While TEE does have the possibility of being deeply contextual, a significant challenge is ensuring that the curriculum is not simply "canned" in one country for export across the world (which, unfortunately, has happened in several instances). Further, in some instances neither the overall curriculum nor the pedagogy has been examined in light of contextualization principles. While TEE might bring the seminary to the student, the challenge remains to contextualize "the seminary" so that what is being brought to the students is situationally and pedagogically appropriate. In other words, changing the delivery modes of education without also changing the curriculum and pedagogy to meet the student's contextual needs runs the risk of simply perpetuating a Western education in a new mode. Because the teaching and learning take place on the students' home turf, however, the implicit demand for relevance gives educators the initiative to rethink not only delivery but also the curriculum and pedagogy.

Conclusion

Perhaps Christian ashrams and other analogues can provide a way forward for a blend of nonformal and formal education that can better train pastors for our globalized world. At the very least they give us space to ask contextually relevant questions of all three modes of learning and education: informal, nonformal, and formal.

CASE STUDY

L'ABRI

As you read through this brief depiction and visit the website for details on one or more branches of L'Abri, reflect on L'Abri as an example of nonformal learning that is contextual. At the same time, it is Western in its structure and function. Compare what you read here with the material on ashrams in the chapter (especially Taylor's depiction) and in online sources (see, e.g., http://www.christianashram.org/what-is-an-ashram.html). After you read through the following description and do your research, answer the questions at the end of the case study.

In 1955 Francis and Edith Schaeffer decided to open their home to become a place where people could ask honest questions and receive satisfying answers. They called this L'Abri (French for "shelter") to identify their home as a shelter from modern life and the secular pressures that came with it. Eventually L'Abri's have been founded in several countries with the same general aims. They identify four main emphases in the teaching of L'Abri:

First, that Christianity is objectively true and that the Bible is God's written word to mankind. This means that biblical Christianity can be rationally defended and honest questions are welcome.

Second, because Christianity is true it speaks to all of life and not to some narrowly religious sphere, and much of the material produced by L'Abri has been aimed at helping develop a Christian perspective on the arts, politics, and the social sciences, etc.

Third, in the area of our relationship with God, true spirituality is seen in lives which by grace are free to be fully human rather than in trying to live on some higher spiritual plane or in some grey negative way.

Fourth, the reality of the fall is taken seriously. Until Christ returns we and the world we live in will be affected by the disfigurement of sin. Although the place of the mind is emphasized, L'Abri is not a place for "intellectuals only."

L'Abri combines an informal learning mode with a nonformal environment. Some workers who are part of L'Abri look after the "students" who come. Each day is roughly one-half study and one-half practical help, and those who come stay for up to one full term (two to three months, depending on the branch).

- How is L'Abri like an ashram?

- How does it differ?

- What makes it particularly Western?

Imagine that you have been challenged to start a L'Abri branch in India. What would you draw from the model of the Christian ashram to ensure local cultural relevance?

Adapted from http://www.labri.org/history.html.

THE SOCIAL DIMENSION AS ORGANIZATIONAL
POLITICS

In every human society, people need to organize the groups that form. In this chapter I explore significant cultural considerations in the ways leadership and the organization of groups and institutions operate in local settings, in religions, and in contextualization. Christian organizations (including churches) are embedded in societies, and considering the ways local cultural values impact everything from church polity to leadership succession and disciplinary actions will help us better contextualize churches and fellowships that form as people respond to Christ. It will also help us better understand why churches that already exist in local settings organize themselves the way they do. In this chapter we explore leadership and organization in societies and then turn to implications for contextualization.

Leadership and Organization in Societies

Leadership

It is widely recognized that approaches to leadership vary across cultures. The challenge is going from this recognition to discerning what in fact determines the way each society understands leadership and what attributes each society values in leaders—and ultimately determining what (if any) roles this plays in contextualizing leadership. As a reminder, at this stage we examine *social* and *cultural* leadership thinking and attributes, not *biblical* ones.

The GLOBE Study

The single most significant set of resources for understanding cross-cultural leadership over the past two decades has been the massive GLOBE study and the various follow-ups (House et al. 2004; Javidan et al. 2006; Chhokar, Brodbeck, and House 2007; House et al. 2014). For their study, researchers defined leadership as "the ability to motivate, influence, and enable individuals to contribute to the objectives of organizations of which they are members" (House et al. 2004, xxii).

In the initial research process, 170 investigators performed in-depth surveys of over 17,000 middle managers from 62 countries representing 3 different business sectors (financial processes, food processing, and telecommunications). They developed a survey of over 700 items long to essentially investigate one question: "How is culture related to societal, organizational, and leadership effectiveness?" (House et al. 2004, xv).

In what follows, I build on selected insights from the GLOBE study. Ultimately researchers identified and investigated 122 leadership attributes (ranging from "administratively skilled" to "worldly"), grouping them into 21 primary leadership dimensions (from "administratively competent" to "team integrator"). They examined which of these 21 dimensions were found in each of 6 "global leadership dimensions" (or approaches to leadership) seen in the business sectors and countries that were studied (House et al. 2014, 20–22).

Cultural Values and Practices

Societies vary widely in their approaches to leadership in ways that can be understood through the lenses of contrasting sets of cultural values and practices. The GLOBE researchers identified and investigated nine such values (in alphabetical order): assertiveness, future orientation, gender egalitarianism, humane orientation, in-group collectivism, institutional collectivism, performance orientation, power distance, and uncertainty avoidance. Table 5.1 offers the definition for each cultural value investigated.

One important feature of the GLOBE research is that the investigators asked the participants to distinguish what they *value* (what is "right") from what they see *being practiced* by leaders (what is "done"). In table 5.1, the high-practice clusters column lists regions that report practices there significantly higher than the norm; likewise, the low-practice clusters column lists those that report practices significantly below the norm.

Table 5.1

Cultural Values and Practices

Cultural value	Description	High-practice country clusters	Low-practice country clusters
Performance orientation	The degree to which a collective encourages and rewards group members for performance improvement and excellence	Germanic Europe Confucian Asia	Eastern Europe
Assertiveness	The degree to which individuals are assertive, confrontational, and aggressive in their relationships with others	Germanic Europe	Nordic Europe South Asia
Future orientation	The extent to which individuals engage in future-oriented behaviors such as delaying gratification, planning, and investing in the future	Germanic Europe Nordic Europe	Latin America Eastern Europe
Humane orientation	The degree to which a collective encourages and rewards individuals for being fair, altruistic, generous, caring, and kind to others	South Asia	Germanic Europe Latin Europe
Institutional collectivism	The degree to which organizational and societal institutional practices encourage and reward collective distribution of resources and collective action	Confucian Asia Nordic Europe	Latin America
In-group collectivism	The degree to which individuals express pride, loyalty, and cohesiveness in their organizations or families	South Asia	Nordic Europe Anglo Germanic Europe
Gender egalitarianism	The degree to which a collective minimizes gender inequality	Nordic Europe	Middle East
Power distance	The degree to which members of a collective expect power to be distributed equally	South Asia	Nordic Europe
Uncertainty avoidance	The extent to which a society, organization, or group relies on social norms, rules, and procedures to alleviate unpredictability of future events	Germanic Europe Nordic Europe	Eastern Europe Latin America

Source: House et al. 2004; House et al. 2014

Christians have long recognized that even though members of a society may value one thing, they may also act against their own values. This is readily seen, for example, in power distance and gender egalitarianism. For both, investigators found that in many countries people preferred small power distance and strong gender egalitarianism. However, they acted in ways that best correlate with large power distance and weak gender egalitarianism. For gender egalitarianism, 61 of the 62 countries in the original GLOBE study positively valued gender egalitarianism but reported that leaders did not practice it (see House et al. 2004, 365–66).

Leadership Attributes and Dimensions

Of the 122 leadership attributes investigated in the study, investigators found that 22 are universally deemed positive (e.g., foresight, motive arouser, honest, and decisive), and 8 are universally perceived as negative (e.g., dictatorial, ruthless, egocentric, and irritable). Of the remaining 92 attributes, 35 had scores varying widely enough to let researchers conclude that perceptions of whether these 35 attributes are negative or positive are contingent on the society or culture. These include attributes such as sincere, self-effacing, risk-taker, enthusiastic, intuitive, status conscious, and independent. It is among these 35 attributes that significant conflict around the ideals and practices of leaders is found. The exercise in sidebar 5.1 gives you an opportunity to explore this for yourself.

SIDEBAR 5.1
CULTURALLY DEPENDENT LEADERSHIP PRACTICES

As you look at the following list, consider whether you consider each attribute to be good, bad, or neutral for a leader. Then imagine a society that views it as opposite of the way you view it. Remembering that others' perspective makes as much sense to them as yours does to you, what do you think might be some reasons for their evaluation?

Ambitious	Procedural	Domineering
Logical	Unique	Habitual
Sincere	Status conscious	Individualistic
Enthusiastic	Formal	Indirect
Intuitive	Risk-taker	Subdued
Orderly	Class conscious	Micromanager
Willful	Intragroup conflict avoider	Elitist
Worldly	Independent	Ruler
Self-sacrificial	Self-effacing	Cunning
Sensitive	Autonomous	Provocateur
Intragroup competitor	Cautious	
Compassionate	Evasive	

Adapted from House et al. 2014, 25

Table 5.2

Styles of Leadership Seen Globally

Style of leadership	Description
Charismatic/value based	Broadly defined to reflect the ability to inspire, motivate, and expect high performance outcomes from others based on firmly held core values.
Team oriented	Emphasizes effective team building and implementation of a common purpose or goal among team members.
Participative	Reflects the degree to which managers involve others in making and implementing decisions.
Humane oriented	Reflects supportive and considerate leadership but also includes compassion and generosity.
Autonomous	Tendency to act independently and without much collaboration with colleagues.
Self-protective	Focuses on ensuring the safety and security of the individual and group through status enhancement and face saving.

Source: House et al. 2004; House et al. 2014, 19

As I mentioned above, the GLOBE researchers identified what they called six global leadership dimensions, which are general approaches to leadership. They are (1) charismatic/value-based leadership, (2) team-oriented leadership, (3) participative leadership, (4) humane-oriented leadership, (5) autonomous leadership, and (6) self-protective leadership (see table 5.2 for descriptions). Space precludes any sort of in-depth discussion, but clearly these styles play roles in both businesses *and* churches around the world today. As you read through the descriptions in table 5.2, consider various contemporary global leaders to see whether you can determine which style of leadership they exemplify. For example, whatever your political persuasion, consider the differences in leadership style of President Obama and President Trump, and you will clearly see that people from the same country are not constrained to use the same style of leadership.

Each of the 6 global leadership dimensions is built on a subset of the 122 leadership attributes and 21 primary leadership dimensions noted previously. For example, the charismatic/value-based leadership style builds on 22 of the 122 leadership attributes and 6 of the 21 primary dimensions. In figure 5.1, I identify not only the attributes and primary dimensions that together comprise charismatic/value-based leadership; I also indicate which attributes are perceived as universally positive and which are perceived as culturally contingent.

To help you better see the cultural variations, in table 5.3 I show which leadership styles are perceived as necessary for successful leaders in the

Figure 5.1: Characteristics of charismatic/value-based leadership

22 Leadership Attributes

6 Primary Leadership Dimensions

Foresight Prepared Anticipatory **Plans ahead**	Charismatic: Visionary
Enthusiastic **Positive** Morale booster **Motive arouser**	Charismatic: Inspirational
Risk-taker Self-sacrificial Convincing	Charismatic: Self-sacrificial
Honest Sincere **Just** **Trustworthy**	Integrity
Willful **Decisive** Logical Intuitive	Decisive
Improvement-oriented **Excellence-oriented** Performance-oriented	Performance-oriented

Leadership Attributes Key:
Bold = Universally positive
Underline = Culturally contingent

→ Charismatic/Value-Based Leadership

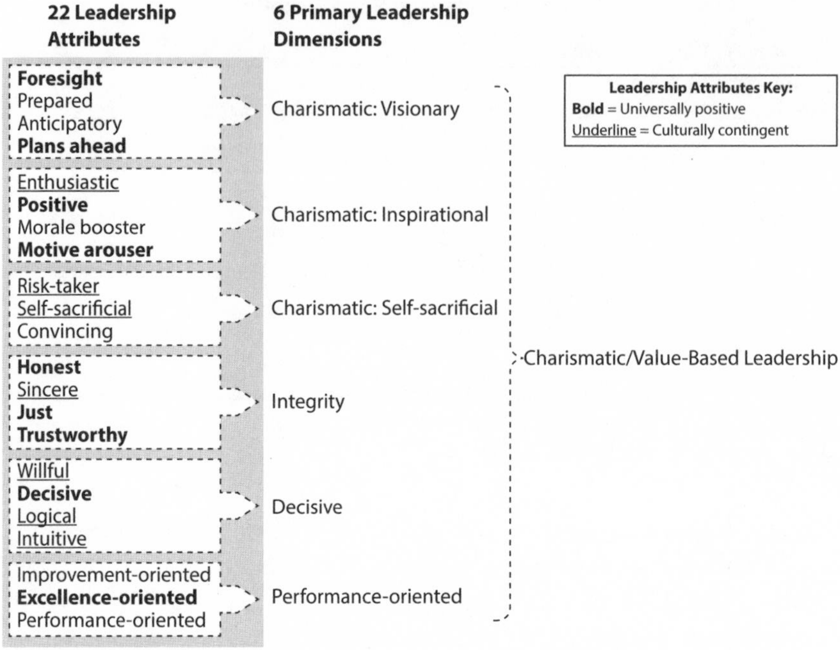

Developed from House et al. 2014, 20–22, 24–25

country clusters of the world grouped by the GLOBE researchers. In this case, examine the rankings of Middle Eastern versus Anglo countries. Successful leaders in the Middle East require significantly different skill sets from leaders in Anglo countries (the US, Canada, Great Britain, Australia, and New Zealand).

Selected Cultural Variances

Given both the massive set of issues related to leadership and the sheer number of cultural values in the GLOBE study, it will help to focus our attention on selected issues to better understand the implications. While the GLOBE study identifies nine values of salience for understanding cultural differences (see table 5.1), in the following I limit my focus to two of the nine (power distance and in-group collectivism). I also add one important cultural value not seen in the GLOBE study but permeating recent missiological literature: honor and justice (adapted in part from Moreau 2017). The central question behind this focus is, In what ways do power distance, collectivism, and honor affect leadership?

Table 5.3

Ranking of Societal Clusters by Value Scores

	Charismatic/ value based	Team oriented	Participative	Humane oriented	Autonomous	Self-protective
Significantly higher than average	Anglo Latin America South Asia Germanic Europe Nordic Europe	Latin America	Germanic Europe Nordic Europe Anglo	South Asia Sub-Saharan Africa Anglo	Eastern Europe Germanic Europe Confucian Asia South Asia Nordic Europe Anglo Middle East Latin Europe Sub-Saharan Africa Latin America	South Asia Middle East Confucian Asia Eastern Europe
Significantly lower than average	Middle East	Middle East	Eastern Europe South Asia Confucian Asia Middle East	Latin Europe Nordic Europe		Anglo Germanic Europe Nordic Europe

Adapted from House et al. 2014, 31

Large and Small Power Distance

Power distance (PD) is a term used to address the reality that in every society people value the fact, distribution, and exercise of *social power*. In large PD societies, members expect those in charge to be the ones who make decisions, guiding and when needed even controlling followers' behavior. In small PD societies, members expect that social power should be more evenly distributed and that the opinions of those of lower social standing should carry the same weight as those of much higher social standing. After all, they reason, the opinions of both are judged on the basis of what is true or right rather than who has more social power.

Collectivism and Individualism

The two general approaches to defining the self are commonly referred to as individualism and collectivism. The GLOBE study identifies and measures two forms of collectivism (noted in table 5.1): *institutional* collectivism and *in-group* collectivism. I refer to the latter in this discussion.

Members of collective societies, such as Korea, believe that the primary unit of society is the in-group. The needs of the in-group take priority over the needs of the individual, though the individual may belong to several in-groups simultaneously (extended family, work, school, church, region, nation, and so on), and the needs of each will be considered in navigating life. By contrast, members of individualistic societies, such as the United States, believe that the primary unit of society is the individual, and the primary group unit is the nuclear family. The interests, needs, and skills of the individual are paramount. People are expected to be independent as adults and not reliant on groups for their identity.

Honor and Justice

The final set of contrasting values is that of justice and honor (see Moreau, Campbell, and Greener 2014, 195–209; plus the material in chap. 3 above). Honor as a culturally constructed value is not investigated in the GLOBE study, though face saving and status consciousness in leadership are, albeit as negative ones (House et al. 2014, 370). The GLOBE authors note that where face saving does make a difference between superior and inferior leaders, superior leaders are surprisingly (their term) *more* face saving than inferior leaders (319; see 378 for the questions reflected in the GLOBE face-saver and status-conscious constructs). In other words, that face saving can be positive in a leader is surprising to the researchers. Beyond this, however, the GLOBE study does not venture.

As noted previously, among biblical scholars and missionaries as well as those who study Christian faith in cultural settings, honor and justice have generated significant discussion over the past three decades, including a few explorations of the role that honor plays in shaping how people lead (see Georges and Baker 2016, 205–8). Both honor and justice are essential cultural values, each with corresponding mechanisms for maintaining social order; shame serves in this capacity in honor-framed societies, and guilt for justice-oriented societies.

At the core of an honor-based approach is *who the individual (or the individual's group) is*. By contrast, at the core of a justice-based approach is *what the individual has done*. Each approach recognizes the value of the other, but members of societies that value one over the other will order their priorities accordingly.

Two Types of Societies

It is helpful to contrast two types of societies based on these three values as seen in table 5.4 (in this case, limited to European countries). At the risk of oversimplification, in table 5.4 I refer to the orientation on the left as CLH and that on the right as ISJ. The "mixed" countries in the middle are those that do not fit the general pattern, whether through being individualistic but large in PD (power distance) or the opposite.

Table 5.4

Two Types of Societies (European Countries)

CLH: Collective, larger PD, honor-oriented societies	Mixed	ISJ: Individualistic, smaller PD, justice-oriented societies
More often seen in southern and Eastern Europe (Albania, Bulgaria, Croatia, Greece, Portugal, Romania, Russia, Serbia, Slovakia, Slovenia, Spain, and Ukraine)	Belgium, Czech Republic, France, Poland, Hungary, Latvia, Lithuania, Italy	More often seen in northern Europe (Austria, Denmark, Estonia, Finland, Germany, Great Britain, Ireland, Netherlands, Norway, Sweden, and Switzerland)

Given these contrasting sets of cultural values, it becomes apparent why societies value differing styles of leadership. ISJ societies, for example, are more likely to value leaders who respect the opinions of subordinates, who tolerate deviation from the norm, who are more democratic in decision making, and who see justice as blind to the person or group. CLH societies, however, are more likely to value followers who respect the decisions of leaders, leaders who promote group harmony and unanimity, who are more autocratic in decision making, and who value a person in light of his or her honor or status.

Given the realities of economic power in our globalized world, generally people from ISJ countries often experience significant educational and economic advantages over people from CLH countries. When unchecked (a frequent occurrence), people from ISJ countries are more likely to assume they should be the primary voice(s) at the metaphorical global table and be holding the "winning" hand. Indeed, they are more prone to come to the table with the perception that their approach is the only viable approach and to devalue the voices of the people from CLH countries during disagreements over leadership, organization, and maintaining order (see, e.g., Bonk et al. 2011).

In fact, given the historical dominance of ISJ countries, people from them often *expect* to be the lead voice at the table and also expect that their model of leadership should not even be questioned. Those from CLH countries, through historical experience, have learned to simply allow the status quo to remain if they want to continue to come to the table and receive the benefits that being present at the table brings.

Conclusion

In sum, leadership style preferences are culturally mediated, and the patterns of preferred leadership vary across cultures. From the GLOBE research we learn that the charismatic/visionary leader is universally appreciated, but the appreciation and exercise of the other five GLOBE-identified approaches is culturally dependent. From the broad perspective of societal values, we see differing models of leadership that can help us better understand how Christian leaders operate in relation to the values of their societies. From table 5.4, we see contrasting approaches based on the alignment of three sets of cultural values, and we will return to that in our discussion on contextualizing leadership.

Organization

Figure 5.2 presents a standard conceptual framework for analyzing organizational culture in a local setting. As figure 5.2 illustrates, there are four major conceptual categories that play a role in organizational culture and leadership: (1) the setting, (2) the cultural system, (3) the sociostructural system, and (4) the individual actor. The first three are systems themselves, and when integrated together each plays a significant role in contextualizing the individual actor and determining the range and types of actions considered appropriate for that person in relation to the organization.

The Setting

The setting includes the cultural, social, political, and judicial systems of the society in which the organization originates, the history of the organization, and the contingent elements that characterize the organization and the larger industry in which it participates. Each plays a foundational role in determining the patterns of the organization and the systems by which it operates. For example, evangelical churches in the United States today exist within a larger society whose mores are shifting, pressuring them to change or find ways to stand firm within the societal system—or to attempt to change the systems themselves. Contextually driven social issues ranging from gender identification to gay marriage to separation of church and state all impact churches, which must choose how (not whether!) to respond to the challenges to traditional beliefs and practices generated by these social issues.

The Cultural System

We have already discussed the cultural systems of leadership; everything that was said in that discussion about cultural values and practices applies not only to leaders but also to *all* members of an organization.

In the cultural system, figure 5.2 also includes the organization's myths. "Myths" refer to the stories people tell themselves and each other about the organization and the people that make up the organization. Think of the legends told about Apple and about Steve Jobs, Apple's storied cofounder and

Figure 5.2: A conceptual framework for organizational culture

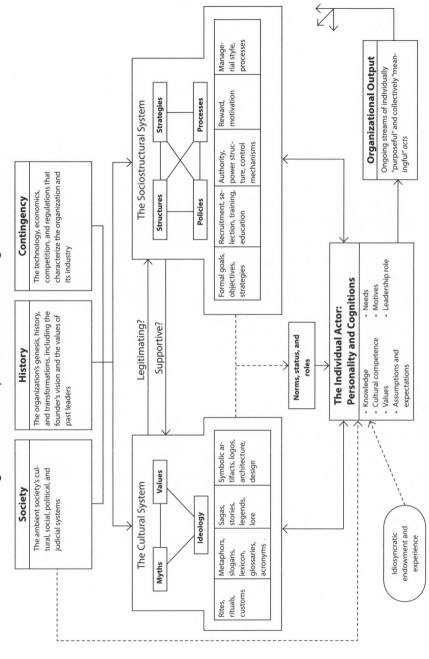

Source: Allaire and Firsirotu 1984, 214. Used with permission.

CEO. The many stories about his life and leadership style and the resulting corporate culture of Apple continue to resonate after his death, indicating his mythic status. Hollywood's portrayal, titled *Steve Jobs* (2015), and numerous documentaries helped cement his mythic status outside the computer industry. We examine myth in this sense in greater detail in chapter 6.

The cultural system also includes both the ritual (from staff meetings to coffee breaks; chap. 9) and the signs and symbols (from corporate logos to dress policies to architecture; chap. 8) of the organization. All of these intertwine with and reinforce one another, and each new employee or member within the organization is expected to either understand the system on arrival or to learn the system over the course of their participation.

The Sociostructural System

In chapter 2 we explored how institutions establish and maintain their identity. Our focus here is less on identity than on the cohesion of the group. Threats to an institution's or even a society's existence come from the competition for power seen in the struggle for control over human, human-made, natural, and supernatural resources. With the exception of supernatural resources (depending on the religious orientation of the members), these resources are all limited. As a result, conflict of control over and plans concerning the appropriate use of those resources is inevitable, and it is within the sociostructural system of the organization (fig. 5.2) that this gets played out.

The sociostructural system includes those elements that keep the organization intact and functioning but that also frame how it responds to challenges (internal or external) to the established order. Together with the cultural system, the sociostructural system provides the set of norms for behavior, the set of statuses available within the organization, and the roles people take on based on their status and the organizational norms. For example, when our entire academic department shifted to a new location within the same building, the allocation of offices was determined by role (faculty first, administrative staff second, part-time employees third) and, within each role, by longevity with the organization (or status). As the longest-serving faculty member, I was granted the right to be the first person to choose the office I wanted. The longest-serving department administrator chose only after all faculty chose. This was assumed to be the "right" way to allocate offices based on the norms, statuses, and roles: it was a "justice" orientation that also reinforced "honor" based on role in the institution. In a different setting a different system would be deemed appropriate, perhaps based on the relationships of the people being moved to those of higher status in the organization. In that case, if the son of the college president served as an administrator in the department, he may well have been given the first choice of office space based on his relational status rather than his job status. And in that setting, people would agree that this is the proper way to allocate space.

The organizational or political system of an institution, therefore, is in many respects the network of positions, individuals, and social roles that exists to regulate or control the competition for resources—and ultimately competition over power.

In many societies, these resources are perceived to be limited such that my success inevitably results in less success available for you, referred to as a zero-sum approach. For example, in a zero-sum–oriented group the amount of goodwill toward leaders may be considered as not having the potential to grow. When a new person joins and begins to win the goodwill of other members, the existing leaders may feel threatened that they will have less goodwill themselves. When they feel threatened, they may well take steps to neutralize the threat (from shaming gossip to expulsion).

The Individual Actor

The final component in figure 5.2 is the individual, who stands within the sets of overlapping systems. Individuals may be both restrained and elevated by the setting, the cultural system, and the sociostructural system. These constraints are conscious as well as subconscious.

In 2010 I participated in a gathering of Korean and North American mission leaders (Moreau 2011). The Koreans initiated the conference to discuss with North American mission leaders issues of accountability in mission. Altogether ten case studies were presented, five by Koreans and five by North Americans. Each case study had a response from the other group. Over our time together, each case and response was presented to the entire group, and time was then given for discussion of the case. At the end of the conference a Korean and I were tasked with summarizing what we had learned from the proceedings.

For my response, I examined the vocabulary used by each group to see which terms each side used far more often than the other side, with the intention of uncovering the subconscious differences between the two groups, since neither was paying conscious attention to the vocabulary they used in their papers. I grouped the terms each group used far more often than the other into "clusters," each with a theme based on the vocabulary each used, illustrated in figure 5.3.

Figure 5.3: Korean and North American "hidden curriculum" illustrated

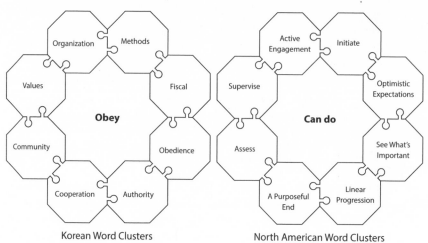

Korean Word Clusters   North American Word Clusters

Adapted from Moreau 2011, 307, 312. Used with permission.

The vocabulary analysis uncovered important differences, especially in areas in which clashes would likely occur, such as the Korean value of knowing one's role and place versus the American value of freedom. Four sets of contrasting values that would more likely lead to clashes between the two are illustrated in figure 5.4.

The following account summarizes the differences I found through the vocabulary analysis (which were also confirmed in the discussion over our time together):

The hidden curriculums uncovered by the analysis in this chapter suggest that Koreans and North Americans who choose to partner together will face significant challenges in developing a mutually acceptable approach to accountability. For example, Korean expectations that are related to hierarchical authority, obedience, and specific organizational titles will mix poorly with North American expectations of initiation, engagement, and optimism about linear progression toward a purposeful end. . . .

A telling example of this point is provided by the expression "relational economics." The term was used in one of the case studies and reiterated during several question-and-answer sessions. For Koreans, relational economics drives accountability, but the exposure of the Korean hidden curriculum enables a better understanding of this concept. The clusters in our analysis help uncover Korean "relational economics" as not egalitarian but hierarchical, the proper form of interpersonal relationship as tacitly understood by Koreans. This hierarchical framing has well-defined constraints that can be seen in the clusters,

Figure 5.4: Areas of Korean and North American culture value clashes in accountability

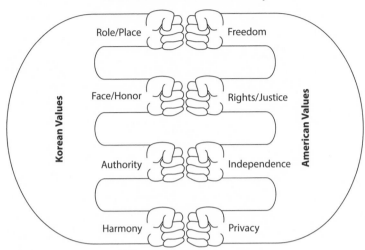

including obligation, harmony, and precise organizational roles—all defined and applied from a Korean perspective.

Thus, Korean missionaries on the field believe that correct behavior incorporates a flexibility that means shame is not brought to the organization or its leaders. For example, they might value contravention of written policy when that policy clashes with the maintenance of harmony and obedience to authority. Generally speaking, Koreans who note such a breach of policy would likely choose not to mention it, knowing that to do so could bring disarray to the ministry both on-site and back home. North Americans, in contrast, would be more likely not only to mention any disregard of policy but even to force an investigation of the matter. This response fits with the ideals identified in the North American hidden curriculum, such as initiative, the identification and assessment of what is important, and progressive steps to deal with significant issues. The American approach, however, would be deemed so offensive by the Koreans that major conflict would be all but inevitable. (Moreau 2011, 312–13)

While both groups value accountability in their respective organizations, they take different approaches to accountability and maintaining order within institutions. Drawing from this example, Koreans working for American organizations will generally be obedient and deferential to bosses as well as flexible in interpreting policy depending on the relationships they have with bosses and subordinates. They will also likely find ways to cover shameful mistakes rather than reveal them.

On the other hand, Americans working for Korean organizations are more likely to focus more on written policy than relationships; they may take the initiative to deal with issues that concern them more overtly even when some may result in losing face. They will be more likely to fight for "what is right" when their bosses ask them to do something with which they disagree. Both must learn to adapt to the constraints of the cross-cultural organization, and each may need to face the sense of betrayal or violation of conscience by the other as part of the reality of working for an organization not of their home culture.

So far we have explored leadership and organization on a societal scale, generally ignoring how they are particularly manifested in religious organizations. It is safe to assume that societal values impact religious leadership values (and in many cases, vice versa). In sidebar 5.1 we note several questions to be considered in any new setting as you explore the social institution of leadership and organization.

Leadership and Organization: Implications for Contextualization

Leadership

In table 5.3, we noted from the GLOBE study the leadership styles perceived as necessary for successful leaders in the country clusters, and we mentioned the differences between the Middle Eastern and Anglo perceptions. Given that Jesus himself was Middle Eastern, to what extent can contemporary Middle Eastern leadership styles and values be mapped onto the values of ancient Middle Eastern (e.g., biblical) culture? The answers are complicated, but this also raises the question of the extent to which we tend to read contemporary Western values onto the biblical text (see, e.g., Bailey 2008; Richards and O'Brien 2012; Georges and Baker 2016, 205–8).

Missionary statesman and thinker Jim Plueddemann (2009, 66) provides a very helpful framework for contextual thinking about leadership through asking the following five questions:

What are my underlying cultural assumptions about leadership?

What are the underlying assumptions of those from different cultures?

Which biblical principles of leadership must be followed in every culture?

When does leadership need to change in order to reflect biblical principles?

When does the Bible allow for flexibility in leadership style?

SIDEBAR 5.1
QUESTIONS ABOUT LEADERSHIP AND ORGANIZATION

Below are some questions to consider as you explore social organization and leadership in your setting. Asking and exploring the answers to these questions will enable you to better understand local examples of organization and leadership—but more importantly help you think more clearly about church and the means Christians may use to organize themselves in light of local societal norms.

As I noted in parallel sidebars in previous chapters, answers to these questions could be used to compromise the gospel or the biblical definition of church. That is not my intention. Rather, the questions equip you to find biblically appropriate and culturally sound ways for Christians to understand local views of social organizing and leading. They help you avoid the danger of simply generating and using only the organizational and leadership approaches that make sense from your own cultural setting. As you ask these questions, also be asking yourself how the answers impact what type of approaches to organizing and leading would make sense to local people without compromising their relationship with Christ.

1. Leadership (secular and religious)
   a. In what ways do leaders operate that follow normal societal values?
   b. In what ways do leaders operate that go against normal societal values?
   c. What types of vision do leaders exercise?
   d. How do leaders motivate their followers?
   e. How do leaders maintain control over their organizations?
   f. What is the normal leadership-selection process and installation?
2. Organizations (secular and religious)
   a. How do insiders categorize the various organizations that exist?
   b. Purposes: What types of positive purposes do organizations serve? What types of negative purposes do they serve? How do people inside the organizations perceive each of these?
   c. What characterizes organizations that separate their members from society?
   d. What characterizes organizations that integrate their members into society?
   e. What revitalization or renewal organizations or movements do you observe? What makes each successful? What are the challenges each faces?
3. Beyond the doctrinal concerns, in what ways does the gospel condone or condemn indigenous leadership practices and styles as well as organizational systems?

He illustrates the issues raised by means of a Venn diagram of overlapping ideas of leadership (fig. 5.5) that displays graphically the areas we need to consider. In the prior sections, we focused on the bottom two circles of the diagram: our cultural values and the values of other cultures. Contextualized thinking requires that we also bring in the top circle, which likewise causes us to consider the overlapping areas among all three circles, plus the areas in which there is no overlap.

Figure 5.5: Overlapping ideas of leadership

Source: Plueddemann 2009, 67. Used by permission of Inter-Varsity Press, PO Box 1400, Downers Grove, IL 60515, USA. www.ivpress.com.

Plueddemann (66) lists the following points that the diagram is intended to illustrate:

1. No culture can boast of leadership values that are completely biblical.

2. All cultures are blessed with some biblical leadership values.

3. Cultures exhibit many differences in leadership values.

4. Cultures have some leadership values in common with other cultures.

5. Most cultures contain leadership values that intersect with those of other cultures and also follow biblical principles.

Many Westerners are conditioned to think that the model they follow is "the" biblical model as a "servant leader." As legitimate as that approach is, it is also easy for us to miss or overlook the cultural constraints inherent in our chosen model(s). Additionally, we often do not recognize that while the paradigm of "servant leader" is a legitimate, biblically based approach, the fact is that "servant" and "leader" are both culturally framed; indeed, the very definition of "servant leader" is culturally framed. Christopher Wright (2015), successor to John Stott as director of Langham Partnership, offers an option that opens up deeper conversation by identifying three biblical characteristics of leaders: humility, integrity, and simplicity. Even using that approach, however, each term is understood in light of cultural framing.

To illustrate, at the end of a trip to Korea being hosted by a Korean mission agency, I debriefed with my interpreter at the airport. For ten days I had been treated like a king—doors opened, luggage carried, taken to meals of my choice, given very nice accommodations with all expenses paid, and so on. As an American, the level of treatment was embarrassing. I simply rode it out, knowing I was the guest rather than the host. However, as we debriefed, my translator stated that I was very humble. He stated that many Americans get angry at Korean hosts after a few days because they want to do things for themselves and they don't want to be so highly honored. He said that I allowed him and the other Koreans who hosted me to be Korean and that this was because I was so humble. It dawned on me that he defined "humble" differently than how I did: he saw it as knowing my place and fitting into the role that was expected of me as an honored guest. Allowing my hosts to treat me in this (to me) very nonhumble way was for him an indicator that I was humble. I realized that he and I used the same English word, "humble," in very different ways. From my vantage point, a truly humble person would not have stood for the treatment I received. For him, humility was about knowing my place and fitting in. For me, it is about not putting myself in a position of honor. Even today, more than a decade later, his declaration to me shouts that even though we spoke the same language, our respective underlying worldviews colored the definitions even of the terms we used.

Given that reality, leaders of Christian organizations or ministries in new cultural settings do not always realize that they do not understand the rules of the new setting. This is especially true of multinational ministries or denominations, since the leaders understand the rules in their own countries, they assume those rules apply in the same way in the new setting.

In a globalized world, we anticipate the continued proliferation of multicultural and multinational teams with an ever-greater diversity of leaders. While there are challenges, there are also opportunities. Cross-cultural partnerships can be far more fruitful than homogeneous partnerships—but they require developing a "third way" of navigating relationships, policies, procedures, and values—especially for Western leaders. What follows are several suggestions to develop a third way of leadership (adapted from Moreau 2017), especially for Western leaders leading majority-world people. In the discussion that follows, we will use the terms ISJ (individualist, small power distance, justice oriented) and CLH (collective, large power distance, and honor oriented) as noted in table 5.4.

Learn to Listen Well

Perhaps the most significant challenge for ISJ leaders is learning how to listen well to those from CLH societies. Rarely does this come through the normal organizational exercises that typify ISJ leadership such as focus groups, performance reviews, or brainstorming sessions. First, CLH people typically were not enculturated into these exercises and may view them through a CLH lens—which means, for example, that they may be trying to read cues from the leader(s) on how they should respond or behave. Once they sense they have discerned the will of the leaders, they will conform to that will as long as it does not cause them to lose face.

ISJ leaders may work to empower CLH people to be able to say what they are thinking even if it is negative. The problem with this approach is that we are in essence trying to train them to behave in ways that make sense to us rather than to them.

A better path is to develop relationships outside the work environment, over meals or other social events. Learning about their lives, their challenges, their aspirations and hopes is better done in informal environments and through long-established relationships than in formal settings with relatively new relationships.

Value Leaders in the Local Image Rather Than a Western Image

A common path to leadership development is to train leaders to lead *as we do*. We might send them for training at an ISJ institution. Alternately, we might train them in-house by using the training methods through which we ISJ folks typically learn leadership. Both are likely to yield the same result: they lead like us rather than as natural leaders in their own CLH societies lead.

An additional concern is that all of us naturally promote those we positively assess, and we are more likely to positively assess people who lead in ways that we value. When we see qualities of leadership in them that we appreciate based on our own values, we choose them as emerging leaders in our organizations. We may even think of this as nationalization without asking whether they appear to behave as foreigners to people of their own societies.

Finally, we should not overlook the various categories and types of leaders in other religions, examining them for styles and patterns that fit local sensibilities and do not contravene biblical leadership models. These approaches become available for adaptation in a local setting. Are guru (Indian), lama (Buddhist), imam (Muslim), and rabbi (Jewish) styles of leadership all to be categorically rejected because they come from non-Christian religions? Contextualization requires that we consider what we might glean from them that still reflects biblical priorities.

Valuing Honor and Face

People from ISJ societies value truth—often above relationships and partnerships. While we certainly cannot compromise on the truth of the gospel, we should be more cautious with the "truths" about leadership that we promote. Respecting the face, or social status, of local leadership is of paramount importance in CLH societies (see, e.g., Thornton 1984).

Certainly there is potential danger in overidealizing leaders, but likewise there is also the potential danger of those from ISJ societies focusing so much on justice that we demean people made in God's image. As noted previously, it is critical to remember that society throughout biblical times was much more CLH than ISJ (see Bailey 2008), and learning to read the Scriptures in light of honor and face opens doors to better biblical understanding (see Mischke 2015).

Knowing When to Speed Up and When to Slow Down

Often ISJ organizations value efficiency and effectiveness in terms of time and money. Less money and shorter time to complete a project are valued positively, even though relationships may suffer and people may be trampled in reaching the goal. While that is less true of Christian organizations, the orientation toward efficiency and effectiveness as measured by time and money often characterizes ISJ-type Christian organizations as well.

An African proverb states, "If you want to go fast, go alone. If you want to go far, go with others." That captures the orientation of CLH societies, in which going alone may get the job done but does not create or sustain the relational capital necessary for the smooth running of an organization. ISJ people need to learn that there is a time when slowing down is better in the long run for their organization, even when donors are unhappy over delays.

Approaches to Policies and Procedures

The idea that efficiency and effectiveness may be measured by relational metrics rather than performance metrics may not make much sense to ISJ leaders. They are often unaware that their CLH subordinates value "policy economics" less than they value "relational economics," as reported in the Korean accountability case mentioned above. In a setting of policy economics, it is the policy that counts, and exchanges are weighted in terms of the specific policies or management techniques. In relational-economics settings, policy still is important, but it is weighted in terms of relational capital and history rather than what the manual actually states.

Conclusion

Clearly much more on contextualizing leadership can and should be explored. For example, insights on leadership from church planting movements (CPM) literature abound and are well worth scouring. David Garrison (2004, 189–91) points out that lay leaders are better at developing CPMs than formally trained clergy. He notes that all CPMs are composed of small house churches planting other small house churches. Within this structure, lay leaders are at the same educational and socioeconomic level as their congregations, they are more willing to hand off a new house church to a lay leader, they do not require full salaries since they are bivocational, and this follows Jesus's model of calling laypeople to follow him and developing them into leaders through apprenticeship rather than formal education.

Organization

From the house churches of the Congregação Cristã no Brasil (CCB) to the largest megachurch congregation in the world, Yoido Full Gospel Church (YFGC) in Seoul, South Korea, the forms and varieties of churches found globally are staggering. Contrasting these two organizations helps us see the breadth of the contemporary contextualizing of churches as organizations.

First is the CCB, perhaps the largest antiorganizational church in existence. Founded in 1910 by an Italian American and established through numerous follow-up trips to Brazil, with an estimated 2.3 million members, it is the second largest denomination in Brazil (Valente 2015, 73). As a church it prohibits normal evangelistic methods (tracts, public evangelism, radio, television, and so on), essentially confining outreach to personal contacts (Nelson 1989, 40). Reed Nelson (40) offered a synopsis of the antiorganizational stance of the CCB in 1989: "Its organization is extremely rudimentary. The CCB has but one small rule book of about 20 pages, and has no formal mechanisms for communication and coordination except for a bimonthly circular which announces the dates and places of upcoming baptisms. The church denies the existence of any formal hierarchy and has only two or three official positions, none of which are salaried positions. It does not maintain membership records, does not levy tithing, and does not take collections during meetings."

While churches are planted in homes, when they outgrow the homes and eventually build buildings, the structures that they build follow a universal architectural plan for all CCB congregations. They are located in peripheral urban areas, where the land is relatively cheap and the presence of the poor is dominant. There are no paid clergy; members supply their own Bibles, hymnals, and musical instruments. The personal-relationship evangelism together with a ban on the use of all normal social outlets (media, sports, clubs) results in a homogenous body that tends to be ingrown in nature. Worship is improvised, though led by an elder (*ancião*) who has veto power over all that happens. While churches are flexible *within* the church service, they are inflexible in church organization and membership commitments (dress code, isolation from media and other churches, and so on). What was once a glue for social cohesion in the organization is in process of becoming a weakness, as Rubia Valente (2015, 76–77) notes: "In the last decade, once social media and higher educational possibilities became widespread in Brazil, the CCB ministry's coherent worldview and its discourse weakened. With the spread and availability of the Internet, members of CCB started to interact with members abroad, particularly in the United States, and inconsistencies were discovered."

Theologically, CCB is Pentecostal, but sociologically it fits Weber's definition of "sect" (see Hiebert, Shaw, and Tienou 1999, 331–32) in that it separates members from normal social life. Maintaining that separation today is much harder than it was just a few decades ago, and how or whether CCB will adapt has yet to be seen.

At the other end of the organizational spectrum is Yoido Full Gospel Church. Founded in 1958 through a worship service of five people (counting Cho's future mother-in-law), today YFGC has 800,000 members (and 200,000 attending one of the seven Sunday services at the main campus). It is a complete contrast to the nonorganizational structure of CCB. With a pastoral staff numbering several hundred, over a thousand elders, and tens of thousands of deacons, YFGC members are organized into home cell groups, just under 17,000 of them in 2004 (Lim 2004, 126), with women leading them (in contrast to traditional Korean culture). Everything about the Sunday service is planned to the minute; with seven services in a single facility holding 12,000 worshipers and translated into more than a dozen languages, YFGC is organized to the hilt. It has to be, just to get one set of 12,000-plus worshipers out so that the next set can enter and be seated—six times every Sunday for the seven services. This same level of organization extends to the church newspaper (with a circulation of some 12 million) and magazines, two universities, Osanri Choi Ja-sil Memorial Fasting Prayer Mountain, and varied social welfare ministries.

Clearly there is no single answer for successfully organizing a church. From a purposeful lack of structure to the extremely structured, between the two of them, CCB and YFGC exhibit characteristics that span the spectrum and are yet both eminently successful in their respective contexts. It appears there is far more flexibility in how Christians can successfully organize than many of us imagine.

Conclusion

In this chapter I have explored the organizational component of the social dimension. Understanding leadership and how organizations operate in light of culture yields insights for contextualization. Biblical values for leadership and organizational operations are the bedrock on which we contextualize, but the Bible presents multiple models rather than a single model. Certainly it is fair to appeal to Jesus, and many of us from the West also appeal to Paul or Nehemiah. But there are numerous other leaders spanning the two millennia of the biblical narrative to whom we can appeal as leadership models—such as Abraham, Job, Deborah, Solomon, Barnabas, Timothy, and Aquila. All are held up in the biblical narrative as people who followed God. Even so, they are far less frequently portrayed as exemplary leaders in Western literature than are Jesus and Paul.

Given that, it seems that multiple approaches to leadership considered in light of local values must be considered a viable contextual approach to organizing churches and other Christian organizations. Even though we are anchored in the biblical text, there is no one biblical, universal, "one size fits all" approach to leadership. The short case study offers you a chance to consider leadership of a multinational team in an all-too-real setting. As you read it and consider what you might say or do, also bear in mind that *how* you implement your solution is just as important as *what* the solution is.

CASE STUDY

TEAM DYNAMICS

It has been a real struggle to accomplish much work during the last three weekly meetings of a multinational team in China. One of the single Brazilian men has fallen in love with a Korean team member, and this has led to some division. The Korean team leader and his wife believe it is better not to encourage this relationship. The other three members of the team, an American couple and their 20-year-old son, see no serious problem with it, provided they go slowly and remain accountable. The leader tries to instruct the Brazilian man privately but they end up arguing. The oldest American tries to act as a mediator between both parties as this issue is brought up during the team meetings. The Korean woman is confused, the team leader feels his authority is being overlooked, the Americans want to move on and focus on ministry issues, and the Brazilian is afraid that he will lose a potential wife. Take the part of one of the seven team members, and describe what you might do to help resolve this situation.

Reprinted from Cho and Greenlee 1995, 182–83.

6

THE MYTHIC DIMENSION

Our God is a storytelling God. As we are made in his image, we too are storytellers. Given that, it is not at all surprising that so much of the Bible is narrative rather than didactic (teaching). In this chapter I consider that storytelling component of who we are and examine some of the implications for contextualization.

What Is Myth?

A significant challenge of using the category of "myth" as a dimension is the common understanding among evangelicals that a myth is an untrue story. Certainly we do not see the Bible in this way, and Smart (1996, 130–31) states that this is a challenge not only for Christians but also for Muslims and Jews.

Contemporary approaches to mythography (e.g., Segal 2015) consider the historicity or veracity of a particular myth as insignificant for it to operate *as a myth*. As a result, it is easier to examine myths in action than to attempt to define them (O'Flaherty 1988, 25–27). In the contemporary approach, "a myth is in principle neither true nor false, but *a useful fiction*" (Barbour 1974, 24). Religious scholar Kenneth MacKendrick (2015, 23) concurs: "As my four-year-old daughter once said, 'Thor and Loki are real when we pretend they are real.' In a sense she's right. Pretend play is when we act as though something is real when it is not. It is a way of acting in the world that posits and sustains a counter-factual reality."

Henry Murray (1960, 355–56) offers a typical contemporary and accessible definition: "Myths are instruments by which we continually struggle to make our experience intelligible to ourselves. A myth is a large, controlling image that gives philosophical meaning to the facts of ordinary life; that is, which has organizing value for experience. A mythology is more or less an articulated body of such images, a pantheon."

From the vantage point of the social sciences, myths are culturally derived instruments that encapsulate ideals of behavior (Eliade 1963). Thus mythographers tend to focus on the *values exhibited* and the *role* of a particular myth (or corpus of myths) as it is used in a society. A primary concern is the role (or roles) played by enduring stories, not their historicity. Typically the role myths play is to express the values, hopes, and fears of the people who pass them on to others. Clearly these stories are important in the local setting. From a contextualizing vantage point, Christians crossing cultures for Christ bring in a new set of (biblical) stories that operate in our lives with the hope that they will come to operate similarly among those whom we serve.

For contextual purposes, by "myth" I refer to the narratives that reflect a society's thinking about itself, humanity, the world, and the laws and values on which these all interact and operate. Mythographers typically focus their work on timeless stories of creation, redemption, and human/divine drama seen in a society's scriptures, epics, and classics. However, and again for contextual purposes, I use a broader definition: *myth is any real or fictional story, recurring theme, or character type that appeals to the consciousness of a people by embodying its cultural ideals or by giving expression to deep, commonly held beliefs and felt emotions.*

The mythic corpus of any society, then, includes its scriptures, epics, and classics, but also proverbs, folklore, fairy stories, and even contemporary stories that incorporate mythic elements (stories of heroism, sacrifice, love, and so on). Contemporary myth includes stories found in contemporary literature, movies (Hollywood, Bollywood, and Nollywood), and the oral traditions of a society. By oral traditions I include not only the stories we tell our children but also the stories that circulate among adults about celebrities, political figures, and religious leaders.

What Does Myth "Do"?

I stated above that it is easier to see myth in action than to define it. Myth is multidimensional, so we cannot confine it in action to a single purpose or function. Understanding how scholars approach myth and the functions it serves in societies helps us best consider what it means to contextualize myth.

At the most foundational level, myth plays a role in the life history of every person and society. It is woven into the fabric of our lives in the informal learning process of enculturation. Ultimately we all see the world through our mythic foundations: myth, worldview, sacred canopy (Berger 1969; by which I intend to indicate religious faith), and the patterns by which we live all interweave together—and all impact one another (see fig. 6.1). Steven Evans (2010), a specialist in cross-cultural communication, posits that we can catalyze changes in worldview and culture through storytelling (or myth). Likewise, I posit that when we change our lifestyle by engaging in new patterns of behavior (whatever the underlying cause), that change may well affect our worldview and (depending on the lifestyle change) the sacred canopy (our religious convictions, especially when the lifestyle change violates religious taboo). Likewise, religious conversion (a change in sacred canopy) impacts all areas: how we live, our worldview, and our myth structures.

Figure 6.1: Interweaving of myth, worldview, lifeways, and sacred canopy

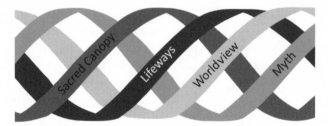

The corpus of myth in a society both contains and constrains the social and personal values of that society, which may be expressed in ritual and ceremony both in daily life and in formal, dramatized performances or rituals (Doty 1986; see chap. 9 below). In addition to seeing how scholars approach myth, examining the functions myth has in societies deepens our understanding. Ian Barbour (1974, 23–28) identifies two major categories of mythic functions: psychological and social.

Psychological Functions

Myths can serve us when we face uncertain circumstances as an individual or on a societal level. They buttress us in the face of uncertainty and help reduce anxiety. In one sense they provide shelter in the storm, contributing to the scared canopy (Berger 1969) that protects us from the vicissitudes of life. Consider how many Christians turn to biblical stories when faced with financial, medical, psychological, or other crises. Similarly, Muslims may turn to the Qur'an or the hadiths (Arabic: ahadith), Jews to the Torah or Psalms, Buddhists to the Tripitaka, Hindus to the Vedas. Typically those who turn to myth during a crisis are more interested in the deeper religious myths than the fairy stories they heard or the platitudes they learned in childhood, though Native American author Leslie Marmon Silko poignantly notes, "The old folks said the stories themselves had the power to protect us and even to heal us because the stories are alive; *the stories are our ancestors.* In the very telling of the stories, the spirits of our beloved ancestors and family become present with us. The ancestors love us and care for us though we may not know this" (Silko 1996, 152, emphasis added). In times of crisis or need, it is comforting to have a mythic, larger-than-life resource to draw on. In one sense Christians recognize this as the draw of all people to connect to their Creator and to the story of redemption, in which God's love for every person offers not only comfort but even salvation.

When we face conflict with other people, mythic paradigms offer images and stories of what an honorable, righteous, just, or good person should do. In terms of this function, whether we utilize mythic framing to justify our actions before or after the fact makes little difference; either way, myth still guides our behavior and either condones or condemns our actions. Stories of characters handling conflict honorably (or dishonorably) provide the grist for our contemplative mills, offering both security in the conflict and, at the very least, intimating that there are viable paths to resolution.

Social Functions

Myths act as a social glue holding a society together. To the extent that they are shared across all segments of a nation, national myths (e.g., stories of national heroes) promote the integration of society as a whole by binding people to a common narrative. As Barbour (1974, 24) observes, "Myth sanctions the existing social order and justifies its status system and power structure, providing a rationale for social and political institutions—from kinship to kingship." Through narrative, myth does this in part by validating the rules, mores, and taboos of a society (Loewen 1978, 303).

While this is certainly true for a single ethnolinguistic group with one mythic corpus, it is less likely true for a nation when that nation is composed largely of a polyglot of peoples or of immigrants from across the world (e.g., the US). As an example, a common mythic orientation in the United States by that subset of the nation known as conservative Christians maintains that the

SIDEBAR 6.1
QUESTIONS ABOUT MYTH

Below are some questions adapted from religious scholar William G. Doty (2000, 466–67) to consider as you explore myth in your setting. Asking and exploring the answers to these questions will enable you to better understand local examples of myth—but also help you think more clearly about church and ways Christians might better understand myths in their contexts and, when appropriate, use them or the cultural insights they offer to better contextualize the gospel.

As I noted in comparable sidebars in previous chapters, answers to these questions could be used to compromise the gospel or the biblical definition of church. That is not my intention. Rather, the questions equip you to find biblically appropriate and culturally sound ways for Christians to understand local views of myth. They help you avoid the danger of simply generating and using only the mythic structures that make sense from your own cultural setting. As you ask these questions, also be asking yourself how the answers impact what types of uses of myth would make sense to local people without compromising their relationship with Christ.

1. Social contexts
    a. How does the mythic material function within the society in which it is indigenous?
    b. To what extent does myth justify social rules, organize hierarchies of social interaction, convey moral values, and express political or other relational interaction models?
    c. Does myth model, idealize, reflect, or criticize social experience?
2. Psychological aspects
    a. What aspects of the psyche/personality/self does the myth or ritual address?

US was founded as a Christian nation. This mythic framing provides those who believe it an anchor in the midst of troubling political times. However, the call to return to our Christian national heritage is only one of the many competing narratives in US political discourse today, and not by any means the dominant narrative.

When new and competing myths enter a society, competing ideals of how that society should operate generate tension. MacKendrick (2015, 23) explains: "Not only do [myths] filter experience, they also shape the selection of which interpretive lens can be applied, and condition the kinds of expressions that are acceptable. Competing myths are part of the creation, maintaining, and dissolving of social structures and social formations." To the extent that

    b. Does it speak primarily to individual issues or to collective self-understanding?

    c. How is it related to issues of gendering, images of maturity, and career modeling?

    d. How does the material function as a means of emotional expression?

    e. How does it relate to cultural patterns of exhibiting and controlling anxiety, anger, joy, the erotic, the religious, and creativity?

3. Literary/textual/performative aspects

    a. What are the literary characteristics of the materials?

    b. How is the ritual or myth related to other similar material in the culture?

4. Structural aspects

    a. What are the innate dynamics of the myth or ritual, and do they correspond to those found in the wider context of the host culture?

    b. How does the material fit within the society's conceptual, aesthetic, and semiotic (signifying) systems?

5. Other interpretive matters

    a. What must we know about the imagery and iconographic conventions of the society to be able to understand the signifying systems of this particular ritual or myth?

    b. What functions does the ritual or myth serve regularly or occasionally in the society?

    c. Who controls access to the ritual or myth, and how much change is acceptable?

    d. How self-evident is its meaning to the hearer/participant?

the competing narrative takes root, those who continue to hold to the autochthonous narrative will be threatened and fight back. This is especially true in countries or societies that share a single, compelling religious narrative, such as "To be Thai is to be Buddhist."

Questions about Myth

All the world's religions have revered stories and texts that serve as foundations for their beliefs and practices. Approaches to those scriptures vary from religion to religion. In sidebar 6.1, I note several questions to be considered in any new setting as you explore myth in that setting.

Mythic Themes or Paradigms

Myth expresses themes or paradigms in narrative form. Globally, scholars have noticed several themes or paradigms found in myth, ranging from adventure (or the quest) to redemption.

Adventure or the Quest

Myth offers us stories of adventure—from Odysseus in the *Odyssey*, to the Knights of the Round Table in search of the Holy Grail, to Luke Skywalker embarking from Tatooine in *A New Hope*, characters (often heroes) in ancient and contemporary myth embark on adventures. Those adventures range from journeys away from home to find themselves and/or restore order to the world (or galaxy), to epic struggles to return home. In the midst of their adventures, they are themselves transformed while numerous mythic themes play out in their adventures. They return from their quest after performing a physical task (e.g., victory in battle; saving a life) or encountering the divine and gaining spiritual insight (Campbell and Moyers 1988, 123), which irrevocably changes them.

Brokenness and Redemption

People are broken but can be redeemed, whether by outside agencies or by exercising internal gifts and strengths. In Greek mythology Hephaestus is lame and hence cast out of Olympus. As the god of the forge, he creates beautiful art as well as clever weapons, one of which is a golden throne that traps Hera, who threw him out of Olympus. Dionysus is sent to retrieve him, and once he gets Hephaestus drunk, he subdues him and brings him back to Olympus to free Hera. Hephaestus is the only exiled Olympian to return to Olympus.

In many quest myths, redemption comes because of hard work or superhuman effort. Less frequently do we see echoes or even shadows of God's grace. While outside forces often intervene in mythic narratives, they typically do so because the central character has done something heroic enough to earn their intervention. People can earn redemption before or after a heroic deed. When it comes before the deed is accomplished, it usually comes with an obligation and the implied warning that the gift may be withdrawn if the recipient does not meet the obligation.

A modern example takes place in the film *Hancock* (2008). The main character, Hancock, is an amnesiac alcoholic with superpowers who uses his powers as a vigilante. He metes out justice in such reckless ways that local officials and even the populace turn against him. While his tactics do save people and effect justice, they wreak havoc, which costs the city (and its citizens) millions of dollars in damage. In the movie we learn the reason for his brokenness: he is estranged from his wife because when they are together, they both lose their superpowers. By the end of the movie he finds a form of redemption, but still on his own terms and still separated from his wife.

Suffering and Sacrifice

Embedded in the motif of brokenness is the universal theme of human suffering. We suffer in no small measure *because* we are broken and flawed, and myths place that in narrative for us to emotionally experience as well as to ponder. Through such things as karma, tempting spirits, or people simply making bad choices, myths tell of our fall and explain why we suffer. In their own ways they describe the entrance of brokenness into the world, much as the Genesis narrative does. Through history, in fact, missionaries have used local mythic stories of humanity's fall and the cause of suffering as starting points for introducing the Gospel narratives.

In contemporary use, to sacrifice is essentially to give yourself or something you value for the benefit of another. Mythic heroes willingly sacrifice themselves and things they cherish. Lily Potter gives up her life to save her son, Harry; Frodo sacrifices his health in his quest to destroy the ring; and Anakin Skywalker (Darth Vader) sacrifices himself so that Luke can defeat Emperor Darth Sidious. In religious settings, sacrifice refers to offerings made in order to placate God or other supernatural powers. In the Christian faith, Christ's suffering on the cross is the ultimate mythological image of suffering.

Coming of Age

Another common theme in myth is about the coming of age of young women and men, who must grow into their place in life. The film *Princess Mononoke* (1997) portrays the intersecting lives of a Japanese village prince (Ashitaka) and a young woman raised by wolves in the forest (San, who calls herself Princess Mononoke). Ashitaka becomes cursed while saving his village from a demonically mad boar, which had been wounded by an iron musket ball. He is exiled and forced to travel west on a quest to deal with the curse given to him by the spirit realm.

He finds a village inhabited by lepers and former prostitutes; this area is the source of the iron. They clear the forest to get at the iron underneath, by which they wage war against nature and the nature spirits that inhabit the forest. San, having been raised by wolves, aids them against the villagers. Ashitaka's quest of dealing with his own suffering takes place through his quest to get both sides to stop the war. By the end of the movie the war is over: both sides have grown and gained wisdom, but not without the pain of struggle by all.

Heroism

As we have already recognized, heroes play large in mythic narratives around the world. Clearly the image of a hero varies from society to society and even from age to age within the same society. Common elements include abnormal physical power or skills, courage to sacrifice themselves or to simply go against societal values when those values are wrong, a sense of honor to do what is right, and the ability to gain victory over all foes.

The American version of the hero, who always wins, is not found everywhere in the world. In many African folktales, for example, the main character is almost as likely to die as to live, but life in many parts of Africa remains unforgiving, and such stories traditionally served to protect children by giving them respect for and fear of their tribal taboos and sanctions.

More recently, American narratives of heroes have taken a darker turn, casting doubt on their purity and even having them reflect on their own nature. The *Civil War* graphic novel series by Marvel Comics offers a fascinating glimpse at the shifting superhero landscape in contemporary myth through the questions superheroes raise and the sides they take after they are required to register with the government and obey legislative agendas. The traditional American hero who does not need to question his or her actions or motivations is becoming a thing of the past.

Christians celebrate heroes of our faith, from biblical characters (Deborah, Barnabas) to martyrs (Janani Luwum), missionaries (Pandita Ramabai), and evangelists (Sadhu Sundar Singh). You likely noticed that the postbiblical examples I provide are not people American Christians would typically recognize.

Love

Love, from romantic to friendship, is the final theme I stress. The popular idea of romantic love as we know it in the West originated in the Middle Ages and was polished in French literature with the development of the concept of "romance." This idea of an individualized love (I love her; she loves me) differs from the impersonal agape (Greek *agapē*, impersonal because we are to have agape for everyone), the bodily driven *eros* (physical love), and the nonerotic *philia* (friendship love). Joseph Campbell identified romantic love with the Latin word *amor* (Campbell and Moyers 1988, 186–87) rather than one of the Greek terms. Mythic stories such as the tragic love seen in *Anna Karenina* and *Romeo and Juliet* embody and define elements of romantic love for many Westerners (whether they know the stories or not). However, this newer mythic ideal of romantic love threatened the practice of arranged or political marriages, which was nearly universal for much of the Middle Ages, and it therefore threatened the church, which sought to stamp it out. Campbell believes that this notion of *amor* is "the essential thing that's great about the West and that makes it different from all other traditions I know" (187). Whether or not we agree about its greatness, it certainly has driven Western tradition and through media is becoming far more of a global phenomenon.

We should be careful not to read contemporary ideals of individual, romantic love into the types of love portrayed through myth, especially when the narratives predate our current notions of individualized romance. A challenge for modern Christians is that many of the notions we have of romantic love, often fueled by Hollywood and Bollywood, are not part of the biblical narrative, and we are tempted to read them into it.

Biblical Example: Jesus Uses Myth (Luke 15)

Jesus himself provides multiple examples of the use of myth to frame important truths about the gospel and his place in it. Throughout the four Gospels, Jesus draws on the Old Testament, the religious mythic corpus of the Jewish people. He cites historical events and quotes from the various sections of Old Testament events. However, he did not limit his use of myth to the Old Testament: he also used proverbs and told parables, through which he connected his hearers to spiritual truths. His encounter with the Pharisees in Luke 15 offers a clear example of Jesus's mastery of myth for communication.

As we look at the broader pattern of Luke's Gospel, we see that Jesus confronts or is confronted by the Pharisees at least a dozen times (this is the ninth). These encounters follow a general pattern typically seen in challenges in honor-framed societies (see Mischke 2015, 237):

Step 1: Pharisees accuse Jesus of a specific violation (trying to discredit him).

Step 2: Jesus responds variously, using metaphors, parables, and actions (such as healing), and he tends to avoid playing to their strengths (e.g., debating the law).

Step 3: Rejoinder or follow-up by Pharisees (not always seen).

Step 4: Verdict (seen in the response of the people): in some encounters Pharisees slink away, in others the people rejoice. For this encounter the reader is left without a verdict.

In societies where honor is at stake, these encounters are used to generate or regain prestige (honor) or to create a loss of face (shame). In the encounters parables, proverbs, and stories are tools, even weapons. Many Westerners have lost this art today; but understanding that it was a valuable tactic at the time helps those of us from justice-framed societies better understand the Pharisaic attacks on Jesus. Those in this type of society can lose their honor. When this happens, that person is likely to become an outcast (e.g., the woman at the well; the Gadarene demoniac).

Luke contextualizes the confrontation by reporting that sinners and tax collectors were gathering to hear Jesus (15:1–2)—a direct threat to the Pharisaic ethic of separation from evil. Luke uses a verb tense for "gathering" that implies this was ongoing practice, not just a one-time event, and this is not the first time in Luke's Gospel that the Pharisees complain about Jesus's associates (see 5:27–30; 7:39).

The Pharisees complain about Jesus eating with unclean people (step 1), implying that he is unclean. They attack him, hoping to discredit him and cause him to lose honor or face. Why? At least on one level, Jesus lives a radical lifestyle that challenges their traditions, which serve as the social glue they use to keep their place of spiritual prominence and maintain the respect they enjoy among the Jewish masses. This rabbi who associates with sinners threatens their social glue; to counter the threat, they fight back to undermine him, make him lose honor/face.

Jesus responds to their complaining by telling three stories, which both audiences (Pharisees and sinners; step 2) hear. The first story is about the joy a shepherd experiences on finding a lost sheep. The parable is a simple story that fits the normal life issues of the "sinners" in Jesus's audience. That the shepherd calls his friends and neighbors to celebrate finding the lost sheep is likely an exaggeration of normal behavior (what self-respecting shepherd throws a party to celebrate finding something he should never have lost in the first place!), but Jesus uses it to make his point. He cements the point by marking it with the words "I tell you" (15:7), which indicate to both audiences that the primary point is that heaven rejoices when one lost person is found. No displeasure with the ninety-nine is implied: they are not the focus of the story. Neither is the method of finding the lost sheep. It is the celebration on earth as a parallel to the celebration in heaven that Jesus wants them to understand.

As a parallel, the second story is about a widow experiencing joy in finding a lost coin. Again, both audiences can relate to the story. In their mental imaginations, they could see the widow's dowry woven into her headdress and imagine one of the ten coins falling out during the course of the day. They can also see her looking desperately for the coin, then being happy to find it. As with the shepherd, that she celebrates by telling her neighbors is likely an exaggeration. But once again Jesus's main point ("I tell you," 15:10) is that heaven rejoices over one sinner who is found.

We can imagine Luke's audience responding, perhaps wondering where this story is going. Jesus brings the confrontation to a close with a final story in which the rejoicing over a lost son is just as clear as in the first two stories, but there is an addition to the story, for which no conclusion is given. The story of joy in the prodigal son's return is the punch line of Jesus's response to the Pharisees. Unlike the other stories, this one is audacious from the outset.

First comes the younger brother's bold request: he is effectively asking that his father act as though he were dead. That the father grants the request is even more audacious! By now both audiences are riveted. Eventually, of course, the lost son gets up and turns from his chosen life, which expresses the core of repentance. This is what the "sinners" with Jesus face: Do they want to turn from their sinful lives and return to their (heavenly) father? But in the third story we have an extra character, the older brother. He is out of touch with the family and certainly not in tune with the father, who declares (15:32), "We had to celebrate"!

Jesus leaves the disposition of the older brother unresolved. In addition to the repetition of celebrating that the lost are found, the conclusion-less component of the story is an invitation to those who scorn Jesus. In effect, they will write the rest of the story through their response to Jesus, . . . and Luke does not tell us how they react (which would be step 3).

In Luke 15, then, Jesus masterfully uses myth to handle the Pharisaic challenge. The first two stories he tells have a common conclusion of heaven rejoicing over the lost being found. The third story has two foci: (1) the rejoicing of the father over his prodigal son's return, and (2) the older brother's grumbling about it. The latter reminds us (and Jesus's audiences) of the muttering of the Pharisees about Jesus. By emphasizing in each of the first two stories that heaven rejoices over one sinner being found, he invites the sinners present to become part of the story generating heaven's party. By adding the older brother into the final story, Jesus indirectly criticizes the Pharisees for muttering against him, but more importantly, he indirectly offers them a choice: get in tune with heaven. In this case, Luke leaves step 3 without a conclusion.

Contextualizing Myth

A missionary anthropologist four decades ago, Jacob Loewen pointed out that when missionaries simply preach against mythic frames without knowing them or understanding them, those beliefs do *not* die out: they simply go underground. Through such preaching and rhetoric,

> The believers had thus been forced into a splitlevel existence. On one level, in the missionary's presence, they denied and disowned everything about their pagan past. On another level, however, behind the missionary's back, they believed and practiced a good number of their tribal myth-based rituals. In fact, the many new good and bad "hard" words [*Christian vocabulary introduced into the setting*] that resulted from the interpreted sermons, actually confirmed some of their pre-Christian beliefs so that people believed, feared, and practised them all the more fervently. (Loewen 1978, 289)

Why Contextualize Myth?

Perhaps the most compelling reason to contextualize myth is that Jesus utilized (and contextualized) myth for his audience, and we should follow his example. In addition, however, Loewen (1978, 325–32) identified eight ways myth can help us. Though his focus was on aboriginal peoples and their narratives, and his reflections are over forty years old, with only minor adaptations his points still demonstrate benefits of contextualizing myth for today.

First, knowing myth enables us to locate "contact points" for witness. The mythic corpus of a people offers starting points for conversations, topics of local relevance, and approaches to problems that people face with which they are familiar. Just as Paul used Epicurean poetry as a contact point with his Mars Hill audience, we may use local mythic references as contact points for a presentation of biblical truths.

Second, myth can help us better communicate. Myths encapsulate the vantage points of a people—their perspectives on life common to all peoples. Understanding the vantage points our audience is likely to share enables us to more clearly communicate on issues of relevance in ways they understand. We can find things God commends as well as things God condemns, though we do well to focus on the former before turning to the latter.

Third, in addition to "contact" points, we can also locate "conflict" points: issues of tension between the gospel and culture. When myth points to something such as an incurable separation from our Creator, we can point out that the Bible offers a different teaching based on the Creator himself speaking to us. When local myth indicates that evil spirits can be controlled and channeled for good purposes, we can offer an alternative narrative.

Fourth, understanding local myth can help us see ourselves as the Other viewed through our host's lenses. All too often we come with our own agendas and packaged approaches to sharing Christ in new settings. Coming to grips with local myth can help us understand points of our agenda that make no sense in the local setting, and points that are critical to them but off our own mental radars. This is the basis for Loewen's fifth point, that we can see the felt needs of the culture more clearly from the emic (insider) perspective. Their stories offer windows to their hearts (see W. Moon 2009, 195), and a wise person will want to see through the local windows whenever possible.

Sixth, myths provide a wealth of information on contextual problem-solving approaches. If you happen to be living cross-culturally, take advantage of that to observe how those around you handle conflict—and how often they bring myth (sometimes stories, other times proverbs and the like) to bear to help them move past an argument or point of conflict (see, e.g., W. Moon 2009, 160–64).

Seventh, when we know local mythology, and the terms and phrasing that are part and parcel of that mythography, we can *translate* the Bible more accurately and thereby enable the biblical myth to more accurately enter their symbolic world. As simple examples, knowing the local versions of the creation story can help us better translate Genesis, just as knowing local poetry and poetic forms can help us better translate the Psalms.

Eighth and finally, we can spot syncretistic tendencies more quickly and facilitate local ability to head them off before they go too far. When we know the uses of mythic vocabulary, when we understand their themes and tropes, we can more readily see them as they show up in Christian life. The goal is not to stamp them out, but to find appropriate ways in concert with local church leaders to co-opt them for the gospel.

All of these points are legitimate reasons to contextualize myth, but doing so is less incendiary in settings where no formal sacred textual traditions exist than in settings where they do. For example, using the Qur'an as a starting point for sharing Christ (as in the Camel Method presented in chap. 4) generates sharp disagreement. Proponents notice Paul's use of Greek poets and philosophers and John's use of the Logos concept in the New Testament; they claim that Paul's and John's use of them demonstrates that we can use non-Christian scriptures, or at least the ideas from them, as contacts or starting points today.

Opponents respond that to use the scriptures of other religions as teaching truth is to validate those other scriptures for their adherents. This is especially true for the Qur'an, since Muslims believe it supersedes all prior holy books, including the Bible. Opponents argue that if we give them an authoritative inch, they will take it a metaphorical mile. They further relate that when we interpret the Qur'an by using Christian principles of biblical hermeneutics, we are applying *our* system of interpretation to *their* text. We certainly object to Islamic scholars using their hermeneutical methods to interpret the Bible; it is not surprising that they likewise object when we use our methods to interpret their text (see Schlorff 1980).

To date no resolution that all evangelicals agree on has been found, and both sides are deeply entrenched in their thinking. We leave that as a point in tension within the larger discussion of contextualizing myth.

An Example: Mythic Themes in American Spiritual Warfare

In this example I consider the role myth plays in a particular area of ministry: spiritual warfare. How do mythic structures—in this case the driving images and values—specifically for North Americans of European descent affect the way contemporary evangelicals understand spiritual warfare? What follows is adapted in part from prior works in which I examined strands of spiritual warfare among North American evangelicals from a variety of vantage points (Moreau 1995, 169–70; 2002a, 2002b, 2006a, and 2015).

For this case study, I limit my discussion to five mythic themes that permeate Euro-North America and how each is seen among evangelicals engaging in spiritual warfare. The five themes are (1) the joy of the fight, (2) good is obvious, (3) the superhero, (4) pragmatism, and (5) millenarian utopianism. As you read through this account, remember that I am not using the word "mythic" to discern right from wrong. Rather, I am showing how the mythic themes that permeate our larger society also permeate the ways evangelicals engage spiritual warfare. This type of analysis could be repeated for other areas that evangelicals engage, from church planting to political participation. While I do have opinions on how each of these themes is operating among evangelicals in spiritual warfare (see Moreau 2002b and 2006a), in this depiction I am not using "myth" as "wrong" but as the driving images, values, and categories that evangelicals harness in spiritual warfare discourse.

First, as a society we attend to the actual fight more than the outcome of the fight (Hiebert 1992). We have so glorified violence that we want our movies (and books and games) to be nonstop action. While we may end our stories with "They lived happily ever after," we never get any extended depiction of what that would be like. We need our heroes to actually fight the villains: can you imagine a movie in which everything is peacefully negotiated? Compromise is not allowed, nor is surrender. Our heroes and villains repeatedly return to the same script: fight, fight, fight (Wink 1992, 18). Spiritual warfare literature is rife with stories, most often of success. I have personally attended several spiritual warfare conferences and consultations over the past few decades, and on a regular basis the keynote speakers are also the best storytellers, regaling audiences with war stories either to support their theological or methodological assertions or to motivate the rapt members of the audience to join in the battle themselves.

Second, at least through the modernist era, Americans tended to believe that good and evil are clearly distinguishable. Millennials today are far less likely to hold to this ideal, but evangelicals generally still cling to it, especially in spiritual warfare issues. We want good and evil to be easily separable; we want our enemies to be easy to spot because their evil intentions are evident. Especially in Christian circles, we rarely bother to explore whether our heroes might actually be in the wrong. One of the ways this shows up in spiritual warfare is our uncritical acceptance of the testimonies of people who testify that they have turned from a "pure" bad (satanic ritual) to a "pure" good (following Christ). While we should rejoice in any such conversion, the good and evil categories are presented in such a way that we often simply ignore the possibility that the person giving the testimony might be lying or glossing over the elements of an account in which good and evil are not as readily distinguishable. We also see this in graphic stories in which deliverance counselors outwit demons to set captives free, and in which the enemies are always the external ones: rarely do we explore whether we ourselves are acting in concert with the enemy (though see Wink 1992). Privately, I've also heard from licensed therapists who worked to clean up the messes generated in people's lives by well-intentioned deliverance sessions in which the counselee was emotionally or spiritually abused. Those stories, which paint a more complex picture of deliverance ministry, are far less often found in spiritual warfare literature or conferences. As I have stated elsewhere, "As in our mythic structure, authors [*and speakers*] rarely question their own motivations and integrity. The trap we may fall into is loving power rather than using the power of love (N. Wright 1990, 173–86)" (Moreau 1994, 17–18).

Third, at least until recently (e.g., Marvel's *Civil War* series, noted previously; see MacKendrick 2015), we characterize our heroes with certain universal qualities (see Wink 1992, 18–20). For example, our heroes *always* make the right choice, snatch victory from the precipice of defeat, never cheat (though the enemy almost always does), outwit the enemy, and typically have to dig deeply for internal resources such as courage or simply dogged perseverance to do right in order to ensure the enemy is overcome. As Wink also declares, the theme of "redemptive violence" pervades our mythic imagery—our heroes use good violence to overcome the bad violence of their enemies. They may seek to redeem the enemy, but ultimately such efforts prove to be futile (unless the enemy is an antihero). Further, the battle is likened to a chess game of strategies within strategies on both sides (Hiebert 1992), with the outcome in doubt throughout the story until the champion reveals the final move that checkmates the enemy. In spiritual warfare this can be seen through the multiple personal stories of victory offered by speakers and authors typically without much reflective self-examination. We often portray ourselves as heroes using good violence against evil enemies without conscious reflection.

A fourth mythic theme is our American pragmatism, which shows up in multiple ways. For example, our self-help literature is filled with titles using vocabulary such as "steps" or "keys" to "victory" or "success." We tend toward a "build a better mousetrap" mentality, selling and trying program after program until we find one that works. When it ceases to work, we embark on yet another search. This shows up in spiritual warfare literature, where war stories of success, distilled to a series of steps, is a typical formula used by many authors and practitioners. In the workshops and literature we can find prayers to cleanse our homes or other important physical locations, to bind or otherwise hinder Satan, to protect people and cherished places or objects, to force a demon to speak the truth, and so on. Many evangelicals eschew ritual for ritual's sake, yet in dealing with the unknown in the arena of spiritual warfare, we tend to move toward ritualistic approaches that have been proved to be successful for others.

The fifth mythic theme is peculiar to Americans: the idea of a millenarian utopia. As I mentioned in my earlier analysis, "The consummation of history is one we must fight for (theme one); it is easy to tell right from wrong in light of our utopian vision (theme two); and our heroes are responsible for bringing it into being (theme three)" (Moreau 1995, 170). Historian William McGloughlin (1978, 19) observed of the United States: "Our history has been essentially the history of one long millenarian movement. Americans, in their cultural mythology, are God's chosen, leading the world to perfection. Every awakening has revived, revitalized, and redefined that culture core."

It should be clear how each of these plays out in spiritual warfare. Theme 1: it's better to be in battle with demons than on the sideline. Theme 2: demonic work and schemes in the lives of people are clear and easy to discern. Theme 3: those involved in deliverance ministry are spiritual heroes who are able to discern good from evil and can avoid the latter while engaging the enemy. Themes 4 and 5: not only do we win in the end; it also is our responsibility to be the ones who bring victory through dramatic and decisive action.

This discussion helps us to clarify how our own mythic structures and framing tend to drive us into deliverance ministries; it can also help give us pause to reflect on the extent to which we buy into these themes. Such reflection also creates space in which we may explore those themes biblically for correction and possible reproof. It also reminds us that all the analytic tools we bring to bear in the dimensional discussions apply not only "out there" but also in the West.

An Example: Builsa Use of Proverbs

In our final example we shift to Africa, for which Asbury missiologist W. Jay Moon (2009) provides an excellent example of informal learning through myth in the form of proverbs. This material is part of his PhD dissertation on the use of proverbs among the Builsa of Ghana.

Moon reports that while traditional proverbs and stories continue to play a role in training children, they are also utilized by adults throughout everyday life in multiple ways, ranging from conflict mediation to theological discussion. In the second half of the dissertation, based on careful and extensive field research, Moon creates a series of discussions in which Builsa church leaders debate questions of traditional cultural values expressed through proverbs that encapsulate those values.

The Builsa Christian leaders gather to discuss problems in light of proverbs they hear and use in order to "pick the meat from the bones" (88–89) so they can eat the meat (those elements or meaning in the proverb that accord with the Bible) and discard the bones (those elements or meaning in the proverb that do not accord with the Bible).

The narrative is rich and lively, interspersed with Moon's analysis. What he clearly demonstrates is that the informal learning of the Builsa, as seen in their proverbs, in many respects conforms to Christian teaching (and in other respects does not conform to Christian teaching). The Builsa church leaders work through the task of figuring out not just the larger, obvious (to them) meaning of the proverb; they also identify less obvious ways the proverb is used by Builsa speakers.

The moral of Moon's dissertation is that, rather than throwing out all the proverbs wholesale, many can be repurposed for Christian teaching and discipleship by the local community. The proverbs that are appropriate for understanding or deepening Christian faith may be utilized so that people see the connection between Christ and their own culture. There are no degrees or formal institutions: there is only small-group, informal discussion by church leaders of proverbs used in everyday-life conversations that are then appropriated (or not) for use in the Builsa church in discipleship.

CASE STUDY

THE POWERFUL LITTLE FLY

Long-term missionary in Africa Eudene Keidel (1978, 60–61) compiled a book of African stories told to children that offer life lessons paralleling biblical teaching. As you read the following example, in which the main character dies through his own foolishness (and Keidel's application), consider ways you might use mythic stories where you minister to contextualize evangelism, discipleship, or other types of spiritual growth.

The fly had just finished feasting on the carcass of a millipede. His tummy felt so full and good that he wanted to find someone to tease. Suddenly he spied Mr. Hippopotamus basking on a sunny sandbank. He buzzed past the lazy hippo's head, tickled his ear, and said, "Do you know I'm stronger than you are?"

The sleepy hippo answered, "Don't be ridiculous. Go away and leave me alone."

"If you don't believe it," teased the fly, "just wait around awhile and you'll see."

He buzzed into the hippo's ear. He tickled his nostrils. The hippo twitched his ears, tossed his head, sneezed, and finally got up and lumbered lazily off into the water where the fly couldn't bother him anymore.

"See. What did I tell you?" boasted the little fly, as he circled over the hippo a last time and headed back toward the forest. He was so happy he'd been born a strong little fly, and not a lazy hippo. All of a sudden BANG! He ran into a wall he couldn't see. It was springy and sticky. His feet got caught in it. He tried every way to get unstuck but couldn't. It was a spider's web.

Sometimes we feel quite proud of ourselves and boast about the big things we can do and the wonderful plans we have. Yet we never know what lies ahead for us. The Bible says, "Do not boast about tomorrow, for you do not know what a day may bring" (Prov. 27:1).

By ourselves we have nothing to boast about. Every day of our life is a gift from God.

7

THE ETHICAL DIMENSION

We grow in environments in which we learn our society's perspectives on what is right and what is wrong—what is the right thing to do, while avoiding the wrong thing. Initial training in right and wrong comes from our parents and other relatives, who teach us to share things, to be kind, to show respect as well as to not hurt others, to not be stingy, to not be greedy. How each of those is implemented is somewhat culturally variable, but as we grow up we learn, albeit imperfectly, to navigate the good things and refrain from doing the bad things. As missiological anthropologist Robert Priest explains (1994), through childhood we develop a sense of conscience from the patterns we see and experience, learning right from wrong, and eventually being either commended for our good actions or condemned for our bad ones.

What Is the Ethical Dimension?

This is the ethical dimension, where the "shoulds" and "oughts" of life reside. As we will see in chapter 11, doctrine answers the question, What is true about the universe, the world, people, and other living beings? Ethical obligations are derived from the doctrines we believe. For example, Christians teach that all humans are made in God's image. What ethical obligations result from that doctrine (see fig. 7.1)? Such obligations are usually encoded into laws (e.g., the US Constitution, Sharia) that discourage unethical behavior and encourage virtuous behavior.

Figure 7.1: Truth, ethics, and law

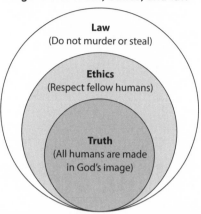

Figure 7.1 illustrates the embeddedness of truth, ethics, and law through an example based on the Christian truth that all humans are made in God's image. Laws are based on ethical injunctions, which in turn are (ideally) based on a perceived truth about the world or human beings; so because all humans are made in God's image, we should (or must) respect fellow humans. Because we have an obligation to respect human beings, we codify and enact laws such as prohibitions against murder or stealing, since either act does not respect humans as those made in God's image. I will deal with the doctrinal dimension (or religious truth) in chapter 11, and I touched on maintaining order (which connects to law) in chapter 5. In this chapter I explore the intersection of Scripture and society in the ethical dimension.

In the approach depicted in figure 7.1, scriptural injunctions such as the Ten Commandments are ethical obligations in the form of laws that are based on underlying truths. Likewise, for Muslims, Sharia is based on the Qur'an and the collected hadiths (see below). The assumed truths underlying ethical obligations and the resulting laws are not always stated or even obvious. The Ten Commandments, for example, are based on at least three primary truths: (1) God is Creator of the universe, (2) God created humans, and (3) God created humans in his own image. Ethically, then, when we violate a human being, we violate the image of God in that person and effectively violate the God who created that person in his own image.

Ethics in Societies

As we grow up interacting with those who raise us, we develop a culturally tuned instinct for right and wrong behavior based on how we are raised and by which we determine how we live. Children raised in collective, honor-based societies develop a conscience framed in those values. Even if they choose to rebel and violate what they learned was right and wrong, they still know what their society expects of them.

Conscience and Ethics

In a widely cited article, anthropological missiologist Robert Priest (1994) details a biblically faithful but anthropologically informed view of culture, conscience, and ethics together with implications for contextual ministry. In this section, I frame his approach; I return to the implications for contextualization that he outlines later in the chapter.

Priest makes his argument through a series of twenty-five assertions, the first of which is, "The faculty of conscience is culturally universal (e.g., Rom. 2:14–15; 2 Cor. 4:2; 1 Cor. 10:25, 27)" (294). Conscience is essentially "a knowing in common" (294). In other words, it is a shared "database" of knowing what is right and wrong—developed as we grow up but even so simultaneously, to use Paul's language, written on our hearts. This conscience is composed of "the actual moral standards and norms used in everyday life in judging others" (294). We constantly judge others and ourselves against this database, at times approving and at times disapproving of the actions of ourselves and others with whom we interact.

Conscience, Priest declares (294–95), is a natural phenomenon and not solely the result of the mysterious working of the Holy Spirit. For example, "Believers also may be bothered by a conscience which condemns for behavior God himself does not condemn. That is, conscience is a natural faculty not necessarily dependent on the special action of the Holy Spirit" (294). In other words, Christians can feel guilty for doing something that God does not condemn, such as drinking in moderation. Such guilt, Priest rightly argues, is not due to the work of the Holy Spirit but due to the believer's own sense of conscience. This does not eliminate the possibility of the Holy Spirit working through our consciences, but shows how conscience is a natural thing that God has given to people and that develops even apart from the direct work of the Holy Spirit. This sense of conscience is God-given and yet natural rather than supernatural. It is, he argues, therefore amenable to study and analysis through empirical methods (psychology, sociology, and anthropology).

Because it is natural, "The content of conscience is fallible and variable (e.g., Rom. 14; 1 Cor. 10:27–32)" and "is directly dependent on learned cultural meanings, norms, ideals, and values" (295). In figure 7.1, for example, I stated that because human beings are made in God's image, it is wrong to steal from them. However, societies differ in their understanding of both owner-ship and theft. Thus, while all human societies may well agree that stealing is wrong, their respective views of stealing are dependent on the culturally constructed definitions of ownership and personhood. For example, land may be believed to be held in trust by the community rather than owned by an individual. If I come as an outsider and make a payment to an individual and receive a legal document identifying me as the "owner," members of the community will still believe that the community actually owns the land: perhaps I'm just leasing it for a time. They may perceive that they have the right to pick occasional fruit that grows on "my" land because they never lost their rights to sharing in what it produces.

To bring it closer to home for me, in the academic world the issue of plagia-rism can seem very convoluted to those from countries that do not recognize intellectual property the particular way we do in the West. Consider how convoluted it would appear to the authors of the New Testament and the early church fathers, who regularly utilized words and ideas from others without at-tribution. According to Priest, in societies that have come to value intellectual property in such a way, guests need to pay attention to the local rules. The bot-tom line? People from one society who expect similar behavior to apply univer-sally overlook the cultural factors that determine the rules and regulations for each setting.

It should thus be clear that when we cross into a new culture, we will find ethical obligations we hold in common with the people there and ethical ob-ligations on which we differ with the people there. However, as Priest notes, it is not the areas on which we agree that I as a cross-cultural worker will notice: I will be struck by the areas on which I disagree with them. In other words, it is the *violations* I see in the new setting that will stand out for me. For example, when I started teaching in a public high school in Swaziland, I was told by many people that Swazi students will not look you in the eyes: I later learned that for a younger person to look an older or more respected person directly in the eyes is an act of pride or rebellion. Further, they should bend at the knees and lower their head when making a direct request to a superior. As a teacher, I was automatically a "superior" to my students. When students needed to make a direct request of me, they kept their eyes to the ground, their heads well below mine, and (typically) whispered their request. I was tempted to tell them to stand up straight, look me in the eyes, and speak loudly enough for me to hear—but thankfully I had been warned not to do so. It took over a year for me to adjust, but since I was a guest in their society, the task of adjusting was mine to take on rather than theirs. Yet the fact that

I remember this so clearly some forty years later is a reminder that it was the violations of my ethical values that stood out to me.

Likewise, American Christians teaching in Asian countries often complain about students copying on exams and other work. Less frequently they question the underlying obligations and motivations behind such actions. Rather, they are consumed with the violation and their desire to fix it. Additional frustration comes when national teachers or even school officials emphatically confirm that cheating is wrong and yet appear to allow said cheating to continue unpunished. Again, it is the violations, the bad behaviors, that stick out to American teachers, not the good behaviors they also exhibit. It seems natural to the cross-cultural workers to want to correct the violations they see. This has been a missionary impulse since the time of the New Testament, during which the early church wrestled with significant ethical boundary issues. These ranged from privileging Hebrew-speaking widows over Greek-speaking widows (Acts 6), to the question of whether gentile believers needed to be circumcised or follow other Jewish regulations (Acts 15), and to claiming the authority of one apostle as a patron over another (1 Cor. 3).

Cultural Values and Ethics

In chapter 5, I identified three sets of cultural values and briefly introduced the role each plays in leadership. In this section, I use the same three sets to flesh out how Priest's presentation of conscience and ethics works in light of cultural values. To simplify the task, and at the risk of reductionism, in each case I assume a uniform adherence by a society's members to what they value. Further, the examples also assume that only one cultural value set is operating at a time, and no other cultural values skew the behavior I note. In reality, of course, members of a society do not uniformly adhere to their society's values, and multiple cultural values are always operating.

Power Distance

As I explained above, in Large Power Distance (LPD) societies such as Guatemala, Serbia, and Indonesia (Hofstede and Hofstede 2005, 43–44), members *expect* those in charge to be the ones who make decisions, guiding and when needed even controlling followers' behavior. Typically the behavior of LPD leaders in Small Power Distance (SPD) countries such as Australia, Canada, and the Netherlands (43–44) sets off several ethical alarms. SPD subordinates see LPD leaders as dictatorial, power hungry, and unethical. They don't consult subordinates and don't respond to legitimate complaints or even ideas that subordinates have. On the other hand, LPD subordinates view the actions of SPD leaders and perceive them as weak and unable to make important decisions without input from far too many people.

In-Group Collectivism and Individualism

Assuming that power distance is not involved, people raised by in-group collective societies such as Guatemala, Serbia, and Indonesia (Hofstede and Hofstede 2005, 78–79) learn that they have an ethical obligation to ensure that they meet the needs of their in-group above all else. Typically the actions of collectivists in individual settings such as Australia, Canada, and the Netherlands (78–79) set off multiple alarms. For example, in-group favoring for hiring and promoting by the collectivist leader will be read as nepotism to the individualist subordinate, who will by definition always be out of the in-group. Conversely, the in-group individualist's hiring and promoting practices will be perceived as strange, or even unethical, to in-group collectivists. They may wonder how their boss dare overlook her own family when hiring or promoting—or otherwise not rely on her family when tough decisions need to be made.

Honor and Justice

Honor versus justice has not yet been measured and quantified for countries as the previous values have been, so there is not a reliable list of the rankings of countries (or peoples) from which to choose an example. However, you may have noticed that I used the same three countries for each side of the spectrum in the first two sets of cultural values. For the sake of this discussion, I will assume that the LPD, in-group collective countries (Guatemala, Serbia, and Indonesia), are more likely to highly value honor, while the SPD, individualistic countries (Australia, Canada, and the Netherlands), are more likely to value justice highly.

To the extent that this assumption is correct, honor-valuing leaders are socialized to pay attention to the honor, or face, of themselves and their in-group and to utilize the social power they have to protect or extend that honor. Further, for them, the obligations of honor are present in *every* social setting. Given that, honor-valuing leaders will set off ethical alarms among justice-valuing subordinates. An honor-valuing leader will always honor the obligations carried for the in-group. It is extremely shameful for them to admit mistakes, and social truths are less important than social face. They expect loyalty even when they are wrong. On the other hand, justice-valuing leaders will also set off ethical alarms among honor-valuing subordinates. They may confront their subordinates in front of others, making them lose face. They might admit to being wrong in front of the group or even in public, making their organization lose face.

Questions about Ethics

The need for adherence to a proper life plays out within religions on the basis of layers of religious reasoning, sensibility, and framing. From threats of divine punishment to honor killings in Muslim settings, people and organizations exercise numerous means of maintaining order in organizations. Sidebar 7.1 offers questions to ask about ethics in local settings.

While the brief discussion in sidebar 7.1 only scratches the surface, it does illustrate the type of thinking we need to carry into contextualizing ethics. One of the challenges is that looking at ethics *only* through the lenses of cultural values leaves us in a more relativistic position than is biblically viable. Jesus's framing of a leader who is a servant, for example, does not fit well in an LPD setting. Cultural values alone do not provide a reliable guide for ethical living. Later in the chapter we will turn to a consideration of the integration of biblical values in contextualizing ethics.

Personal, Group, and Systemic Ethics

In societies we can distinguish ethical obligations into three different levels. The first level is personal, that of the individual who chooses (or not) to live a moral life as defined by that individual's society. People who refrain from societally perceived sins and engage in societally perceived virtuous behavior as individuals are deemed to be virtuous people. Those who do not may be perceived as shady or worse.

The second level of societal ethics is the group dimension. This level is much more visible in collective societies than in individualistic societies but is present there as well. We have obligations to kin, to those with whom we associate, and to our organizations. Collective societies see these as part and parcel of what it means to be human ("We relate, therefore we are"), but individualistic societies read group ethics in light of individual rights and obligations.

Third is the systemic level. It is the most complex level, at the same time right in our faces and yet hidden from our view. The systemic level of ethics is worked out in individuals and groups, but it serves to anchor a society as a whole—often to the detriment of those on the margins. We condemn racism in the United States even as we practice it. We move heaven and earth to save a child trapped in a well, and we weep over the death of another child, and yet one out of every six pregnancies in the United States ends in abortion (https://www.cdc.gov/reproductivehealth/data_stats/abortion.htm). We

SIDEBAR 7.1
QUESTIONS ABOUT ETHICS

Below are some questions to consider as you explore ethics in your setting. Asking and exploring the answers to these questions will enable you to better understand local examples of ethics—yet also help you think more clearly about church and ways Christians might better understand ethics in their contexts and, when appropriate, use them or the cultural insights they offer to better contextualize the gospel.

As I noted in the sidebars in previous chapters, answers to these questions could be used to compromise the gospel or the biblical definition of church. That is not my intention. Rather, the questions equip you to find biblically appropriate and culturally sound ways for Christians to understand local ethics. They help you avoid the danger of simply generating and using only the ethical approaches and values that make sense from your own cultural setting. As you ask these questions, also be asking yourself how the answers impact what ethical values and stances would make sense to local people without compromising their relationship with Christ.

1. Levels of ethics: What are the "musts," "oughts," and "shoulds" found within the society?
   a. For the individual?
   b. For the group?
   c. For the society as a whole?
2. Living ethically . . . or not
   a. In what areas do people indicate that they are able to successfully adhere to the ethical virtues?
   b. In what areas do people see disconnects between their cherished virtues and how they live their lives?
   c. How do individuals internalize the reality that they do not live up to their own society's ethical ideals?
   d. In what ways do their ethical values speak to group or collective issues?
   e. In what ways do their ethical values confront or support systemic injustices?
3. Ensuring adherence
   a. What control systems are in place to ensure adherence, especially in prohibiting unethical behavior (as locally defined)?
   b. What structural justices are present? For example, what ethics or laws exist to protect the marginalized or helpless members of society?
   c. What structural injustices are present? For example, what ethics or laws exist that disfavor the marginalized or helpless members of society?
4. In what ways does the gospel condone or condemn indigenous local ethical values and practices?

wring our hands over poverty, and yet in 2015 executives were paid 335 times the wage of the average worker (http://time.com/money/4339078/ceo-pay-compare-workers). This type of snapshot is not just true for the United States: it can be found globally. From the Dalits in India to the mestizos in Brazil, injustices against the marginalized everywhere are seemingly intractable due to their systemic nature.

These levels are deeply intertwined. Individuals can feel powerless to act in virtuous ways when the entire organization they are in encourages or even enforces unethical behavior. Groups and organizations are part of the systems of their societies, and when an organization stands against the system, it risks being crushed. The systemic level is built on and strengthened by the ethical actions of individuals and the behaviors and policies of groups. All three are intertwined and feed into one another, ultimately strengthening the system and fighting against any change, which is perceived as a threat.

Personal, Group, and Systemic Ethics in Religions

On the personal level, Buddhists meditate to gain mastery over thought and action such that the practitioner gains an unfettered insight on the true nature of reality and thus attains complete harmony with self and environment. Among some contemporary Buddhists, it is believed that a person who has attained this also gains control over cosmic and magical forces. Right thought plays a critical role in Buddhist ethics, which tend to be inward focused and achieved through proper discipline and meditation. Buddhists value four "large virtues": benevolence, compassion, joy in the joy of others, and equanimity (see Smart 1996, 209). As with mastery over thought, they pursue these virtues through meditation and acting properly.

For the Muslim, honor and submission are perhaps the paramount virtues and are integrated across personal, group, and systemic ethics. Muslims honor God (and his glory) by submitting to him. They honor Muhammad by confessing him as God's prophet and submitting to the Qur'an he revealed, to the patterns of his life seen in the ahadith (Arabic plural for hadith) and Sharia. Finally, they uphold the honor of fellow Muslims in relation to non-Muslims, the clan in relation to other clans, the family in relation to other families, and oneself in relation to other individuals. This is somewhat less true for Western Muslims than for Muslims from other parts of the world.

The ahadith provide excellent examples of human enforcement of norms at the personal, group, and systemic levels. Together with the Qur'an, they are the foundation for Sharia law. For most Muslims, the ahadith are not understood as divinely revealed, as is the Qur'an, but they are nevertheless revered as authoritative sources for ethical living. Building on more than thirty years of living among Muslims, Edward Hoskins (2011, 424) explains:

> Muslims believe the Qur'an is heavenly, mysterious, and only fully understood by Allah. It does not completely address all the minutia of life. The only way to completely apply the Qur'an to daily life is to emulate Muhammad—the only man to have perfectly lived out the Qur'an. I like to think of the Qur'an as the skeleton, with Muhammad being the flesh on the skeleton, applying all of Islam to life. . . .
>
> One Muslim told me, "The Qur'an tells us to pray, but it doesn't tell us how. The hadith gives us the details of how to do it."
>
> From the early seventh century A.D., every word and deed of Muhammad was observed and memorized by his immediate family and close friends (companions), then told to others who related them to still others. These stories include every deed, gesture, and act of Muhammad, from dressing to dining, marrying to mating, dreams and visions, crime and punishment, buying and selling, and even sneezing and passing gas. Every aspect of Muhammad's personal life was under scrutiny.
>
> These narrations were related person-to-person over many years; each tradition consists of two parts, an *isnad*, or chain of transmitters, and a *matn*, or main text. The chain appears like this: "I heard so-and-so mention that he heard on the authority of so-and-so, who related to him that he heard such-and-such companion say that the prophet said . . ."

Hoskins relates, "I have never met a Sunni Muslim who did not accept the hadith as authentic and authoritative for practical living" (2011, 424).

Enforcing Ethical Norms

All religions have ethical norms, and ensuring that adherents conform to those norms, practicing virtues and avoiding taboos, is seen universally. Adherents typically see two different types of enforcers of their ethical norms: *supernatural* enforcers and *social* enforcers.

Supernatural Enforcers

In numerous traditional religious societies, the supernatural powers in one form or another are responsible for maintaining order. The panoply of the supernatural, which maintains order, includes personal beings such as God, other gods, angels, demons, nature spirits, departed ancestors, ghosts, witches, and sorcerers. It also includes nonpersonal forces such as magic, mana, or karma. The supernatural may punish or reward. In many traditional

African stories that I have encountered, the main character dies because of foolishly violating a taboo or is punished by a supernatural being or a person using supernatural power (a prophet, a witch, or a sorcerer).

As an example of the supernatural maintaining order, spirit possession can be a vehicle through which the differences in the social power of the genders play out (Lewis 1966, 316–18). In such cases, typically, spirits or powers come to the aid of women who face situations of deprivation. Whether genuine or feigned, the possession of the women and their subsequent pronouncements against the treatment they received at the hands of men are used to balance social power and ensure that ethical obligations are followed within the group. Among the Taita in Kenya, for example, spirits may spontaneously possess (typically) married women in an event called *saka*. The women, while possessed, may speak syllables in what is thought to be another language. Even so, they are able to communicate—typically to announce conditional judgment on their husbands, judgment that may be avoided only through meeting prescribed conditions (e.g., giving gifts to the women, paying more attention to them, the men submitting to some punishment by the women; Harris 1957). In this way ethical order is maintained.

The supernatural may also entice people to maintain order through a system of rewards. Many religions hold that practitioners who do something that gains merit or favor for self or the in-group will be blessed by a supernatural power. This includes such things as making right choices when facing temptation, but also offering worship or performing sacrifices and the like as tributes to one or more of the supernatural powers. The powers so honored then offer blessings in this life (prosperity, good fortune, success), in a future life (through reincarnation), or in the next phase of existence (access to or greater status in the afterlife).

Social Enforcers

Religious organizations also use methods that do not appeal to the divine or supernatural for direct intervention, though normally the approval by the powers is assumed (or at least claimed) by the person maintaining order, especially when it involves disciplinary measures against what is perceived as sin or taboo violation.

Proper behavior and maintaining order may be motivated by fear of physical punishment, social punishment (shunning or ostracism), and psychological pressures (guilt or shame). Ostracism or persecution for a change in religious belief is commonly seen; at times this escalates into violence or even murder, justified in the name of religion.

On the other hand, as we noted with the supernatural, proper behavior may also be motivated by hope of reward, though natural means are limited to offers in this life (e.g., social recognition, a place of honor in the religious structure).

Punishments and rewards, whether divine or natural, are typically codified in some way, either through legislation or ideals for living, such as Sharia for Muslims, the Ten Commandments for Jews, dharma for Hindus, and the Eightfold Path for Buddhists.

For example, practitioners of Confucian social order were deeply linked with a political order in which the state was the enforcer of social norms. Ultimately, Confucianism is a religion of social order founded on *jen* (respect, benevolence) and *li* (propriety, etiquette), in which each person has roles to play and is expected to play those roles appropriately (Carroll, n.d.). People demonstrate *jen* when they live respectfully and empathetically toward others. *Li* frames proper behavior in terms of ritual, from the palace to the marketplace. It is seen more as acting with propriety in all settings than as being ritualistic (though that is included). Through *li* "life is properly ordered and harmony is established" (Carroll, n.d.).

In Confucian thought, *proper relationships* are societal placeholders in which every person must live and behave harmoniously (contrasted with the American ideal of rebellion against tyranny). These relationships start at the level of the ruler in relation to the subject and extend to the level of friend to friend. The Confucian ideal is relatively simple to summarize: if all people maintain the right ways of living in relationship with each other by practicing *jen* and *li*, society (and the individuals in society) will be in harmony (see also Tran 2009).

In light of the ways the ethical dimension shows up in societies and in religions (when they are not integrated across the society), how do we contextualize the ethical dimension? That becomes our final focus in the chapter.

Ethics: A Biblical Example

A somewhat startling reality to American Christians is that in the New Testament Epistles the vast bulk of the emphasis is on how Christians are to treat *each other in the church*—not on how Christians are to treat those outside the church. A refrain throughout the Epistles is the term "each other"—and it consistently describes some aspect of how Christians *should behave* in relation to each other. For example, we are to serve (Gal. 5:13); honor (Rom. 12:10); love (Rom. 13:8; 1 John 3:11, 32; 4:7, 11); forgive (Eph. 4:32; Col. 3:13); encourage

(1 Thess. 5:11; Heb. 3:13); agree with (1 Cor. 1:10); submit to (Eph. 5:21); be kind to (Eph. 4:2; 1 Thess. 5:15); live in peace with (1 Thess. 5:13); spur on (Heb. 10:24); be humble, gentle, and patient with (Eph. 4:2)—the list is extensive. We are likewise given several prohibitions: don't lie to (Col. 3:9), bite or devour (Gal. 5:15), provoke or envy (Gal. 5:26), slander (James 4:11), grumble against (James 5:9), or pass judgment on (Rom. 14:13). Perhaps this is best summed up by the simple phrase "Live in harmony with one another" (Rom. 12:16; 1 Pet. 3:8). This is group-level ethical living practiced by individuals.

One of the messages of Ephesians is that the heavenly authorities (angels and demons) will learn of God's plan when they observe Jews and gentiles united with each other as a single body *in the church* (Eph. 2:11–3:10). Jesus declared that others will know we are Christians by our love (John 13:34–35). As that reality is fleshed out in the New Testament, the primary focus is on our love *for each other*. Certainly this does not exclude our love for unbelievers, but that is not the primary focus in the New Testament. According to John Nugent, professor of Old Testament at Great Lakes Christian College, "Scripture teaches us to love fellow believers—not all humans in general. The evidence is so clear and overwhelming that it is hard to believe it is not common knowledge" (2016, 90). If Nugent is correct, what are some implications for contextualizing ethical "churchness"?

Bernard Adeney's brilliant and challenging book *Strange Virtues* (1995) explores cross-cultural ethics, and I am deeply indebted to his thinking through significant issues in ways far more deeply than I am able to do in this chapter. In digging into this example, as he points out, "the commandments of Scripture must be understood for what they meant to people in a specific time and place before we can begin to understand what they might mean in our time and place" (82). Though Adeney is specifically referencing the Old Testament commandments, his admonition applies equally to the one-another commands. To flesh this out, consider that when I, as a twenty-first-century Anglo-American, read Jesus's and John's commands to "love one another," my instinctive thought is of love as a positive emotional response to someone rather than the unconditional commitment behind the Greek word. I instinctively think having this love means I need to feel good about fellow believers. My instinct, as we have seen in the discussion of Priest (1994) on conscience, comes as a result of what I learned that "love" meant as I grew up. Later in life as I studied Scripture, I realized that my idea of "love" needed some radical readjustment!

Following Adeney's (1995) insight, to ensure that I properly contextualize the many one-another admonitions, I need to explore each one with three questions in mind:

1. What did the New Testament author intend to communicate as seen by the wording and the contextualizing of the admonition?

2. What did the author's audience understand when they read the admonition?

3. What are appropriate ways to apply that in this particular setting?

I already reported my instinctive reaction to the "love one another" command and how it is not the same as the New Testament framing. But contextualizing the ethical one-another admonitions requires much more than simply doing a series of word studies to ensure I have the correct interpretation. As Adeney (1995, 85) explains, "The primary way we learn goodness from the Bible is by making the story of the Bible the interpretive framework through which we view all of life." I also need to better understand my own cultural framework so that I can better see how the framework of the Bible both challenges and commends my cultural instincts. Only when I grasp both the biblical framing and my own cultural instincts am I positioned to partner together with local Christians to contextualize the ethical dimension.

What are my cultural instincts? Geert and Gert Hofstede claim that no country is more individualistic than the United States (2005, 78). When our cultural individualism also reigns in the church, as missiological trainer Jackson Wu states, "the church becomes a collection of individual Christians who gather for worship. This is what individualism asserts: I the individual am most basic, not the group. When Christians see themselves fundamentally as individuals, *the church is merely one among many choices when deciding to join a group.* Social divisions also creep into the church. Individuals form cliques, small groups, and organizations united by something other than Christ" (Wu 2017, 7, emphasis added). If you are an American, how well does this describe your attitude toward church? The follow-up question that contextualization requires is even more important: How well does Wu describe the attitude of the typical American missionary?

When I honestly assess myself, I see how my individualistic penchant (described by Wu) guides me into a privatized faith, which sees the church I attend as only one option among many. As you can imagine, when I bring my own individualistic ethics into what is an "each-other" community, I do not follow the New Testament ideal. Bernard Adeney declares, "We learn ethics from the biblical story by allowing its way of seeing the world to become our own symbolic structure of meanings" (1995, 88). For example, I learn how to frame the "one another" commands contextually by seeing them as they were intended, and then I align my life in light of them. Given that God intends to use the church to demonstrate to the powers his plan of reconciling all people, and that living one-another lives is a top priority for those who love Jesus, it must also be a top priority for me, and those like me, when I work to contextualize ethics at the church level.

Contextualizing Ethics

Understanding the various ways that religious practitioners maintain their ethical ideals in your setting is an important first step toward contextualizing a Christian response. How do they know ethical behavior? How much variance between their ideals and their practices will they allow? Some of their ethical ideals will be compatible with the gospel; others will not. To understand cross-cultural ethics, we cannot separate the study of *their* ethics from *their* theological or philosophical commitments and how they understand what the adherence to those commitments entails.

For example, the belief in reincarnation "brings about a more educational attitude to morality: that is, it is something learnt over more than one life." For adherents who believe in reincarnation, "wickedness is not completely fatal: there is always hope, since hells are not permanent—in effect they are purgatories. Moreover, the gradualism of moral progress seems realistic to people. You do not need to be a saint straight off" (Smart 1996, 198). In other words, living a righteous life is less urgent because it is believed that you will get multiple chances to do better in the future. While reincarnation is clearly not biblical, we still need to understand the perspective of those who do believe in it if we are to best communicate the good news among them. As we have done in the previous sections, we will explore the contextualization of ethics at the personal, group, and systemic levels. But before we do that, we need to examine and better understand the idea of syncretism.

Syncretism

Evangelicals have generally defined syncretism as "the replacement or dilution of the essential truths of the gospel through the incorporation of non-Christian elements" (Moreau 2000c). Concerns over syncretism through contextualization are expressed through blogs, books, and social media (for more extensive exploration, see Van Rheenen 2006). "Syncretism can be exceedingly complex to distinguish from contextualization, as the differences between them are often more fuzzy than binary. . . . It is even more complicated when we realize that shifts in culture make syncretism a moving target; what is 'seeker-oriented' contextualization in one generation becomes 'market-driven' syncretism to the next generation if society has shifted while Christianity has not" (Moreau 2012b, 125).

Given the complexities, I limit discussion to ethical syncretism, which can be seen in two directions. The first direction is to add anti-Christian practices or obligations to Christian faith. For example, using magical means of healing or protection (charms, amulets, magic rituals), calling on the ancestors for help, and the like are syncretistic. These practices add something inappropriate to the Christian message.

Among missionaries, those who "become like Muslims in order to win Muslims" are accused of this type of syncretism (compare Woodberry 2007 with Smith 2009). Missiologists have yet to agree on where the line of syncretism should be drawn. Today we argue less over missionaries keeping the Muslim fast of Ramadan and debate more over increasingly radical practices such as missionaries participating in mosque rituals and calling themselves "Muslims" (as "ones who submit") (e.g., Parshall 1998; Schlorff 2000; Tennent 2006; Woodberry 2007; http://biblicalmissiology.org). While it is true that missionaries are in many senses "cultural chameleons" (Poston 2000), we have yet to agree on where and how to draw lines that demark syncretism from contextualization.

A second direction syncretism can take is that of forbidding practices that are not forbidden in Scripture, such as forbidding the consumption of *any* alcoholic beverage. At my own institution (Wheaton College), for example, activities such as card playing, going to movies, social dancing, and any drinking were variously prohibited over the history of the school, even though there are no specific scriptural injunctions against any of them. The declaration of these as taboo was culturally imposed as a result of historical experiences of evangelicals; they were banned to protect students from the influence of a secular society.

One of the important challenges is not just that these were prohibited at Wheaton College: it was also the potential for Wheaton College alumni to carry these prohibitions with them wherever they served. As previously noted, missionaries are more likely to ban practices about which native conscience does not have taboos, and thus more likely to move in this second syncretistic direction.

Contextualizing Personal, Group, and Systemic Ethics

How should we contextualize ethics on the personal, the group, and the systemic levels? Our ultimate goal is acting *wisely*. Bernard Adeney maintains that "cross-cultural wisdom combines biblical knowledge, the power of the

Holy Spirit, and cultural experience to produce the fruit of goodness" (1995, 72). As you read through this section, consider how you might cultivate cross-cultural wisdom.

Personal Level

Robert Priest's framing of conscience offers us important insights. After arguing that conscience is developed in the context of culture, and that we are far more likely to notice the discontinuities we have in cross-cultural settings, he points out that we are far more likely to offer moral condemnation for those things on which we disagree than those on which we agree (1994, 297).

However, he also points out that across human societies there are both areas of overlap and areas of discontinuity with other societies—and also with God's morality as revealed in Scriptures. Missionaries, then, who seek to live an exemplary life will do so in light of *their own* cultural values rather than in light of the local cultural values. They will be misunderstood at best—and seen as immoral at worst.

While I taught in Kenya, I asked the students in my cross-cultural communication course to identify the things other African Christians said when they talked about the behavior of missionaries, and notably those things that they considered to be strange behavior. The list I compiled has 110 items from 6 countries! The following examples typify what the students observed:

- Imposing "Christian" practices wrapped up in Western culture to the exclusion of accommodating African cultural practices that in fact enhanced observance of morals (Zambia).
- Alienation from the people: this seems to be a tradition for all missionaries; they always isolate themselves from the Africans and live far away from them (Liberia).
- Several missionaries refused to give their Christian friends rides in their cars even when they needed assistance to be taken to the hospital when they were sick because the backseat was already occupied by their pet dogs (Uganda).
- In the area of dressing, some missionaries dress in a way that large portions of their bodies remain unnecessarily exposed. Such kind of dressing is normally associated with tourists who are seen as rich and irreligious (Kenya).

The missionaries described in these observations tried to live exemplary Christian lives, yet they were judged by their hosts as falling short. They were not bad missionaries, but they lived out their own cultural values, some of which were seen as unethical/immoral by African Christians. I could have similarly compiled a list of complaints I heard the missionaries make about African Christians. It is not surprising, as Robert Priest comments, that "missionaries, whose message entails ideas of sin and judgment, will naturally tend . . . to speak of sin with reference to matters about which *their* conscience speaks and native conscience is silent—with the result that native conscience does not work to support the message" (1994, 302, emphasis added).

One result is that nationals who accept missionary ethics without challenge experience a new set of rules and norms. These new taboos are then added to the national taboos already extant (305), creating a system of dependency and paternalism. After all, only the missionaries know the new rules, so the local church depends on them for guidance.

Further, nationals who are chosen for leadership roles may well tend to be those who best conform to the missionary's conscience. Clearly this is less than ideal. In light of this, Priest argues, "in initial evangelism the missionary should stress sin, guilt, and repentance principally with reference to native conscience—*particularly that aspect of their conscience which is in agreement with Scripture*" (309, emphasis original). That takes hard listening work: listening well enough to local people to see the world as they see it, and to understand their moral compasses well enough to address what they see as violations rather than what we see from our moral compass.

What are the options we have when we find ourselves in settings of conflicting ethics? Once we take the time to understand what the conflict is, we face five possibilities of response, as outlined in table 7.1. As you work through the case study at the end of the chapter, try to consider which option you would choose.

Table 7.1
Options in Coping with Value Differences

Nonacceptance	Reject the new value and behave as you would in your own culture.
Substitution	Replace your native values with the new values appropriate to your new context.
Acceptance	Retain both sets of values, using whichever is most helpful in a given situation.
Combination	Combine and integrate elements of both sets of values.
Synthesis or combination/ integration	Create a new, innovative value system that draws from the values of both cultures.

Source: Adeney 1995, 68

Group Level

Richard Gehman, missionary with Africa Inland Mission, developed the model for local church theological development currently used by the Africa Inland Church in Kenya. He defines the process of contextualizing theology (each number represents a step in the process): "Contextualizing theology is that (8) dynamic process whereby (1) the people of God (6) living in community and interacting with believers throughout time and space, (4) under the illuminating guidance of the Holy Spirit, (9) proclaim (7) in their own language and thought forms, (5) the Word that God has spoken to them (3) in their context (2) through the study of the Scriptures" (Gehman 1987, 77). A critical step in his approach is to establish what he calls a "Theological Advisory Group" (TAG), which oversees research on the question for which the TAG is established and, on the basis of their research, develops tools to guide the church. The TAG appoints a research team to study the crucial needs, exploring things rooted in the people's past, those found today, those in the church and society, and any additional doctrinal issues.

Systemic Level

Historically, evangelicals (and missionaries) have typically focused on the individual level of personal morals. The oft-quoted phrase "Don't drink, don't smoke, don't chew—and don't go out with those who do" captured the personal ethical narrative of many early to mid-twentieth-century conservative Christians. (It does not capture millennials, however!) Larger societal issues such as civil rights were not on their mental maps the way personal moral issues were. I vividly remember repeatedly hearing that the best way to change society was to change individuals and that only a society of changed individuals could itself be changed (see the critique in Hunter 2010). Evangelicals are in need of better tools to understand—and struggle against—the systemic powers that permeate our societies and that we all too often unwittingly perpetuate (e.g., by policies of separation and marginalization).

Conclusion

Contextual ethics presents numerous challenges to the cross-cultural Christian. Maintaining the tension between going too far and not going far enough has presented a challenge. So has explaining decisions you make "over there" to your home audience, especially when they do not have a context to understand your decisions. In our case study for this chapter, we are asked to consider how or even whether to help a woman in need when she is under duress to get an abortion in a country that requires her to do so. One complicating factor is that she is not a believer. Which of Adeney's five options in table 7.1 would you choose? How might you implement your choice?

CASE STUDY

TEACHER LEE'S ANNOUNCEMENT
GAIL STROMBERG

Few ethical issues weigh heavier among American evangelicals than abortion. It is a violation of Christian teaching in so many ways, and yet when we live in another country with different morals, how should we respond? Earlier missionaries denounced widow burning in India, foot binding in China, twin killing in West Africa, and the like. In what sense does abortion fit into those categories? As you read this case, consider how you would wish the class would respond to Teacher Lee's announcement.

The American cohort class held an emergency meeting after their Mandarin conversation class to talk about what Teacher Lee had announced and how best to respond to her in a way that would be truthful, loving, gracious, and life giving.

The small cohort of ten students had been studying Mandarin intensively for about eight months. Each of them had taken a break from teaching English in order to study language full time, with the goal of building closer and more meaningful relationships with Chinese people and to share truth in their heart language of Mandarin. They spent time weekly together in prayer for each other and their teacher. Even with this prayer and fellowship, they were all worn down by the exhaustion of memorizing characters and tones and struggling to express or understand concepts in conversation.

Teacher Lee had taught American cohorts in years past and knew what to expect. Since the cohort spent two hours every day with their teacher in class, working on conversational Chinese, they got to know their teacher fairly deeply. Teacher Lee was married to an important government official, and they had a toddler. With obvious pride and joy, she often talked about her toddler in class. The class knew that Teacher Lee had struggled with infertility and that a previous American cohort had prayed for her and let her know they were doing so. Teacher Lee then conceived and gave birth, crediting the previous American cohort's prayers for this miracle. Although she professed to be atheist, she was impacted by this event and the love she felt in her American students. She clearly felt at ease with the current cohort based on relationships built with previous American cohorts, and she often shared small details from her life and listened as the students reciprocated as best they could in their still-developing Chinese.

Suddenly in class one day, Teacher Lee made an announcement in the middle of a lesson. "I won't be here Friday or for the next two weeks because I need to have a surgery," she said. Seeing the blank stares of incomprehension, she wrote the Chinese word "surgery" on the board, and the students looked it up. Once the class understood, they immediately expressed concern for her through facial expressions and follow-up questions. A surgery sounded serious, and the class could tell from the teacher's troubled eyes that this was a big deal. Teacher Lee then poured out the rest of the story. "I am pregnant again, but it is illegal for me to have a second baby. The law only allows me to have one baby. We had so much trouble becoming pregnant that I haven't been careful since then. But now through my carelessness I'm pregnant, and if I have another baby my husband and I will both lose our jobs. Besides, it is illegal for me to have a second child. This surgery will fix the mistake I made. I wish I could have a second child, but I can keep my job and obey the government if I have this surgery. So I won't be here for class. I will arrange a substitute who can teach you all very well in my absence."

The class sat in stunned silence, processing what Teacher Lee had just told them. Teacher Lee didn't realize how emotional an issue abortion is for many Americans, especially for evangelicals such as her students, but her sad eyes showed she felt sorrow on a deep level. This was the first time anyone in the American cohort had encountered the effects of the one-child policy this closely. Before anyone could frame a response in Chinese, Teacher Lee brushed away the tears clustered in her eyes and abruptly switched back to the interrupted lesson.

After class, the students lingered around Teacher Lee, letting her know in their broken Chinese that they would be praying for her and asking whether there was anything they could do for her. Teacher Lee responded with gratitude but assured them that she was fine and not to worry. She reassured them that she would find a good substitute in her absence, and that the doctors and her family would take good care of her.

The class said goodbye to her and went to their American cohort room downstairs, where they immediately began discussing the situation together. Several people in the class were adamant about doing something to save Teacher Lee's unborn baby. A few others were concerned about the spiritual and emotional impact an abortion would have on Teacher Lee. A few others pointed out that there really wasn't anything the class could do. They were outsiders and could neither change the law nor provide adequately for Teacher Lee and her family in the serious consequences that could follow having a second child. They also didn't know her husband at all and had no way to influence him, since his job and opinions were also important as playing into Teacher Lee's decision. "But shouldn't we fight to save her unborn baby?" was the response some classmates gave. After an intense discussion of the issues, the class finally decided to . . .

8

THE ARTISTIC AND TECHNOLOGICAL DIMENSION

I use two parallel terms for this dimension: art and technology. I will set the stage by briefly introducing what I mean by each term before exploring how they appear in society and in religions, and how we might contextualize in each area of this dimension.

After the unimaginable act of creating the universe itself, with all its beauty and functionality, the first mundane act of art found in the Bible is when God makes garments out of skins for Adam and Eve after the fall (Gen. 3:21). God is infinitely creative (from the universe to garments), and part of being an image-bearer for us is that we, too, are creative. This creativity flows in at least two directions: creating things simply for their beauty (fine art) and creating things that we use to extend ourselves (applied arts). While we do not know what fashion statement was made in the first garments, it is hard to imagine them being ugly since God created them! In any event, the garments serve as examples of art in both beauty and functionality.

Ninian Smart used the word "material" to refer to "the way religions reflect themselves materially" (1996, 275). By this he meant such things as their architecture (e.g., temples, shrines), their objects of religious devotion or worship (e.g., idols, altars), their functional and symbolic religious instruments (e.g., religious clothing, jewelry, icons), and so on. I utilize his core concept of the material, but by "art" I broaden Smart's "material" dimension by incorporating the nonmaterial, such as religious performance (e.g., music, drama, and speaking).

The second term for this dimension is "technology," using twentieth-century cultural commentator Marshall McLuhan's framing most famously captured in the phrase "The medium is the message" (1964, 1967). For Mc-Luhan, "technology" refers to anything made by people that extends us in physical, cognitive, or sensory ways, by which he intended things we use that change us as we use them (Knippa 2016, 374). From simple tools (hammer, pen) to spacecraft, from the telegraph to the internet, technology is whatever humans make that amplifies our strength, increases our senses, or accelerates our abilities.

In a rather large nutshell, then, in this dimension I blend the overlapping categories of art (including Smart's concept of the material component of religion) and technology (following McLuhan). That makes it a very large dimension! Given the reality of space limitations, I will offer only very broad brushstrokes for the sections on art and technology in society and religions, leaving space for greater depth in the section on contextualizing this dimension.

Art and Technology in Religions and Societies

Art and technology are part of every society. There is extensive overlap between them, and they are deeply integrated with the religions found in societies. Before turning to contextual thinking about them, I explore some of the contours of art and technology in relation to societies and religions.

Art

In his discussion of the material dimension of religions, Smart explores several important questions about religious adherents' use of the material:

1. How do they portray their deities?
2. How do they symbolize important religious truths?
3. What do they use to denote spaces of religious significance?

Though Smart's questions are specifically focused on religious concepts, they are easily broadened to society as a whole. For example, the first question can be reframed as, How do societies portray the powers they recognize? In answer, we notice that they use material items such as flags, paintings of symbolic scenery or important cultural events, and statues of cultural icons or heroes. They construct revered symbols such as Mount Rushmore, the Lincoln and Vietnam Memorials, the Taj Mahal, the Tower of London, the Eiffel Tower, palaces, parliament buildings, and the like. With regard to the toppling of the statue of Saddam Hussein in Firdos Square in Baghdad (Iraq) and the contemporary American debates over whether to topple memorials to southern Civil War figures, reactions to these monuments show how powerful such symbols can be even when they are not framed religiously.

Smart's second question can be reframed as, How do societies symbolize important truths? Items noted in answer to the first question reflect what powers are recognized by the society, yet they also symbolically express perspectives on truth. To these we can add cultural artifacts such as the Magna Carta, the Declaration of Independence, the Statue of Liberty, the Liberty Bell, patriotic pledges, national anthems, and mottoes on official national seals and emblems, all of which symbolically capture truths that people of a society believe.

Smart's third question becomes, What do societies use to denote significant cultural spaces? These include historical locations such as the Great Wall, Gettysburg, country and regional capitals, official buildings such as the White House, national parks, game reserves, cemeteries, and the like.

Smart's discussion of the material is limited to the physical. Art incorporates the physical but also includes the nonphysical. For the purposes of contextualization, I distinguish four types of art that merit contextual considerations: (1) performing art, (2) literary art, (3) visual 2-D art, and (4) visual 3-D art. In table 8.1, I list selected examples for each category (in alphabetical order).

To be human is to have an artistic bent; whether or not you are gifted artistically, you still are able to develop an appreciation for art. I see this as one

Table 8.1
Categories and Examples of Visual Art in Societies

Performing	Literary	Visual 2-D	Visual 3-D
Acting (movies, television)	Comics	Animation	Architecture
Dance	Poetry	Calligraphy	Body art (scarification)
Drama	Prose	Cartoon	Carving
Mime		Design	Ceramic art
Musical (instrumental, vocal)		Drawing	Decorative (e.g., banners)
Opera		Etching	Design (e.g., furniture)
Oral (e.g., comedy, poetry, storytelling)		Graffiti	Environmental
Theater		Painting	Fashion (e.g., clothing)
		Photography	Sculpture
		Printmaking	Virtual Reality
		Typography	
		Website design	

facet of humans reflecting our artistic image of God. While we all are able to appreciate art, we also have preferences ranging from Marvel to Michelangelo and from country music to opera.

Arts are seen everywhere in society, from so-called high arts of opera and national museums to children's plays at school and folk art. Advertisers depend on art—as do politicians, religious leaders, civic leaders, social clubs and groups, and so on. On a large scale, societies utilize art to infuse members with values such as patriotism, loyalty, respect, and obedience (the line between patriotic literature and propaganda is often blurred). Groups use art to convey their messages to society, to attract new members, and to motivate existing members. Individuals, in addition to making a living from art, use it to express themselves, to promote personal causes, and to make statements (from approval to judgment) to their societies. Art entertains, challenges, cajoles, pacifies, preaches, warns, and admonishes—and can do all of that at the same time.

Although this dimension includes more than art, a more focused examination of religious art, which encapsulates and promotes religious values (see Smart 1996, 278–84), will help us distill important insights for contextualization.

Some societies—Bali, for example—are so deeply infused with religious art that it binds them to one another and to their religious community. As Wayan Mastra explains: "Balinese . . . are extraordinarily visual. They can understand things after they have seen them. They want everything to become concrete, visible, and tangible. That is why they look for signs of their faith in significant happenings in nature and human life. It is important for them to symbolize their faith in action—drama, dance, painting, carving, and architecture, which are seen in temple ceremonies as well as in the temples themselves" (Mastra 1978, 11). Today Bali still remains a Hindu island stronghold in Muslim-dominated Indonesia, maintaining its Hindu identity in part because it is so infused with Hindu-framed art; to date it has provided the fortitude to successfully hold off competing religious influences from Islam and Christianity (see Mastra 1978).

Space constraints limit this section to a cursory overview of two artistic categories: performing arts and 3-D visual arts (specifically architecture). However, these two areas well illustrate significant implications for contextualizing in this dimension—and show why study of all the arts, not to mention the material and technological, is critical for evangelicals.

Religious Performing Arts

The performing arts include such things as drama, music, and speech acts. They blend both content and delivery and are typically evaluated on the basis of both. We find multiple types of performing arts across religions.

Among the Balinese, dance plays a critical religious role. It is a national pastime that is as popular among the Balinese as baseball is among Americans. However, dances are not simply for entertainment, as entertaining as they are. Rather, Balinese dances play out story lines of Balinese history, similar to historical theater in the West. They also present mythological events and themes (complete with elaborate costumes), especially seen in performances such as the Barong dance, a dance ritual in which the Balinese re-create a mythological battle between good (the Barong) and evil (Rangda the witch), including spirit possession of many of the participants. In relation to the artistic dimension, Knapp (1984, 56–58) describes Rangda, whom the Balinese believe is the personification of evil: "Rangda fascinates; she haunts; she intimidates. . . . [Her face] is white—spelling evil. Her bulging eyes, the tusks jutting forth from her inflated jaws, the long pieces of heavy rope all over her body hanging down to the ground—all these make her an unforgettably nightmarish vision." Between the ritual dance and the costume, this event is saturated with components of the artistic dimension. Dance is so deeply embedded in Balinese life that sometimes they dance where no one observes simply as an act of devotion to their deities (Volf 2003).

Muslims have been perceived and portrayed historically to be skeptical of the performing arts (Shiloah et al. 2017). Performances such as the Sufi whirling dervishes have existed from the thirteenth century, but those in particular are means of generating personal religious ecstasy rather than public performances. Folk dances in societies that had such before becoming Islamic were perceived as nonreligious entertainment. The call to prayer (e.g., https://www .youtube.com/watch?v=ppt3BugCulQ) and reciting the Qur'an are artistic events, but for conservative Muslims, viewing them as such puts too much emphasis on the performer and not enough on submission to Allah. In today's globalized world, however, attitudes and practices are changing, especially in settings in which Islam is not the dominant religion. Rap (e.g., https://www .youtube.com/watch?v=SGbvyoFtfwo), soap operas, and plays are all being produced in the contemporary Muslim world (Nieuwkerk 2011).

Among Buddhists, chanting is ubiquitous. Typically used in preparation for meditation rather than for public performance, recordings of Buddhist chants are readily available online through services such as YouTube (https://www .youtube.com/results?search_query=buddhist+chant). Recent technological innovations have enabled the development of "Buddha-recitation devices" as well as apps on phones and the like that endlessly reproduce the name of Buddha as a form of chanting (Heller 2014). Early Shinto rituals became the contemporary *noh* plays of Japan, embodying the living mythos of Japan and evoking religious experience among audiences and participants (Pilgrim 1989).

Each of these represents only a few examples of performing arts presented by religious practitioners; each in its own setting offers opportunity for consideration for contextual purposes. However, simply trying to infuse Christian sensibilities into religious visual art poses a significant challenge. The danger of syncretism lurks, and knowing how your audience understands what you communicate requires intimate knowledge of local idiom as well as a continual feedback loop between participants and audiences.

Religious Visual Arts: Architecture

From drawings to sculpture to architecture, visual art across the religious landscape is a massive topic. Religious faithful who build dedicated structures construct "places of worship that respond to particular ritual and social needs" (Renard 1997). Understanding architecture in religious framing will help us better connect places of worship with their particular religious practices and beliefs.

Hindu temple architecture varies across geographic regions, but Hindu temples are generally not considered places to host "congregational" meetings the way mosques or churches are. They have shrines with deities in place for direct devotional practices, but the architecture is typically more accommodating to individual worshipers than groups, by utilizing, for example, smaller worship spaces inside the temple. From the images of the idols in the temple to the images of deities that often decorate the outside and the rich symbolism worshipers engage as they offer pujas to their deities, visual art is woven into the fabric of Hindu temples.

Architecturally, Hindu temples typically depict the underlying doctrine that the universe is manifested through a series of emanations—a progression from one reality to today's many realities portrayed through visual elements such as the layered roofs, the internal layers within the temple, and the depictions captured by statuary (Hardy 2016). Adherents are thus reminded of this orientation toward the universe whenever they see a temple, and it is reinforced more deeply when they enter and worship in one.

Muslim mosques are patterned after Islamic worship ideals, including regular geometric form, an orientation to Mecca, a minaret to ensure the call to prayer is heard far and wide, stations for washing, and plenty of empty, well-lit space inside for practitioners to engage in the bodily motions that are part of Muslim ritual prayer. Those motions symbolically portray submission to Allah, and when done en masse offer vivid visual confirmation that the community as a whole submits. Within this general frame of reference, multiple regional styles of accomplishing visual submission to Allah are seen

across the Islamic world (Renard 1997, 64). There is a commonly held theological framing underlying mosque architecture—namely, that Allah is One
and transcendent—seen through such symbolism as infinitely repeatable patterns (arabesque) and found in mosque calligraphy, geometry, or other design
elements (Renard 1997, 71).

Islamic practice forbids art depicting people and animated objects, so
calligraphy and geometric designs typically adorn mosques. In contrast to
Hindu temples and Buddhist shrines, mosques host regular congregational
meetings for group worship and civic meetings, and the open architecture
inside the mosque enables group prayer and also works for holding large
assemblies.

Buddhists worship in temples, but they also construct pagodas, stupas,
and shrines for worship purposes. Pagodas, usually associated with temple
complexes, are monuments in the shape of towers or pyramid-like structures
using vertical repetition of ever smaller shapes (e.g., in Japan). As monuments
rather than houses of worship, they commonly have little interior space, if
any at all. The devout circle them from the outside rather than kneel before
or within them.

Buddhist stupas are edifices that house relics, typically of Buddhist monks
or nuns. People appeal to the departed for good luck or merit, or they seek
absolution by walking clockwise around the stupa. Buddhist shrines range
from massive constructs to small shrines in and around the house. Those
who construct and use the shrines see them as locations for spirits or deities. Dotting buildings across cityscapes in countries such as Cambodia,
their myriad styles, designs, and offerings more commonly reflect animistic practices than formal Buddhism—even in Buddhist monasteries (Ang
1988).

Buddhist temples vary widely in architectural style; in contemporary times
they host not just religious adherents but also increasing numbers of casual
tourists. For religious adherents, ideals of Buddhism are found in the architecture and layout of the temple complex, as observed in an ethnography
of adherents at perhaps the most important historic and scenic Bulguksa, a
Buddhist temple in eastern South Korea (Bendle et al. 2014).

The temple captures the harmony of opposing forces, a prominent thought
in Buddhist cosmology, as the ethnographers note: "Together, the halls, pagodas, staircase, terraces, masonry walls and surrounding gardens express a
harmony between Yin (passive energy) and Yang (active energy). As a monk
remarked: 'This Temple . . . reflects the ideology of original Buddhism and
represents the well matched meanings of Yin and Yang'" (Bendle et al. 2014,
205).

Understanding practitioners' experiences in places of worship is a critical step for contextual thinking. A Korean female tourist recounted her experience at the temple: "I enjoy fresh air, beautiful scenery, and the handsome architecture that expresses Buddhism to me. I visit Daeungjeon and show my good manners by bowing with a respectful mind to Buddha. Next, I meditate in Geuknakjeon [the Hall of Supreme Bliss] where I confess my mistakes and then brace myself up in front of the Buddha sculpture" (208).

I am left with several considerations stemming from these observations about places of worship among three religions. First, understanding the local idioms of worship gives us insights into architectural elements, and vice versa. Second, when it comes to contextualization, understanding that the architectural elements are not divorced from religious thought and beliefs stands as a reminder that simply adopting the architecture of local places of worship in constructing churches can be laden with unintended consequences. Third, understanding the embedded explicit (and implicit) symbolism enables us to make wise choices in utilizing (or rejecting!) local idioms for meaningful Christian worship.

Technology

As we mentioned at the outset, technology refers to what we create that extends us in some way. McLuhan (1964, 1967) identified a critical consideration for this component: we create a medium, and then the medium (re-)creates us. He coined the oft-quoted but somewhat cryptic phrase, "The medium is the message." In simple terms, we invent a writing instrument such as a pencil, and it in turn changes how we view writing, remembering, remarking, and thinking. The "medium" of the pencil becomes the "message" in that it reshapes us in significant ways. In more contemporary terms, think of how the invention of the cell phone and the associated apps has reinvented us. Together they dramatically change how we connect with each other (social media), how we remember events (videos and pictures), how we conduct business (email), how much we are available (24/7), how we learn (from blogs to online courses), how we get news (newsfeeds), how we get and/or stay healthy (counting steps), and so on. Just as the printing press remade European intellectual societies hundreds of years ago, so cell phones reshape us today.

I conclude this discussion, as I have in previous chapters, by posing several questions in sidebar 8.1 to be considered in any new setting as you explore art, material, and technology.

This concludes our very cursory overview of ways this dimension can be seen and understood in societies. Next I turn to the ways we see it in Scripture.

SIDEBAR 8.1
QUESTIONS ABOUT ART, MATERIAL, AND TECHNOLOGY

Below are some questions to consider as you explore art, material, and technology in your settings. Asking and exploring the answers to these questions will enable you to better understand local examples of art, material, and technology—yet also help you think more clearly about church and ways Christians might better understand religious uses of art, material, and technology in their contexts and, when appropriate, use them or the cultural insights they offer to better contextualize the gospel.

As I explained in parallel sidebars in previous chapters, answers to these questions could be used to compromise the gospel or the biblical definition of church. That is not my intention. Rather, the questions equip you to find biblically appropriate and culturally sound ways for Christians to understand local views of art, material, and technology. They help you avoid the danger of simply generating and using only the art, material, and technology that make sense from your own cultural setting. As you ask these questions, also be asking yourself how the answers impact what types of uses of art, material, and/or technology would make sense to local people without compromising their relationship with Christ.

1. Art
   a. What uses of art in belief and ritual do you observe?
   b. How is art used to support or possibly subvert ideals and messages?
   c. How does art model, idealize, reflect, or criticize social experience?
2. Material
   a. What uses of material elements in belief and ritual do you observe?
   b. How are material objects used to support or possibly subvert ideals and messages?
   c. How does the material you observe model, idealize, reflect, or criticize social experience?
3. Technology
   a. What uses of technology in belief and ritual do you observe?
   b. How is technology used to support or possibly subvert ideals and messages?
   c. How does the technology you observe model, idealize, reflect, or criticize social experience?
4. Other matters
   a. What must we know about the imagery and iconographic conventions of the society to be able to understand the signifying systems of art, material, and technology?
   b. Who controls access to art, material, and technology and their creation?
   c. In what ways does local art fit the gospel, and in what ways is it in conflict with the gospel?

Art and Technology in the Bible

Understanding the artistic and technological as things we make and that in turn remake us, we see numerous examples in the Bible, ranging from the grandeur of the universe itself to the mundane garments God made for Adam and Eve. They include the temple in Jerusalem as well as Jerusalem itself descending from heaven, but they also include performance through dance and speech. In this section I limit myself to two examples, the tent of meeting found in the book of Exodus and some of the speeches found in Acts.

Exodus 31:1-11

In Exodus 31:1–11, God informs Moses that he has chosen Bezalel of the tribe of Judah and endowed him "with the Spirit of God, with wisdom, with understanding, with knowledge and with all kinds of skills—to make artistic designs for work in gold, silver and bronze, to cut and set stones, to work in wood, and to engage in all kinds of crafts" (vv. 3–5). He has also appointed Oholiab of the tribe of Dan to help him; together these two (who were able · to teach others; Exod. 35:34) are to oversee the making of the tent of meeting and all that goes into the tent—from the temple garments to the incense they are to use and the ark of the covenant itself. Exodus 35:10 states that God has called "all who are skilled among you" to participate in making the items needed for the tabernacle, including the tabernacle itself. Exodus 36:8–39:32 offers a detailed account of each major item made, culminating in their being brought before Moses for inspection and subsequent blessing (39:33–43). Certainly the most magnificent component of the tabernacle is that, upon completion, God's glory comes to fill it, and a cloud rests on it in daylight, changing to a pillar of fire at night. The cloud (and pillar of fire) serves as the travel guide for Moses and Israel. When it lifts from the tabernacle, the Israelites, all of whom can see it, pack up their goods and follow where it leads (40:34–38).

Thus this "portable" tabernacle was a magnificent piece of functional art, providing a physical location for God's visible presence among Israel as they traveled the wilderness. They looked to it for direction, and it continually challenged their self-directed frame of reference. In the account, we find that God endows some people with artistic gifts, which are not listed as spiritual gifts in the New Testament. The artistic gifts are to be used for God's glory. Even though the tabernacle is functional art, this does not indicate a position of art simply for the sake of beauty. It does show that functional art that is beautiful has a place in God's heart and his interaction with his people.

Speeches in Acts

In the New Testament, speeches given by Jesus, John the Baptist, and the disciples are contextual performance acts. Andrew Prince (2017) examines four of the speeches recorded by Luke in Acts. In the first of these, Peter responds to the accusation of drunkenness after tongues are distributed among the disciples at Pentecost (Acts 2:14–31). In his speech, he draws on Scripture to explain to the Jews of the Diaspora that what they are seeing is a fulfillment of their shared story—one they did not expect—through the life, death, and resurrection of Jesus the Christ. As Prince comments, "The sermon before Jews in Jerusalem is an exemplary model of someone contextualizing their message to suit their audience. Using the tools of ancient rhetoric, Peter sought to persuade his audience through drawing on common ground, drawing on their own Scriptures, and interacting with their Jewish worldview" (86).

Second, Stephen gives a long speech to his Jewish audience, which has accused him of blasphemy, and his "counter to the charges through the constraints of forensic rhetoric is in many ways a classic argument of defense" (91). In his defense he extensively rehearses Israel's history through the lens of their tendency to kill God's messengers and prophets, climaxed historically by their betrayal and murder of the "Righteous One" (Acts 7:52). He boldly declares that his accusers stand in continuity with their prophet-killing ancestors. Given the strength of his argument and their subsequent loss of honor, it is not surprising that Stephen is stoned to death (7:1–53)—which itself further substantiates his claim. Luke portrays Stephen's speech as a successful witness to the gospel message; perhaps we need to reconsider the contemporary Western "positive results" orientation on evaluating sermons!

Third, Paul speaks to a Jewish audience in a synagogue in Pisidian Antioch (Acts 13:13–47). It comes at the turning point in Acts, where the focus shifts from Peter and Jewish audiences to Paul and gentile audiences. This speech comes at the invitation of the synagogue leaders. Paul shapes his narrative to the traditions and mythic story line of the Jewish people, from Moses to John the Baptist, concluding that the latter identified Jesus as the Messiah; this Messiah was ultimately put to death and then raised from the dead. He connects God's early promise to their ancestors with the person of Jesus by quoting from the Psalms and the Prophets as the texts that Jesus fulfilled. As with Peter and Stephen in their speeches, Paul identifies Jesus as the interpretive key to understanding the story arc of God's promises to Israel. The initial reaction to Paul's speech is curiosity and a request to come back the following week. At the following meeting, "almost the whole city gathered" (13:44).

Seeing this response, the Jewish leaders became jealous, contradicting Paul and verbally abusing him (13:45), so Paul and Barnabas respond that they will turn to the gentiles, who rejoice and believe (13:48).

Fourth, Paul also gives a speech to a sophisticated gentile audience in Athens (Acts 17:16–34), the "intellectual, cultural and philosophical heart of Greece" (Prince 2017, 98). As Dean Flemming (2005, 72) notes, "Paul's address to the Athenians in Acts 17 is perhaps the outstanding example of intercultural evangelistic witness in the New Testament. This makes it a pivotal text for our study of New Testament patterns of contextualization."

Paul's preaching in Athens so intrigued the Athenians that they brought him to the Areopagus in Athens. In his speech, he interacts with his audience's worldview and identifies that he has common ground with them. He bridges from their worldview to God's story arc, addressing the topics of God, humanity, and divine judgment (Prince 2017, 104–6): "Paul's use of philosophical language, common ground, and interaction with the Hellenistic worldview had a purpose beyond simply providing information or even a personal defense against the accusation that he was preaching about foreign divinities. Rather, Paul garners all of these rhetorical devices in order to bring about a transformation of his audience's worldview" (104).

In summary, Prince extensively rehearses in depth the setting, the audience, and the message for each speech as well as the patterns of rhetoric present at the time and how each speech utilizes rhetorical devices (2017, 72–107). Most importantly for contextualization purposes, he summarizes the contextual framing of these four speeches in eight principles (108–12):

Principle 1: The early establishment of common ground provides a platform for the gospel to be heard.

Principle 2: For contextualization to be effective, the gospel needs to be explained in ways that engage the worldview of the target audience.

Principle 3: Faith in Jesus Christ does not necessarily mean social dislocation.

Principle 4: There is no fixed presentation of the gospel since contextual sensitivity requires flexibility.

Principle 5: There is a core content to the gospel, applicable to all cultures.

Principle 6: Cultural pressure must not lead to a dampening down of the challenging demands of discipleship.

Principle 7: Existing cultural terms and forms can be used and imbued with new meaning in light of the gospel.

Principle 8: Culture is both positive and flawed and needs redemption through the gospel.

As seen in these eight principles, Prince's approach to contextualization is concerned not only with the speeches as performance acts, but also with the message given in the speeches. He observes that while there is a core content to the message (principle 5), there is not a fixed presentation (principle 4). All of the speeches examined draw on existing cultural worldviews, forms, and terms (principle 2, principle 7), but that does not mean that God approves all elements of a society (principle 8) nor that the demands of discipleship may be lightened because of cultural pressures (principle 6).

Contextualizing Art, Material, and Technology

Art, material, and technology are all amenable to contextualized thinking and application. Aesthetic and functional art, whether performed or visual, must be part of our evangelism, discipleship, church planting, and church development. As summarized in the Lausanne Occasional Paper "Redeeming the Arts,"

> Every people group reinforces and passes on its story through the arts. Generation after generation, people find themselves through the artistic legacy of story. Art has its own unique way of "speaking" and "meaning." It does not function well when we try to make it into something it is not. To put it directly, art is not a good preacher—it is by nature allusive, indirect. The arts should therefore not attempt to evangelize per se, but they can "bear witness" to truth. For example, stories, contemporary parables, and allegories are very creative, art-friendly, and meaningful ways to engage the imagination, highlight the human condition, and allow the Holy Spirit to "point" people toward transcendent realities. (Harbinson et al. 2005, 31–32)

From Bibles to Bible study materials, from church architecture to musical instruments, from clothing to social media—all are most effective when framed with indigenous perspectives in mind. At the same time, each is a potential vehicle for culture transformation, enhancing the communication of the gospel message. Limiting focus to the arts, ethnomusicologist Brian Schrag (2007) identifies five characteristics of arts that demonstrate their connection to mission, and I add, to contextualization:

> First, artistic acts are special kinds of communication, consisting of the processes and products associated with a person's skillful exploitation of a medium's formal characteristics to create, modify, expand, and shape messages. . . .

Second, artistic activity draws on and is embedded in cultural patterns and symbolic systems. Applications of the arts to local contexts thus rely on understanding the meanings ascribed to them by the communities that produce them.

Third, artistic expressions seldom occur alone. Ethnographic literature abounds with examples of expressive events that simultaneously draw on multiple forms. . . . A single art's perspective—such as dance, music, costuming, or drama—almost never describes a performance adequately.

Fourth, artistic rendering enriches the experience of a message. Tapping into existing arts allows new messages of truth to be marked as particularly important, uniquely memorable, and distinctly engaging. Artistic expressions are often the most powerful and enduring means of communication within a culture.

Fifth, and finally, local arts exist, well, locally. Community members already master these media, in contrast to writing systems that often require the acquisition of completely new skills and cultural patterns. (Schrag 2007, 200–201)

It is clear that the artistic dimension offers significant strategic advantages in contextualization. Locally produced arts draw on the local worldview, as Kenyan artist Elimo Njau states: "Art 'makes Christianity African,' provides a new context for worship, stimulates devotion, and teaches the meaning of the Bible through imagery" (cited in Stinton 2007, 20). Arts appeal to all that we are: body, soul, heart, and mind. Creating art can be a transformative process, and viewing created art can touch the deepest parts of who we are.

Art and the Bible

Our understanding of contextualizing art will be enhanced by a brief synopsis of the perspective on art and the Bible presented by Christian philosopher and apologist Francis Schaeffer (1973; also cofounder of L'Abri, the subject of the case study at the end of chap. 4).

First, Schaeffer declares, a work of art has an intrinsic value. God is creative, he made humans to be creative, and the creation of art connects us to the one who created the universe. This does not mean that all art is good, however. Good art reflects God's creative work. It is not just cognitive: it accesses the full range of our emotions, from intense joy to intense sadness. Finally, it embodies messages that reflect the perspective or worldview of the artist. Schaeffer adds that art forms add strength to the worldview that shows through, whether the worldview is true or false. The artist's worldview, and how it changes through time, is captured not in a single work of art but in the gathered works of the artist.

While art forms have varied across history (and continue to shift and change), there is nothing wrong with such changes. However, Schaeffer argues that art should show some form of symbolic continuity with the normal syntax and style of the medium. When the artist divorces the style from symbolic convention, the message is lost since none of the audience has access to the artist's "language."

Schaeffer further notes that the greatness of the constructed art is not the basis of the truth of the art's message: separate criteria are used for evaluation of the message (namely, Schaeffer declares, the Word of God). Art has no limitations on its message, which can be historical or the product of imagination. Therefore, Christian art is not restricted to religious art.

We can apply Schaeffer's framing of art to *The Pieta of Kwangju* (fig. 8.1). In this lithograph, Taeko Tomiyama strikingly portrays suffering Korean mothers crying over their children in Kwangju, South Korea, just as Mary suffered over Jesus in Michelangelo's famous statue *Pieta*. In 1980, students in Kwangju rebelled against the authoritarian South Korean regime. In response, the Korean army killed and injured hundreds. If you travel to Kwangju today, you can tour the monument, read the story, and see videos of the events that took place—which are commemorated as the birth of contemporary democracy in South Korea. In the lithograph, Tomiyama aligns the suffering of the mothers with the suffering of Mary after the death of Christ. Suffering is a human condition to which we respond viscerally. Adding to the poignancy, Tomiyama herself is Japanese. Japan brutally annexed Korea from 1910 to 1946; that a Japanese woman captures the Korean historical moment of suffering, given their mutual history, adds to the emotion of the work.

Thus Tomiyama brings together the historical moment, her country's shameful history, and the biblical story in a visually compelling way that stirs the soul. This example of contextual art captures and connects the then-current setting with the timeless biblical narrative and offers a message of intermingled pain and hope. The hope of something good coming out of something evil comes not from the immediate Korean context (Tomiyama created it at the time of the event, before the outcome was known). A hope for good comes from the title, which connects the work not only to Michelangelo's work but also to the biblical narrative of the disciples' suffering between Jesus's death and resurrection; the title burns that hope into our imaginations.

With Schaeffer's framing in mind, I turn to two selected examples of contextualization in this dimension.

Figure 8.1: *The Pieta of Kwangju,* by Taeko Tomiyama

Source: Takenaka and O'Grady 1991

Christian Folk Songs of Tamil Nadu

The first example comes from the performing art of singing in India. Theodore Baskaran, from Bangalore, reports that people from Tamil Nadu have
been singing in their work contexts for centuries. In 1870, Charles Gover,
an Englishman who wrote several books on Indian folk music, heard workers singing a song portraying the story of the fall of humankind. This style
of folk music was popular in Tamil Nadu, and people who came to Christ
through Catholic missionaries learned to apply Christian themes to their
cultural musical framing. As Baskaran (1989, 85) observes, "Folk music was
learnt by listening and so was simple in form, composed without notations.
The words used were often colloquial and the lines short so that the song
could be memorized easily. This feature facilitated group singing. It was not
basically meant for entertainment but was always functional, associated with
other activities. There were work songs, songs for games and lullabies and
these could be sung without any accompaniment."

Using local folk songs for evangelistic purposes began in the early eigh-
teenth century, when Ganapathi Vathiyar (an early convert of Bartholomäus
Ziegenbalg) began putting selected biblical stories to song in order to attract
people for street preaching (Baskaran 1989, 86). Over a century later, from
roughly 1880 to 1920, groups of Indians came to Christ in a series of mass

movements. Evangelists and church planters recognized that indigenous songs were a potential vehicle for transmitting Christian truths to the new converts in a way that they would remember, and they began to compose simple, memorable songs that common people could use to learn about their new faith. Some compiled songs into short songbooks and published them in a style that paralleled the style for Hindu devotional songs. Collections were published by Protestants and Catholics, laypeople and clergy. The longest of these songs ran 1,600 lines in forty sections and chronicled the story of the exodus. Others chronicled the stories of Indian believers, with some parts biography and others hagiography. But not all styles of Indian music lend themselves to this type of contextualization:

> An analysis of these Christian folk songs in Tamil shows that the song-writers were quite aware of the different uses of these songs and tunes. I think that such an awareness is crucial both to the study of folk music and their possible use for purposes of communication.
>
> In a culture that has evolved varied music styles to meet the needs of different situations, a modern communicator has to understand their specific usage in order to handle them effectively. (Baskaran 1989, 92)

Over the 1920s, publications of Christian folk music declined as songs with more sophisticated wording set to classical music appeared and gained popularity. This shift was enabled by a rise in Christian education, which supported the classical style and the use of the more sophisticated songs being used in church and other Christian services.

But the development of Indian Christian music should not stop there. Chris Hale, for example, urges the development and use of Christian bhajans, songs that are part of the devotional life of Hindus. He maintains, "Clearly, with Hindus, the bhajan is the most helpful musical form, especially in North India, where Christian and Western influence is most strongly opposed. These songs have Indian lyrics, Indian tunes and an Indian worship format. Historically, they are taken from Hindu devotional practice, but there is nothing unscriptural about these forms" (Hale 2001, 17).

Over the past decade more missionaries and missiologists have been engaging in an artistic discipline with a new name: ethnodoxology (https://www.worldofworship.org; see also Krabill et al. 2013). Dave Hall, international worship arts leader for the mission agency Pioneers, defines ethnodoxology as "the study of how and why people of diverse cultures glorify the true and living God" (Hall 2000, 51). He argues that every church planting team needs a worship arts leader because ultimately God seeks worshipers rather than people who know the theology of worship (50). Essentially ethnodoxology focuses on enabling people to worship God in ways that make sense to them in their own cultural idiom. In today's world, however, the reality is that as globalization continues to grow in influence, worship in urban settings has the potential to move one of two directions: either it will become a fusion or hybrid of local and global worship practices, or the local will be subsumed by the global. Church planters, developers, and pastors—not to mention worship arts leaders—need to be consciously aware that they have the role of determining the direction their churches will go.

Australian Indigenous Visual Art

Irving Tucker worked among the Warlpiri in central Australia for thirty years before teaming up with Frank Jordan, himself a missionary in Papua, to illustrate an artistic expression of the gospel in Warlpiri idiom as portrayed in figures 8.2, 8.3, and 8.4 (Jordan and Tucker 2002).

The Warlpiri use art for religious purposes rather than purely aesthetic or functional ones. Through their symbolic imagery drawn on sand, the body, rocks, and wood, they draw to "release the creative powers of the primal spirit beings in the present and to communicate this with other people" (303). Their art is iconographic: icons represent beings, movement, locations, and objects. Figure 8.2 shows a sampling of the icons they use; they are from the perspective of looking down from above rather than looking from the side. Often they tell stories through the icons, arranged so that the viewer can trace the story through the images.

The Warlpiri do not have idiomatic symbols representing Christian persons or ideas, so they—together with Frank Tucker—developed a set of icons to use in communicating Christian stories. These icons are depicted in figure

Figure 8.2: Range of Warlpiri symbols

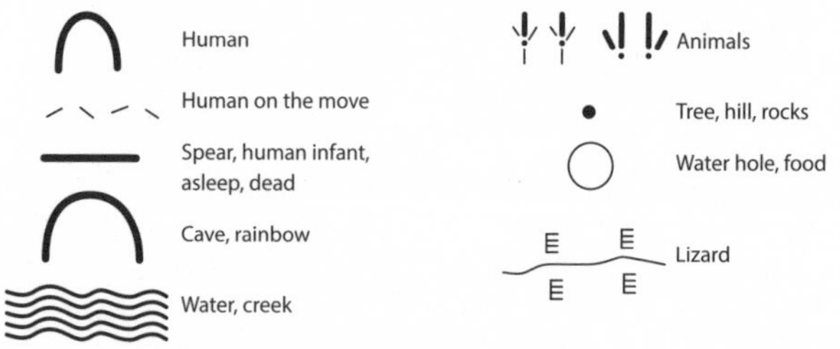

Source: Jordan and Tucker 2002, 304. Used with permission.

Figure 8.3: Warlpiri symbols for Christian communication

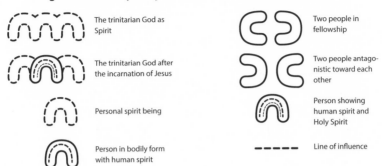

The trinitarian God as Spirit

Two people in fellowship

The trinitarian God after the incarnation of Jesus

Two people antagonistic toward each other

Personal spirit being

Person showing human spirit and Holy Spirit

Person in bodily form with human spirit

Line of influence

Source: Jordan and Tucker 2002, 304. Used with permission.

8.3; they have been used in worship and training since 1975. As you can see, there are symbols representing the Triune God (as Spirit and after the incarnation), spirit beings, people, Christian and non-Christian, people in fellowship, people out of fellowship, and so on.

The images are used in figure 8.4 to present the life of Christ in Warlpiri idiom, with English explanations for those of us who do not yet understand that idiom. The authors note that while the traditional medium is used, the developers did not seek to repurpose traditional religious symbols for use by Christians, thereby hoping to avoid syncretistic elements creeping into the message.

Similar examples can be found in many settings. Since 2000, I have been collecting images of Christ from around the world; the collection stands at more than 5,000 images as of 2018. From Bali to Tibet, Christians are representing the gospel story in ways that touch their hearts and minds. Evangelicals, however, have been more reticent than Catholics or conciliar Protestants to encourage the development of indigenous art. Some are concerned with the creation of images representing God or Christ; others are not willing to look beyond the historical Jesus.

Conclusion

Wayan Mastra, Indonesian artist, asks the following question: "But if we look at the village temple, it is beautiful from the artistic point of view; it fits the tropical climate, it is cheap because local materials can be used; and the village artists have a chance to glorify their deities through their artistic talents. Why does not the church give a chance to the newly converted people

Figure 8.4: Warlpiri life of Christ

1. God the Trinity is sovereign over history and determines to send the Son into the world.
2. Jesus is born of Mary through the ministry of the Spirit.
3. Jesus is baptized by John.
4. The temptation in the wilderness by the devil.
5. Jesus calling the disciples, his teaching ministry.
6. The raising of Lazarus from the dead.
7. The crucifixion.
8. Burial of Jesus in the tomb.
9. Jesus's descent into the world of the dead.
10. The resurrection of Jesus.
11. Jesus reveals himself to his disciples.
12 The ascension into heaven.

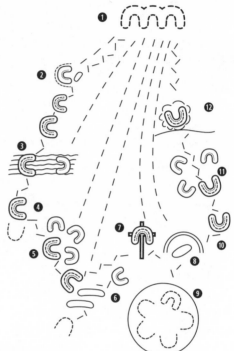

Source: Jordan and Tucker 2002, 306. Used with permission.

to glorify their God through their artistic talents which have been inherited from their ancestors?" (Mastra 1978, 15).

In this chapter we have explored the need for contextualizing the arts. It's an area evangelicals have generally been slow to develop, though that is changing. As you read the case study, consider Hale's appeal and what you might do to contextualize arts in your setting.

CASE STUDY

WORSHIPING CHRIST WITH THE BEST OF EAST AND WEST

As you read the following appeal by Chris Hale, consider your response. With what do you agree? With what do you disagree? What would it take to accomplish? Hale published this appeal in 2001; do a search on YouTube to check out the panorama of Indian Christian music available today.

In 1990, I went to India after graduating from Berklee College of Music with a degree in classical composition, jazz, and rock guitar, with a vision to reach modern Indian youth with a rock band that sang songs in Hindi and English. Within the first year there I discovered Christian bhajans, devotional songs addressed to Christ and having a lyrical and melodic style that was truly Indian and drew me into worship. Our rock band, Olio, which was performing in university campus rock music festivals, began singing some of these bhajans, using the instruments in the band as well as Indian percussion. We found that the young people loved these songs the most, although at that time it was not common to mix Western styles such as rock music with the traditional Indian styles.

Now, ten years later, Hindi songs with Western instrumentation, both devotional and secular, are very popular. Andrew Lloyd Webber is presently working on a new Broadway musical with India's top popular song composer, A. R. Rahman [first performed in 2002 as *Bombay Dreams*]. Rahman popularized the use of Western instrumentation and rhythm in Indian songs.

Indians, both young and old, love their own melodies and poetry. The time is ripe for Christian youth to begin composing worship songs to Christ that blend Indian melody and lyrical style with Western instrumentation. There are many composers of Indian music in the church in India, but many of them feel that the younger generation is not interested in their music. What is needed is a freshness that will attract the young people to the Indian melodies, and that freshness is Western instrumentation and rhythm. There needs to be an exchange of musical ideas between the older and younger generations in the Christian church.

Adapted from Hale (2001).

9
THE RITUAL DIMENSION

Humans are creatures of ritual. Everyday rituals such as greetings, good-byes, and coffee or lunch with a friend act as social glue in our relationships. Completion rituals such as graduations indicate changes in social status. As a whole, rituals are necessary to build and maintain social order (Hiebert, Shaw, and Tienou 1999, 284). It is not surprising that we find rituals in every society since "such rites are central to the lives of people and communities around the world" (283). Scripture clearly portrays humans as deeply ritualistic people. We will continue to participate in rituals in heaven, including corporate worship of our Creator (Rev. 15:4).

As I grew up, I was socialized into the religious ritual of the churches my family attended. However, based on my experiences as a young boy, lodged in my memory is the idea that ritual is boring, meaningless, and empty. Clearly my personal experience with religious ritual was not positive! Over the past several decades of teaching, I have seen that my story is not unique; I know many evangelicals of my age who have had similar experiences. When we came to Christ, we wanted worship that did not repeat our childhood torture sessions.

However, my children have a completely different vantage point. Our family attended churches that did not have a formal liturgy. My children missed out, such that as they grew up they began to seek out churches that practice the very rituals I wanted to avoid. They explained to me that they want to participate in something that has centuries-long roots rather than something that was developed over the past few decades. Within contemporary Western societies, such a change in attitude from one generation to another is not uncommon: the children reject the rituals and practices of the parents, then they create practices that their children in turn also reject. This is less true of children who grow up in majority-world settings, where ritual is often more living than (apparently) dead. How then should we contextualize ritual today? To help us, in this chapter I walk through what ritual is and then explore ways it needs contextual consideration so that it may continue to play a critical role in Christian faith.

What Is Ritual?

Ritual has been widely recognized as a "'window' on the cultural dynamics by which people make and remake their world" (Bell 1992, 3); it is not surprising that there is a deep connection between myth and ritual, with rituals enacting myth and myth in turn reinforcing ritual (see Doty 1986, 11).

Ritual is a symbolic expression of belief through which the participants gain satisfaction (see Malefijt 1968, 189–95) in part because it identifies their place in the world (see Segal 1983); religious ritual establishes their place in the entire cosmos (Hiebert, Shaw, and Tienou 1999, 290).

Ritual has been variously defined as "a social encounter in which each participant has a well-rehearsed role to act out" (Goodman 1988a, 31) and "a patterned activity with symbolic meaning" (H. Anderson 2010, 42). This patterned acting is a reminder that ritual is theater or drama, with actors, settings, and audiences. As such, rituals require performance on the part of participants (Hiebert, Shaw, and Tienou 1999, 292–95). Further, they always have purpose; they are not abstracted actions devoid of intent (Euba 2014, 98). In fact, they "drive meaning into the bone" and become a significant venue for discipleship (W. Moon 2010, 131; see also Courson 1998; and W. Moon 2017).

At the most general level, and following Herbert Anderson (2010), by "ritual" I refer to *scripted actions that have symbolic value*. By "scripted" I mean that the actions have been learned and follow a set, though not always exact, pattern. Some are exacting in their patterns (formal, high-order rites), reminding participants that the world is ordered. Others require participants to let go of normal decorum and release themselves to chaos (antiformal, low-order rites). The latter remind participants and onlookers why the world needs to be ordered: a permanent state of chaos would be devastating to any society (Hiebert, Shaw, and Tienou 1999, 284–87).

Ritual actions are embedded in every culture at all levels and for all walks of life. As pastor and research professor Herbert Anderson (2010, 41) explains, "We employ rituals for establishing courtship, diminishing powerlessness, organizing the hunt, caring for offspring, sending children off, avoiding

life-threatening conflicts, and closing the story of a life." As Hiebert and
colleagues note, rituals reinforce social structures (mutual greetings serve to
reinforce that we have a relationship), cultural structures (weddings reinforce
in us the ideals of marriage), our personal identity (initiation ceremonies
reinforce who we are and to which group we belong), and cosmic structures
(teaching reinforces religious truths; divination rituals reinforce the reality of
the spirit realm) (Hiebert, Shaw, and Tienou 1999, 287–90).

Religious rituals involve scripted symbolic actions that demonstrate and
reinforce religious belief and enable adherence, change, or transformation of
the participants. We use ritual to connect to God, to Christ, to the Spirit—and
to one another. Rituals serve to cement us into a community even as they
transform us as individuals. For followers of Christ, rituals include the gamut
of our faith activity: baptism, Communion, prayer, worship (whether private
or corporate), marriage, funerals, small-group meetings, church events from
meals to Sunday school. In multiple ways each is amenable to contextualization. We can better understand the role that rituals play in religion and in
contextualization by first exploring three categories of ritual and then discussing several important functions of ritual.

Ritual Categories

Scholars identify three major categories of rituals: intensification, transition, and crisis.

Intensification Rituals

The first category of ritual includes those that strengthen or intensify
participants' identity or bonding in some fashion. Over the course of time,
social order and relationships inevitably begin to fray; intensification rituals
reestablish and reinforce both (Hiebert, Shaw, and Tienou 1999, 302). We
use these types of rituals to maintain order and ensure that our world or our
lives do not degenerate into disorder or chaos. At the same time, rituals also
provide us with a renewed sense of order and purpose. When we celebrate a
birthday, we not only commemorate the day the celebrant was born; we also
strengthen their ties to the celebrating community by firming up their identity
as a person who is connected with others.

Other types of intensification rituals for individuals include pilgrimages,
healing, success (e.g., love, children, business, money), personal devotional
times, anniversaries, and the like. Groups also use intensification rituals to
maintain group identity. Examples of group intensification rituals include festivals (Carnival in Brazil; Mardi Gras in New Orleans), fiestas, fairs, national

holidays, celebrations (e.g., parades for victors), regular religious services, commemorative religious services (Easter, Christmas Eve), memorials, prayer meetings, Communion, Bible studies, and the like. In each intensification ritual, people bond to one another and to their common beliefs.

Transition Rituals

In the second category of rituals are those enabling people to change from one state to another—marking and/or activating a transformation in their beliefs, status, or being. Through rituals of transition the community sanctions the process of transformation as well as the new status for those who have made the transition successfully. An American sixteen-year-old who passes the appropriate test and is granted a driver's license has the legal right to drive a car without supervision by a licensed adult. The test is intended to confirm readiness to drive, and American society recognizes the granting of the physical driver's license as the confirmation that the person has passed the test.

Though physical paraphernalia such as a marriage license, a diploma, or a certificate often provide proof of the transition, transition rituals (e.g., religious conversion) do not always require such physical proof. Transition rituals in which an individual is transformed (with the community as witness) include life-cycle rites such as fertility, naming, adoption, initiation, debutante, *quinceañera* (celebration of a girl's fifteenth birthday), and retirement. Transition rituals also include such things that effect or mark religious conversion or transformation: pilgrimage, baptism, citizenship, graduation, ordination, and inauguration. Transition rites in which a group is transformed include such things as group conversions, induction, revivals, retreats or conferences, village purifications, graduations, and age-grade rites.

Transition rituals have three distinct and identifiable stages: (1) separation, (2) transformation, and (3) reincorporation into society with a new status. The first stage is separation from ordinary life. In preparation for the transformation that is about to take place, the person or group must be separated from others. Separation can occur through public identification or selection of candidates, who are then sequestered physically, socially, symbolically, or some combination thereof.

Physical separation takes place when participants are separated from their families and societies. They may be removed and placed in the wilderness or a symbolic location such as a boarding school. Social separation may take place by the participant being marked and then shunned or ignored by others (e.g., the Amish practice of rumspringa). Symbolic separation may be displayed through special clothing (a bride's dress, sackcloth, graduation gowns), body markers (shaven heads, piercings, circumcision), and actions (fasting or other food restrictions, symbolic kidnappings, ritual leave-takings). Depending on the nature of the transformation, the separation may range from minutes (baptism) to years (college).

The second stage is when the transformation of the participant happens. In this stage it is anticipated that the participant will focus on the central responsibilities of the ritual (e.g., students study for a test, warriors-in-training fight each other, and apprentices practice the skills of their craft). In many cases, until this stage is completed, the person remains either physically or symbolically separated from normal social life. They lose their normal social status and may even be considered a nonperson—the term "liminality" is used to refer to this state, and the participant is a liminal being (V. Turner 1977). Thus this person is in limbo, a nonperson removed from the normal course of life who is in the process of transformation to the new form or stage of life.

At a Christian men's retreat I attended, our connections to normal life were removed: watches, phones, anything electronic except for medical devices. At the outset, we chose symbolic names by which we were addressed. We slept together in dorm-style rooms in which the windows were taped over with black plastic sheets so that we had little sense of time. We ate what the leaders prepared for us when they told us it was time to eat. We maintained a discipline of silence except when engaged in group exercises. Our liminality was both physical and symbolic, and I experienced it deeply.

In some transition rituals, participants may be allowed to violate normal social taboos: swearing, drinking, engaging in sexual activities, wearing provocative or no clothing, and so on (swearing was the only one of these allowed at the men's retreat!).

Participants' old status no longer applies, but they have not yet attained their new status. Family members of the no-status participant may perform rituals, don symbolic apparel, or behave in ways indicating to everyone that the participant has no status with them. The participant's transformation may be physical (e.g., trained as a warrior) or symbolic (e.g., being given a new name). People who undergo their transformation as part of a group develop communitas, "the deep sense of oneness with other humans that runs deeper than surface social differences of gender, class, ethnicity, and office" (Hiebert, Shaw, and Tienou 1999, 298).

Having lost all status, they become a community forged by their shared experience in which normal social roles no longer function. They meet others at the most basic level and develop ties that are sometimes stronger than family ties. I experienced this communitas at the men's retreat. We had no titles, no status markers, not even our normal names, only basic food, no way to connect with the outside world, little sense of time, and we were completely at the scheduling mercy of the retreat organizers. We bonded together as much as twenty-first-century Western men who have never met before can bond over a single weekend.

The final stage of a transition ritual is the reincorporation or reintegration back into normal life, albeit at a new level of status and responsibility. After her *quinceañera*, the young Latina acts as an adult; likewise for the Amish person after baptism, at the conclusion of rumspringa. There are often symbolic homecoming celebrations, with special meals and presents indicating to the transformed person and to the larger society that this person has returned. From the relatively mundane (e.g., a driver's license) to the more esoteric (new names, titles, tattoos, specialized jewelry or weapons, symbolic clothing, etc.), successful participants are given means by which they may identify their success to the rest of their society.

As Hiebert explains, "The power of these pedagogical rituals lies in the anticipation and openness to the new that they create in the novices and in the public. At their best, they can change a person or society by providing, in one transforming experience, a new and vital vision and faith" (Hiebert, Shaw, and Tienou 1999, 307). The organizers of the men's retreat warned us at the end to be careful how we entered back into normal life. Many men were transformed by the weekend, and some were so energized that they were ready to proselytize their wives and/or families into their transformed social patterns of honesty and transparency.

As Hiebert notes of people who have been transformed, however, "Their return is fraught with danger, and may be hedged around by further rites of reincorporation. They have experienced power in their transformation and are often seen as hot, dangerous, and needing insulation and time to cool down, or they can be harmful to others" (307). In our case, four days after the retreat the further rite of incorporation was a dinner with families and significant others in a church building. After the dinner, the participants were invited to speak to the guests and share what they had learned on the retreat. Additionally, the organizers contextualized the testimonies of the men by discussing the changes they themselves underwent the first time they were participants. This ameliorated some of the "hotter" elements of the transformation.

Crisis Rituals

The final type of ritual is the crisis ritual, which we use to protect from or deal with unexpected situations. Crisis rituals are typically performed as needed when the participants seek to prevent a looming crisis or after the crisis has already arrived; they are performed to restore order when chaos reigns (Hiebert, Shaw, and Tienou 1999, 316).

Individuals face illness, lack of money or job, loss of love, accidents, spirit possession, or other tragedies. The mirror image of rituals to cure or restore are those performed to create or ensure success in such things as love, business, farming (crops or animal fertility), or exams. Crises can come for a variety of reasons, and many people in the majority world ascribe them to the work of spirits and people of power. As we will see in the Jalari case later, the spirits may be angry because of a family dispute. Alternatively, my neighbor may be jealous of my good luck and visit a shaman or sorcerer to put a curse on me so that my neighbor's luck may increase. Perhaps someone with the evil eye has used their power (whether intentionally or unintentionally) on a victim, or a witch has cast a spell. In cases where the source of the crisis is a spirit (whether an ancestor, a nature spirit, a ghost, an evil spirit, or a deity) or a person with spiritual power, only a ritual calling on the assistance of a more powerful spirit or casting a more powerful spell will be effective.

Groups also face crises such as drought, epidemics, wars, famines, weather disasters, and social upheavals ranging from civic unrest to civil war. The mirror image of group rituals to cure or restore are rituals to ensure group success in sports or other competitions, or to bring rain, war, and social transitions. Every year in Swaziland, a ritual dance to bring rain is held; cyclical rituals like this, intended to prevent a crisis or to bring success, may be classified as either intensification rituals, crisis rituals, or a mix of both. In this case, if the rains came the preceding year, it serves to intensify social order. If the rains did not come or were deficient, the rite becomes more of a crisis ritual.

Christians also use crisis rituals. We confess our sins; pray for protection or rescue; ask respected Christian leaders for counsel and/or prayer; ask our church body to pray for us; go to deliverance specialists; perform a pilgrimage; offer a generous gift to our church or a Christian organization; attend a weekend retreat or workshop; or pledge to become a minister, a missionary, or a monk or nun. When faced with crises, Christians have used all of these and more over the two millennia the church has existed.

Functions of Ritual

Scholars of ritual have identified at least five functions that ritual serves for individuals, groups, and societies. The following synopses offer starting points for understanding the functions of ritual rather than presenting comprehensive examinations of them.

The first significant function of ritual is to establish and maintain individual and group identity (personal, psychological, social, cultural, and religious). As Hiebert writes, "In rituals a group experiences itself most intensely as a unified community, and members recognize themselves as belonging to one another" (Hiebert, Shaw, and Tienou 1999, 301). One of the saddest stories of the global church is the Japanese persecution of Catholicism in Japan, which essentially wiped out the nascent Catholic Church there. After the missionaries were expelled or martyred, as portrayed in Shūsaku Endō's novel *Silence* (1966), the remaining converts were sought out and, when identified, brutally tortured, forced to recant their faith, or martyred in appalling ways. Roger Vanzila Munsi, professor at Nanzan University (founded by the Catholic order Divine Word Missionaries), writes about the Kakure Kirishitan (Hidden Christian) communities (2012). These small groups of secret adherents trace their faith back to the Portuguese missionaries and are still found in Nagasaki Prefecture. The reason I mention them is the role that ritual played in maintaining their identity, as Munsi (2012, 355) reports,

> Left without priests, underground *Kirishitan* communities developed their own rituals, liturgies, symbols, and a few texts, adapting them from remnants of 16th century Portuguese Catholicism and often camouflaging them in forms borrowed from the surrounding Buddhism and Shinto. In short, during the persecution periods (1587–1873), the underground *Kirishitan* communities strove to keep their Christian faith by following the tenets of a variety of religions, especially Catholicism, Buddhism and Shinto, and their religious practices were also imbued with local customs and values.

Rituals enabled this persecuted group to maintain its identity and pass that identity on to future generations through almost three centuries of persecution.

Second, and linked to the first function, rituals prevent individuals and societies from falling apart by restoring order or generating a new order. This runs the gamut from the personal to the cosmic level. Annually the Huichol shaman of western Mexico goes on a pilgrimage with some of his people; the purpose is to restore balance, hunt the magical deer (in this case, harvesting peyote), and ensure that the universe remains in balance. In the annual *incwala* ritual, the Swazi king and other political leaders offer thanks to God for the preceding year's crops and dance so that rain will come for this year's crops. Traditionally during the Qingming Festival, the Chinese feast on special meals and commemorate their ancestors in a variety of ways. For example, they pay their respects to their ancestors by bowing from the oldest male down through the lineage. They also provide wealth that the departed need in the spirit world by burning offerings of money, clothes, homes, and cars made of paper printed for the occasion. Together these and other rituals maintain order in the family and the family's world, building an important foundation to ensure good luck in the coming year.

Third, rituals enable individuals and societies to transition from one way of living to another. In the case of social transition, for example, rituals pave the way for people to keep some level of continuity with the old ways while simultaneously stepping into the new ones. In this function, the rituals often act as a form of social catharsis, and participants express powerful emotions (anger, fear, sadness, and the like). They also encourage acts of reconciliation (Hiebert, Shaw, and Tienou 1999, 301) through which significant healing takes place (H. Anderson 2010). As noted in chapter 3, church leader Desmond Tutu led the Truth and Reconciliation Commission meetings, offering South Africans of all races and tribes opportunities to speak truth in public. Victims and victimizers came forward to air their stories in public; some were seeking forgiveness, others were seeking justice. The commission meetings played an important role in helping South Africa transition from an apartheid regime to a democratic government. The Velvet Revolution in the Czech Republic (then Czechoslovakia), a series of relatively peaceful protests by hundreds of thousands of citizens, led to mass resignation of Communist Party officials and elections of new leaders in a span of just six weeks. The Christian men's retreat I previously described as a transition ritual allowed me (and the other participants) to open the doors to deeply seated emotions such as fear, anger, and sadness; yet rituals during the latter half of the retreat also brought healing and empowered us to return to families as transformed individuals. Another example is an African Christian rite of passage that Tanari Trust (Kenya) developed (http://tanaritrust.org/our -programs/rites-of-passage-experiences) for Christian children to make the transition from adolescence to adulthood. With such rituals disappearing in urban Africa, Muhia Karinjahi created the process of enabling church leaders to develop their own ritual and implement it among their youth. Without it, Christian children were increasingly unable to discern the dividing line between adolescence and adulthood, generating confusion and tension in their homes.

Fourth, rituals serve as symbolic repositories that maintain important cultural values and traditions for individuals and groups. In serving that function, they also indoctrinate people into their personal, group, or cultural story. All rituals employ symbols and symbolic acts through which cultural knowledge is stored and reinforced. Thus rituals serve as living, dramatized cultural libraries. The rings that bride and groom put on each other's fingers at a Christian wedding symbolize that their love is eternal. Symbolic scarification of aboriginal Australians, tribal Brazilians, and traditional Congolese displays, for all who are able to read the scars, important identity information about the one so scarred. According to anthropologist Terence Turner (2012, 486), the bodies serve as "social skin" in which "the surface of the body . . . becomes the symbolic stage upon which the drama of socialization is enacted, and bodily adornment . . . becomes the language through which it is expressed." The trend for younger Americans to get symbolic tattoos shows that this is not simply a rural or traditional phenomenon.

Fifth and finally, rituals enable people to experience the transcendent, to directly connect to the spirits, ancestors, and gods in which they believe (expanded in chap. 10). As mentioned earlier, in the Barong dance the Balinese participants anticipate and experience trance, in which they are taken over by spirits. Likewise, when the Kenyan traditional diviner consults the spirits on behalf of a person or a community, the spirits give guidance. When voodoo practitioners in the Caribbean dance, they become possessed by the *loa* (spirits), who ride them like horses. When a Yanomami shaman (of the Amazonian rain forest) takes *ebene* and goes into a mystical trance, he enters the realm of the spirits. Globally, Christians also encounter transcendence through rituals in which they pray for healing, prophesy, speak in tongues, interpret, offer words of wisdom and knowledge, expel demons, and otherwise experience and demonstrate God's power.

Ritual and Social Scripts

We all learn cultural and social scripts as we grow up. Greetings, running errands, and dealing with a problem are all areas in which we have learned a variety of scripts to handle the necessary interactions. When we cross into another culture, we have new experiences for which we never learned social scripts (e.g., our car gets stuck on a muddy road on a rainy day), or we find that the scripts we learned while growing up are inadequate (or even wrong) in our new settings. Rather than shaking hands, people bow. People drive on the other side of the road, and how they drive is radically different from how we drive.

Rituals follow these types of social scripts, and one tool that we can use to study ritual is script analysis, which requires that we identify the scripts, learn how they operate, and then choose whether to use, reject, or modify them. When people come to faith in Christ, for example, they inevitably learn new patterns of social behavior that identify them as those who follow Christ. They no longer visit diviners to deal with illness, they forgive rather than seek revenge, they participate in fellowship with other Christ-followers, and so on.

SIDEBAR 9.1
QUESTIONS ABOUT RITUAL

Below are some questions to consider as you explore ritual in your setting. Asking and exploring the answers to these questions will enable you to better understand local rituals, yet also help you think more clearly about church and ways Christians might better understand religious rituals in their contexts and, when appropriate, use them or the cultural insights they offer to better contextualize the gospel.

As I noted in parallel sidebars in previous chapters, answers to these questions could be used to compromise the gospel or the biblical definition of church. That is not my intention. Rather, the questions equip you to find biblically appropriate and culturally sound ways for Christians to understand local views and practices of ritual. They help you avoid the danger of simply generating and using only rituals that make sense from your own cultural setting. As you ask these questions, also be asking yourself how the answers impact what types of uses of ritual would make sense to local people without compromising their relationship with Christ.

1. Rituals of intensification
   a. What rituals of intensification do you observe?
   b. How are these rituals used as social glue for individuals and groups?
   c. Which of these rituals may be amenable to contextualization for use in local churches?
2. Rituals of transition
   a. What rituals of transition do you observe?
   b. How are these rituals used by individuals and groups to change from one state to another?
   c. Which of these rituals, or components of them, may be amenable to contextualization for use in local churches?
3. Rituals of crisis
   a. What rituals of crisis do you observe?
   b. How are these rituals used by individuals and groups to deal with threats?
   c. Which of these rituals, or components of them, may be amenable to contextualization for use in local churches?

Questions to Ask about Ritual

In sidebar 9.1, I conclude this overview of ritual, as I have in prior chapters, by posing several questions to be considered in any new setting as you explore rituals where you serve.

Contextualizing Ritual

Rituals of normal social engagement (how to greet someone, how to thank someone, and so on) are typically the domain of intercultural communication rather than contextualization, though the sojourner must learn these as part of the cultural adjustment process. Contextualization of ritual focuses most closely on rituals connected to religious observance (from initiation to burial, from conversion to ordination, and from confession to purification). Contextualizing the ritual dimension is founded on a general understanding of ritual that is applied in the local setting through a deep understanding of the function, actions, symbolism, myth(s), and effects of a ritual. Once these are understood, examining the ritual in light of biblical teachings and framing gives us the orientation local Christians need for deciding whether they should use the ritual as is (e.g., secular, patriotic celebrations), adapt it for Christian use (e.g., rites of passage), or replace it altogether (e.g., traditional exorcisms). With that overall orientation in mind, I explore two rituals for contextual purposes: the first comes from Nepal, the second from South India.

Modified Participation in Bhai Tika in Nepal (Perry 1990)

Cindy Perry, a medical doctor working in Nepal, discusses how Christians in Nepal need to face contextual questions about important festivals that come from their Hindu heritage. In the earliest years of the Nepali church, in no small measure due to missionary influence, the young church categorically rejected everything related to Hinduism. More recently, however, Nepali Christians have begun to rethink their "reject it all" approach. Some have started to reengage in their traditional rituals, albeit in modified forms, and especially in rituals through which family bonding is strengthened. Having rejected them for years, church members lived with the effects of damaged or broken bonds with their families. Perry identifies the primary question driving this change in thinking: "How can we retain our integrity as Nepalis and affirm the positive values in our culture, especially those consistent with biblical values?" Perhaps more importantly, "How can we see and portray Christ incarnate in the Nepali culture rather than as a foreign Christ?" (1990, 178).

Perry documents how one Christian tried to provide an alternative event for the Bhai Tika day of the Tihar Festival, which takes place in late fall. The festival stems from a Puranic myth in which the sister (Yamuna) of the god of death (Yama), who has been separated from him for some time, sends messengers to her brother, requesting a visit. She sends a crow, a dog, and a cow before finally coming herself. During her visit, she worships Yama with a puja that includes applying a tika, circling him while sprinkling oil, and placing a garland of everlasting flowers on him. This she follows by making him a special meal. Before she leaves, she gives him a special gift. In turn, he gives her a special gift. At the end of the visit, Yama declares that any man who participates in this ritual of mutual respect will not die on that day. The Tihar Festival celebrates this event over a five-day span. Over the first three days, participants successively worship the animals Yamuna sent (crow, dog, cow). On the fourth day, participants engage in three acts of devotion (to oxen, to cow dung, and for self-purification), representing the extent to which Yamuna wooed Yuma. And on the fifth and final day brothers and sisters worship each other (http://www.weallnepali.com/nepali-festivals/tihar).

To participate in the Bhai Tika ritual, married women return to their birth home. Following the story line, in addition to applying the tika dot on each other's foreheads, siblings exchange blessings and gifts, cementing their mutual affection and respect. If a woman has no brother, a substitute will be chosen from among relatives or close friends and adopted to take that role.

Perry explains two key meanings found in the event (1990, 180–81). First, a sister offers spiritual protection to her brothers, possibly connected to the sacred status that women have in their birth home, which comes with the ability to confer blessings on their kin. Second, brothers offer honor and economic protection to their sisters by giving concrete financial or material support. In this process they effectively offer puja (devotion or worship) to each other. In the ritual, men demonstrate that they accept their role as benefactors and women their role as sources of blessing. It should be apparent that a Nepalese who comes to Christ and chooses to reject the ritual will cause a significant social rift in his birth family, especially if he is the only brother the sisters have (or vice versa).

Perry relates the case of Sahadev, a respected church leader who rejected the Tihar Festival and the Bhai Tika ritual after coming to Christ. Several years after his conversion, he began to reflect on how he might communicate God's love to his family by using culturally available channels. Further, given the damage he had already caused by avoiding the festival, and especially the Bhai Tika, he wondered whether he could find a way to repair the damage, especially given the biblical teaching on the connectedness of the family.

Sahadev decided to return to his home on the day of Bhai Tika, after the four days of Hindu pujas was concluded. He explained to his family that his Christian convictions allowed him only limited participation in Bhai Tika, which the family accepted. He brought gifts for his sisters and accepted gifts from them. However, he did not participate in the fifth-day puja (e.g., placing/receiving the tika). Instead, he prayed for his sisters in the name of Christ and later joined the family in the traditional meal. Though he limited his participation, his family was delighted that he participated at all. The shame his sisters had experienced when he refused any participation was removed, and he himself regained face with his village because he had come for the ritual.

But what might his participation mean for the Nepali church? There are several things to note. First, the Bhai Tika is a ritual of intensification, restoring and strengthening the bond between brothers and sisters. After rejecting it altogether for several years, Sahadev's decision to participate, albeit in an altered way, was accepted by the family. It may be that his refusal to participate for several years made it easier for his family to accept his modified approach. Second, it was a Nepali who initiated the participation without external influence. He recognized that he was missing ties to his sisters and wanted to reconnect with them, with the hopes of being a viable witness to them. Third, Sahadev made a thoughtful decision to avoid elements of the ritual that he believed contradicted his faith in Christ. Fourth, he did not just ignore the puja: he substituted prayer for his sisters in the name of Christ. Fifth, his family accepted his modified participation, and his relationship with his sisters was reestablished. Sixth, his village accepted his modified participation, perhaps opening a door to witness that had previously been closed. Seventh and finally, Perry does not indicate that Sahadev made his decision through discussion with other Nepali church members: it appears that he was on his own (neither does Perry indicate the response of his church). This illustrates only one of the ways Christians may choose to participate in pre-Christian traditional rituals.

An Example: Jalari Medium Divination

The second example is a Hindu cluster of rituals that the Jalari, a Telugu fishing-caste people who live on the south coast of India, use to effect healing of a pregnant woman who develops a fever. Anthropologist Charles Nuckolls (1991) provides an anthropological analysis of the functions, actions, and symbolism of the rituals. His depiction provides our jumping-off point for contextual considerations.

Background

Nuckolls (1991, 3–4) notes that Jalari diviners use ritual to match conditions such as physical, emotional, and social illness or brokenness to cultural "maps" of underlying causes. He details two categories of reasons behind spirit attacks: *sufficient* causes and *precipitating* causes. Both categories are based on Jalari scripts by which the Jalari understand the malady and treatment. Table 9.1 explains the differences between them with examples of each causal level.

Table 9.1
Jalari Scripts and Examples

Type of script and cause	Example
Primary scripts describe the reactions of spirits to human transgression. They explain the simple or *efficient* causes of the most common maladies in Jalari society, such as illness and poor fishing.	A pregnant woman has a fever because spirits have attacked her.
Secondary scripts describe disruptions in social relations; Jalari diviners use them to explain more complex *precipitating* causes.	Due to a family dispute, two of her brothers failed to contribute to the family "goddess money," so the family itself is unable to make its normal contribution. The spirit attack is the result.

Using this analytic framework, we can examine a hypothetical (yet common) case in which a pregnant woman develops a fever. Following the diagnostic procedure outlined below, the family discovers that her fever is the result of a spirit attack. But they also discover that the attack is not due to something she did. Instead, the diagnosis is that the spirits are upset and attack her, an innocent person, to send a message to the guilty parties of her family that they (the spirits) will not tolerate divisions in the community. In this case, two of her brothers are divided such that both refuse to provide the normal contributions to the "goddess money" (Nuckolls 1991, 17) that the patriarch collects for the extended family. As a result, the entire family is unable to make their normal contribution.

Diagnosing Illness

The diagnostic procedure follows these widely held social scripts: (1) family spirits respond to taboo violations within the family (seen as "mistakes") by punishing the family, and (2) nonfamily spirits respond to taboo violations of one family member to another (seen as "disputes") by punishing the offender's family. When a nonfamily spirit causes the illness, it indicates that the family of the ill person has a dispute with another family in the village, and that family's spirit is coming to their assistance.

In either case, the family calls the diviner (a male) to their house. He examines the victim by feeling her pulse. While feeling it, he essentially asks the household spirits whether they are the ones responsible for her fever, though the form of the question may not be a simple yes/no question (it may include several subcomponents). If the household spirits are the cause, the pulse quickens. If they are not, the pulse does not quicken. In that case, using the same format, spirits from outside the household will be queried. If the final result of this diagnostic script is inconclusive, the diviner may decide that the illness is a "doctor illness" and advise the patient to seek physical medical treatment or to do nothing at all. In our hypothetical case, it is the family spirits that are the cause of the illness.

Once the spirits admit responsibility, the diviner asks for money, which he wraps in a cloth and waves around as an indicator to the spirits of the intention of the family to deal with the problem through an appropriate offering. This signals to the spirits the family's intention to make the offering, which they will do only if the illness remits, typically within a prescribed time frame.

Once the sufficient cause is confirmed by the healing of the victim, but *before* the family presents the prescribed offerings, they need to determine the precipitating cause. Only after this is finalized will the family make its offering.

In the Jalari worldview, the spirits know the precipitating cause for the attack, which the healer seeks to determine through divination in which he asks them to identify the social breach that generated their anger. There are two primary means of divination to determine the precipitating cause: *cupa rayi* or *kaniki*. In both, the diviner asks a series of yes/no questions, the answers to which yield the precipitating cause.

In *cupa rayi* divination, the family gives the healer a "seeing stone" that they keep for such divination. With the stone suspended from his right hand, he asks questions of the spirits, who answer by swinging (= yes) or not swinging the stone (= no). This method is used for less severe precipitating causes (Nuckolls 1991, 8).

In *kaniki* divination, the healer and the family visit a *kaniki* practitioner (who is not a Jalari). This practitioner also asks a series of yes/no questions and discerns the answers by whether a grain of rice thrown into a container of water floats (= yes) or not (= no). This is done in public in the view of those with honest reputations, who validate the diagnosis. Because this method airs the family division in public, it is only used as a last resort (8).

In the hypothetical case, through *kaniki* divination, the healer determines that the precipitating cause was two brothers who had such a sharp disagreement that they did not bring their offerings to the patriarch, and as a result the "goddess money" is insufficient for the normal extended family offering.

Contextualization Analysis

The phenomena fit very naturally into the social system of the Jalari, following their worldview and social scripts and rituals; they make complete sense to the participants. The divination practices reinforce the Jalari understanding of the spirit realm: that spirits are real, that they are engaged with the living, and that they do not tolerate disputes and thus uphold Jalari social norms.

There are at least four contextualization considerations for this case. First, the traditional cultural explanation for sickness of the pregnant woman is that a spirit has attacked her. People who come to Christ often come with their worldview transformed but still loaded with traditional elements. The biblical world also reports spirit attacks on the innocent, and in those stories the Jalari will find justification for their beliefs in the spirit realm. Simply denying that this was a spirit will not erase their traditional beliefs.

Second, the means of dealing with spirit attack are spiritual and ritual in nature. We will need to find appropriate means to meet the felt needs of the community and thus show that we honestly care about their problems. Simply sending a fever-ridden woman to a doctor will begin a process of secularizing the Christians in the community (so that they will no longer see spiritual issues as cause agents for the illness and consider illnesses only biological or psychological). Additionally, this will not stop her (or her family) from going to a diviner on the side, out of sight of the missionary.

Third, for the Jalari, it seems inevitable that the precipitating cause for the disease will be a violation of cultural norms or values, what the society itself will identify as wrong behavior. This moral wrong may have been committed by the ill person, but more likely it will be perceived as a moral wrong done by other members of the community rather than the afflicted. A contextual approach to illness will take not only the ill person into account (the sufficient cause), but also the social relationships that surround the ill person (the precipitating cause). As I explained in chapter 7, this is where biblical prohibitions against what the Jalari consider to be sin can be addressed. The Bible and the Jalari both agree that disputes and fights among relatives are wrong, and yet they still happen. This appears to be a great contact point for communicating biblical ethics in contextual fashion.

Fourth, the Jalari church must take the lead role in determining what to do with these cultural rituals and how to help a Christian face this crisis. Given that the rituals involved require a medium who communicates with spirits, clearly they cannot be brought unmodified into the church. Should the rituals be rejected altogether, or modified in some way, as with the Bhai Tika ritual presented earlier? The local Jalari church will be in the best position to both ask and answer this question. The following considerations help us unpack this contextualization question.

Jalari who come to Christ as adults are already socialized to expect *both* sufficient and precipitating causes when calamity strikes. This orientation to calamity will likely not change, so the church will look to explain calamity in terms of both sufficient and precipitating causes. They will likely resonate with 1 Corinthians 11:27–32, in which Paul declares that people have become sick and even died because they flippantly or falsely participated in the Lord's Supper. They will also find relevance in Ephesians 4:20–31, which calls us to live lives worthy of Christ, including forgiving and reconciling with those who have hurt us. They will be challenged by Job, who fell ill not because of human sin but because God had his own purposes.

Traditionally the Jalari perceive that some illnesses stem from the spirits. The passages cited above may be important for them. In what ways do they need to recast their interpretation? After community study, they may conclude that the spirits are only rarely the cause of illness, and they will come to realize that they now have authority over spirits and can claim Christ's healing power. They may develop a modified ritual in which a church leader prays for God's wisdom on the cause of illness, anoints and prays for the victim, and leaves the results to God. In many majority-world churches, certain Christ-followers recognized as prophets and healers have replaced traditional diviners. Jalari believers, compared to those of us from the West, would find it easier to accept a church leader's conclusion that some type of dispute is the precipitating cause.

Conclusion

In this chapter we have explored contextual issues related to ritual. Like many who grew up in mainline churches, I learned to dislike and even distrust ritual. Even though I was discipled through a ritual of small-group Bible study, I did not see it as ritual (nor would I have wanted to see it that way!). My adult children, on the other hand, have sought to capture meaningful rituals for themselves. Many people from outside my context readily recognize the need for ritual to maintain and sustain a healthy faith. As with the arts, Western evangelicals have gaps in understanding and utilizing ritual. As you read the case study for this chapter, how would you have Rajasekaran respond? Participating in the ritual clearly contradicts his Christian faith. Should he simply refuse, or is there a way he can modify his participation such that he does not compromise his faith? In answering those questions, you are working through real-life issues of ritual that many in majority-world settings continue to face today.

CASE STUDY

FOOD OFFERED TO IDOLS
SIMON P. DAVID

Rajasekaran looked across the room at the large picture of the blue-faced god Krishna, heavily garlanded with marigolds and tinsel, and then at the printing-press workers gathered around the small shrine set up before the god. It was Friday, and Rajasekaran realized that he had arrived just at the completion of weekly prayers to Krishna, the patron god of the press. Like many businessmen in this city in South India, the proprietor provided money to purchase coconuts, bananas, and sugar to offer to the deity at the weekly puja. He believed that the prosperity of his shop was due to the blessing of the god for his faithful offerings.

As assistant editor of a Christian magazine, it was Rajasekaran's responsibility to work with the press workers in order to make certain that the publication was properly printed on schedule. Today there had been some urgent matters to take care of, so he had come earlier than usual. He had hurried into the room, and Mani, the press foreman, had seen him before he realized that the puja ceremonies were still going on.

Over the past months, Mani and the editor had developed a close friendship as they worked together. Rajasekaran hoped someday to win his friend to Christ, but right now Mani was pulling him by the hand toward the group receiving the food that had been offered to Krishna and having *kunkumam* (colored powder) placed as spots on their foreheads to signify that they had been purified by eating the leftovers of the god. Rajasekaran knew that for many Hindus, including Mani, eating the food offered to a god was a sign of goodwill, much like receiving a Christmas present. But he also knew that for orthodox Hindus, partaking of the food and the *kunkumam* was part of the worship of an idol. Rajasekaran did not want to harm his relationship with Mani, but he also did not want to compromise his Christian witness. He saw Mani hold out the platter of food, and he . . .

Reprinted with permission from Hiebert and Hiebert 1987, 38–39.

10

THE EXPERIENCE DIMENSION
THE SUPERNATURAL

Our Christian faith is not just an academic or social enterprise, although it includes those aspects. It is also a spiritual and mystical enterprise in which Christians experience God and the supernatural. We are loved by and serve a living God who—as Father, Son, and Holy Spirit—continues to interact with people today. In addition to experiencing such things as the beauty of our created world and the entire cosmos, people around the world encounter things that are beyond "nature": they are supernatural.

As the Bible so clearly portrays, our universe is not just populated by humanity, but also by spiritual creatures known as angels and demons. People experience the transcendent through dreams, visions, glimpses, supernatural encounters, and the like. Humans themselves are immortal beings; those who belong to Christ will be with one another and Christ eternally. We are created with the capacity to have glimpses into that reality—though, as Paul declared, "For now . . . only a reflection as in a mirror. . . . Now I know in part" (1 Cor. 13:12).

The secular worldview, which denies the supernatural, has been found inadequate on a global scale. Western Christians who were raised within a secularized worldview or buy into it (whether intentionally or unintentionally) have often lost the intellectual and spiritual resources to grasp what it means to personally encounter things beyond the natural world, whether angels, demons, or God himself. Even when they do encounter or study such things, they find secular ways to explain them rather than spiritual ways (see, e.g., Goodman 1988b). For example, a current popular topic among social scholars is the phenomenon of Pentecostalism and how Pentecostals frame their faith in light of supernatural experiences (e.g., Cox 1995; Haynes 2013). However, those writing for audiences of fellow social scientists (anthropologists, sociologists, psychologists, and the like) have tended to analyze the phenomena they study through psychosocial lenses, not dealing with claims for the veracity of supernatural phenomena.

For Christian contextualization, it helps to consider several questions beyond the phenomena themselves. For example:

1. Do we cultivate supernatural experiences or avoid them as best as we can?
2. Do we talk with others about our own supernatural experiences or simply remain quiet?
3. What do we say when someone comes to us with questions about supernatural experiences?
4. What is your theology of supernatural experience?

Incorporating this as a dimension in contextualization does not indicate that we somehow constrain how the Spirit is going to work or try to find new ways to force the Spirit to work. I anticipate that by specifically identifying this as an important dimension of Christian faith, we are in a better position to explore it, understand it, and participate as opportunity arises. It is a global phenomenon typically seen far more in majority-world settings than in secularized Western ones (see Jenkins 2006, 2011). Exploring the contextual issue is critical if we hope to understand what's taking place in addition to seeing how people of other societies and branches of Christian faith understand supernatural experience. Despite the reality that religious experience "is construed a thousand different ways to cover a vast and confusing variety of cases" (Plantinga 2000, 182), the contextual exercise of identifying supernatural experiences, being puzzled by some and simply rejoicing at others, enables us to do a better job of framing what we ourselves think and practice in contextualization of supernatural experiences.

However, it is not just what we're thinking: it's how also we might better understand the worldview and experiences of others and how that might even cause *us* to go back to the Scriptures with fresh eyes to potentially rethink our own theology.

This is especially significant if we come to acknowledge or recognize that others' worldview (and/or experience) may well conform more closely to the Scripture than ours does. Certainly that can be threatening to us! But it's a story I hear repeatedly from missionaries: they find themselves going back to Scripture because they have been challenged by the perspectives of those who are culturally and experientially different from them. With this in mind, we turn to supernatural experiences seen in societies globally.

Supernatural Experience in Societies

In what ways do people experience the supernatural? Frankly, there is no simple way to categorize them. From encounters with visible spirit beings to feeling a presence, from dreams and visions to shamanic voyages, from miracles to healings, people report that they encounter the supernatural in a bewildering multitude of ways. In this section I offer three very short introductions. I start with North America, then turn to the majority world, and conclude with a separate discussion on possession phenomena.

Supernatural Experience in North America

From my vantage point, the data on North Americans is surprisingly univocal. Surveys over the past several decades have repeatedly shown that North Americans in general (Abernethy 2002) and evangelicals in particular (Reimer 2003) commonly report regular experiences of supernatural phenomena. As pointed out by *Religion and Ethics News Weekly* anchor Bob Abernethy (2002), "Eighty-three percent say they have experienced God's presence or a spiritual force that felt very close, and 46 percent say they have felt this many times." For evangelicals this number rises to 98 percent (Reimer 2003, 63), many of whom typically describe their encounters as life changing and the very basis of their relationship with God (58). They report encountering God in special meetings (such as revivals or concerts), during worship services, during devotional times, when in nature, and especially in times of trial.

Sociology professor Sam Reimer's analysis is particularly fascinating: he states that "whatever else they are, religious experiences are socially mediated and culturally understood" (56). Since this is crucial for contextualization, Reimer provides an indispensable sociocultural lens through which we can examine supernatural experiences. Evangelicals have tended to rely more exclusively on a biblical/cultural lens, which certainly is the one we use as our norm in relation to every other lens we apply. However, like putting an additional lens on a microscope, the sociocultural approach adds important insights not always found in the biblical text, insights that we may then bring back to the Bible for better understanding.

Reimer offers five reasons why religious experiences are sociocultural (56–58). First, "Religious experience is social . . . because such experiences are interpreted on the basis of culturally available symbols and meanings." When people encounter the supernatural, they draw on permissions and sanctions of their social groups as they determine how to respond. Second, "religious experiences can be evoked by certain religious settings," such as celebrations, prayer meetings, worship services, and the like. Additionally, stimulants used in religious settings, such as music, incense, decor, and lighting, as well as psychotropic drugs (e.g., peyote for the Navajo or Huichol)—all act to initiate encounters. Third, these experiences are shared events. Even in private experiences, people report that the experience did not come from within them but from an external force or power. Thus, even private experiences are shared by the supernatural Other the adherents encounter. Fourth, their supernatural experiences have social consequences. People may gain or lose status. They may feel more deeply connected to their social groups or more dissociated. For North American evangelicals, Reimer focuses on the fifth sociocultural aspect of supernatural experiences: "the ways in which the evangelical subculture supplies the cultural 'tools' . . . needed to evoke and interpret religious experience, and how religious experience strengthens identity and commitment to evangelicalism" (58). The sociocultural "tools" Reimer identifies are contextual tools that have been developed within societies and subgroups. Understanding those tools and how they are used in supernatural experiences plays an important role in contextualization. Reimer (70–71) concludes:

> Evangelical religious experience establishes the "realness" of the individual's religious identity (or calls it into question) and endows it with meaning. Experience is personal and, in the modern world, uniquely legitimate. Experience is "spiritual," not "religious." It moves faith from the cold sterility of doctrine and duty to the heart. Largely absent . . . is any evidence that evangelicals became convinced of the reality of their faith through an intellectual defense of the faith in light of opposing religious claims. An intellectually defensible faith was not a key component in the salvation of any evangelical I interviewed. Evangelicals did not report changes in their theology or denomination, or any increase in their commitment for intellectual reasons. Nor did they emphasize apologetics in their accounts of witnessing to the "unsaved." In fact, it was hardly mentioned at all. Instead, evangelicals "know that they know" their faith is real because of experience.

Though it might be presumed that American evangelicals would have little to do with supernatural experience, actually such experiences are vital to their commitment to Christ. Theology does not have this impact, nor do other intellectual exercises such as apologetics. It seems clear that effective contextualization for a North American audience will provide opportunities and social space for supernatural experience.

Supernatural Experience in the Majority World

People in majority-world settings are often characterized as connected to the supernatural in ways their secular Western counterparts are not. Muslims, Buddhists, Hindus, and adherents of other global religions believe in and, on a reasonably regular basis, seek out supernatural encounters to help them in life. Practitioners look for answers to practical questions (How can I protect myself from the evil eye?), seek to gain success in their lives or careers (How can I get more business?), and search for ways to cope with challenges or calamities (Why is my daughter ill?). While their questions all have theological components, they are not looking for theological answers. Rather, they want pragmatic answers that will either ensure success or stem calamity. Figure 10.1 illustrates the types of daily needs that people use supernatural experiences to address.

Figure 10.1: Felt needs met through supernatural experiences

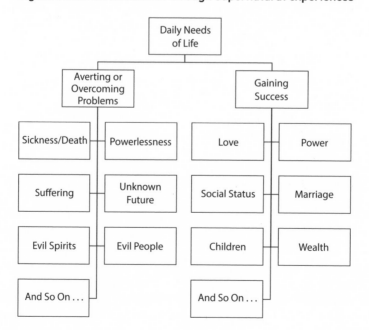

Frequently the type of supernatural activity used to meet these daily needs—consulting with diviners, traditional healers, shamans, psychics, and so on—is lumped together in the category of religions referred to variously as folk religions, popular religions, primal religions, and ethnic religions. Historically, "animism" was coined in 1873 by anthropologist Edward B. Tylor to refer to the belief in animating powers (spiritual beings) and the practices associated with placating them, taming them, or worshiping them (Van Rheenen 1991, 19). These powers, whether personal (spirits) or impersonal (mana, karma), are commonly part and parcel of local belief systems.

In addition to folk or popular religions, people who follow folk religious orientations are found within many of the religions of the world: Buddhism, Hinduism, Islam, Jainism, Sikhism. Even Christians are not immune. In numerous places, including the West, many Christians still hold to folk beliefs and engage in folk practices.

For those who seek supernatural experiences and supernatural powers, the powers serve as a type of "one-stop shop" integrating a spiritual security firm, a police force, and a judiciary. Practitioners use the supernatural to protect themselves from evil, to identify (and apprehend) perpetrators of wrong, and to judge and carry out the sentencing of the guilty, with the sentence ranging from illness or other misfortune to death. The powers also serve as the forces behind local healthcare systems, providing diagnoses, guiding practitioners to local plants or items to use for healing, and offering supernatural restoration to health when illness or calamity strikes (or justice/vengeance when healing is unsuccessful). With such a widespread system meeting so many areas of need, it should not surprise us that people who have come to Christ bring with them the beliefs and practices that characterized their lives prior to conversion.

Possession Phenomena (see Moreau 2000b)

When I was teaching science in a public high school in Swaziland, a student collapsed in class one day and writhed on the floor. I was able to take her to the administrative offices and have her lie down on a sofa. Other Swazis who saw this immediately knew the cause: a young man wanted to have a physical relationship with her, and she had rejected him. He went to a traditional diviner, who called up a spirit to afflict the girl with the malady so that she would change her mind. This was completely outside my experience and worldview: I could not even imagine such a possibility before journeying to Swaziland. When I asked Christian female students about it, one confirmed she herself had experienced this type of possession, and the only solution she found effective was entering into a relationship with Christ. She saw coming to Christ as the key to escaping the affliction of Swazi spirits.

The phenomena Christians refer to as "possession" is found almost universally across the planet. Symptoms may include a trancelike or catatonic state, trembling, sweating, groaning, screaming, speaking in a different voice or an incoherent language, taking on a new identity, inordinate strength, and inexplicable knowledge. Often, but not always, those who have been possessed have no memory of the events of the possession after they have returned to normal life.

Over the last century people have offered a variety of explanations for possessive phenomena in three general clusters. Some explanations focus on the physical: fever, hyperventilation, drug-induced condition, chemical or hormonal imbalance, and so on. Other explanations focus on the psychological, from attention-seeking behavior to projection or group hysteria. The third cluster of explanations focuses on the spirits themselves that, whether beneficent or evil, take control of people to offer messages, commune, reward, or punish the person or the person's community.

Where possession is recognized, non-Christians may see it as beneficial and/or detrimental. Societies have mostly learned to posture possession as a type of "necessary evil"—hard on the possessed but helpful to the family or community. Benefits believed to accrue from possession include, but are not limited to, receiving messages from the departed, healing, warding off attacks from other evil people (witches, sorcerers) or spirits, elevated status (for the possessed and/or family), and/or economic gain. Detriments include the physical and psychological damage done to the possessed—even up to death, if that is the judgment of the possessing spirit(s). Spirits, whether capriciously or maliciously, at times also deceive people for their own purposes, or they may be sent to punish or cajole (as with the Swazi woman).

As reported in the discussion of the Jalari diviner in chapter 9, separating sufficient causes (a spirit attacked a person) from precipitating causes (the person violated a taboo, angering the spirit) is not only possible but also essential in treating the possessed. In some cases a certain type of possession indicates that the possessed is to become a medium who cultivates the possessed state so that the spirits can communicate with the community through the medium.

Conclusion

The need for supernatural experiences plays out within religions on a daily basis. From dreams and visions to possession phenomena, people engage

SIDEBAR 10.1
QUESTIONS ABOUT SUPERNATURAL EXPERIENCE

Below are some questions to consider as you explore how people experience the supernatural in your setting. Asking and exploring the answers to these questions will enable you to better understand local explanations of the supernatural in people's lives—yet also help you think more clearly about church and ways Christians might better understand supernatural experiences in their contexts and, when appropriate, use them or the cultural insights they offer to better contextualize the gospel.

As I noted in parallel sidebars in previous chapters, answers to these questions could be used to compromise the gospel or the biblical definition of church. That is not my intention. Rather, the questions equip you to find biblically appropriate and culturally sound ways for Christians to understand local views of supernatural experiences, and thereby to better communicate a biblical framing of such. They help you avoid the danger of simply explaining supernatural experiences in ways that make sense from your own cultural setting. As you ask these questions, also be asking yourself how the answers impact which Christian teachings about, and experiences of, the supernatural make sense to local people without compromising their relationship with Christ.

1. Supernatural experiences
   a. What types of supernatural experiences do you observe or do people talk about?
   b. How do they view these supernatural experiences?
   c. What *personal* supernatural powers do people talk about (e.g., ancestors, nature spirits, deities, fairies, angels, demons)? What roles do these personal supernatural powers play in everyday life?
   d. What *impersonal* supernatural powers do people talk about (e.g., luck, magic, mana, karma, fate)? What roles do these impersonal supernatural powers play in everyday life?
2. Possession phenomena
   a. What types (if any) of possession phenomena do you observe or do people talk about?
   b. How do they treat the possessed? In what ways does possession mark people as separated from the rest of society?
   c. From the insider's vantage point, what positive purposes do possession phenomena serve?
   d. From the insider's vantage point, what negative results come from possession phenomena?

supernatural experiences in a variety of ways for a variety of purposes. Sidebar 10.1 offers starter questions for you to learn more about supernatural experiences in your setting.

Supernatural Experience in the Bible

There are so many examples of supernatural experience in the Bible that I do not have space to simply list them all. There are both positive and negative experiences. By "positive" I mean experiences that are God-given and deepen the faith of the person(s) having the experience. By "negative" I mean either encounters with negative supernatural powers (Satan, demons, or evil people) or encounters of people being judged (by God, angels, or prophets). In the latter case, the supernatural agent is good, but the person's experience of the encounter is not.

Positive Experiences

In the Old Testament, God's people experience dreams and visions (e.g., Gen. 28:10–16; Num. 12:6; Daniel; Joel 2:28; Zech. 3:1–5), though it does not always go well for the one recounting the dream to others (Gen. 37:5–11). We also find ecstatic prophecy and worship (1 Sam. 10:10–13; 19:20–24), sometimes accompanied by music (1 Sam. 10:5; 1 Chron. 25:1). While God typically speaks to his people through dreams or visions, with Moses he speaks "face to face" (Num. 12:6–8). God gives the Urim and Thummim, which the priests use to determine God's will for Israel (Exod. 28:30; Deut. 33:8). In one instance Saul has bound his army with an oath not to eat before he has avenged himself on his enemies (1 Sam. 14:24). Jonathan, Saul's son, who is unaware of the ban, eats honey in violation of the prohibition. When Saul inquires of God whether to continue an attack the following day, he receives no answer. Having decided that someone is to blame for this, Saul asks the priests to use the Urim and Thummim to determine the guilty party. Jonathan is chosen as the culprit, and he readily confesses that he has eaten in violation of Saul's prohibition. As Saul is ready to kill Jonathan, the army cries out in Jonathan's defense, and his life is spared (1 Sam. 14:45). Daniel has visions of angels who protect him and Israel (Dan. 10–12).

In the New Testament, through the power of the Holy Spirit, numerous supernatural experiences are seen. The most concentrated time frame of supernatural experiences found in the Bible comes in the Gospel accounts. Among other things, Jesus heals (Mark 3:10), restores sight to the blind (Luke 18:41–43), multiplies food (Matt. 14:15–21), walks on water (Matt. 14:25–27), stills a storm

(Luke 8:23–25), raises people from the dead (John 11:17–45), and drives out demons (Matt. 8:16). As a result, some believe, but some do not (John 11:45–53).

Followers of Jesus also encounter the supernatural after his resurrection. In Acts we read of numerous such encounters. The disciples speak in tongues after the Holy Spirit comes upon them (2:1–4). They heal (3:1–8), raise people from the dead (9:40; 20:7–12), go into trances and have visions (10:10), are miraculously rescued from prison by an angel (12:1–12), perform signs and wonders (14:3), heal the lame (14:8–10), cast out demons (16:16–18), prophesy (21:9–11), are compelled by the Spirit to act (20:22–23), and survive snakebites (28:3–5). As in the time of Jesus, supernatural experiences do not convince everyone to follow Christ (e.g., 14:4). The Epistles and Revelation mention supernatural experiences ranging from the peace of God guarding our hearts and minds (Phil. 4:7) to deception by Satan or his demons (2 Cor. 11:3; Rev. 13:14; 20:8, 10), various miraculous gifts (1 Cor. 12:28–31; 2 Cor. 12:12; Heb. 2:4), and out-of-body experiences (2 Cor. 12:2–4).

Negative Experiences

We also find numerous negative experiences of the supernatural. In the Old Testament, Aaron helps lead Israel into a festival of idolatry when Moses does not come down from Mount Sinai soon enough (Exod. 32:1–6). On multiple occasions, God sends an evil spirit to afflict Saul as a judgment (1 Sam. 16:14–23; 18:10; 19:9). When this happens, David seeks to minister to him by playing the lyre so that he will feel better, though at best this provides only temporary relief (1 Sam. 16:16, 23; 18:10). The kings of Judah and Israel also participate in negative supernatural experiences. Manasseh is one of the worst examples: "He sacrificed his children in the fire in the Valley of Ben Hinnom, practiced divination and witchcraft, sought omens, and consulted mediums and spiritists. He did much evil in the eyes of the LORD, arousing his anger" (2 Chron. 33:6; see also 2 Kings 21:5–6). However, later he repents and humbles himself before God, unlike his son Amon, who follows in his father's negative footsteps without ever repenting (2 Chron. 33:21–23). Elijah pronounces God's judgment on Ahaziah after Ahaziah consults another god to discover whether he will recover from an injury (2 Kings 1:1–17). Ahaziah sends three sets of his army to capture Elijah, who calls down God's fire on the first two in judgment (1:9–12). He lets the third group take him to Ahaziah, where he repeats the word of God's judgment (1:16–17). God's angel kills 185,000 members of the Assyrian army to defend Jerusalem against the king of Assyria (19:35). Finally, the prophets—especially Jeremiah (14:14; 23:16, 27, 32; 27:9; 29:8) and Ezekiel (12:24; 13:6–9; 21:29;

22:28)—rail against those who use false dreams and visions to lead God's people.

The most detailed Old Testament account of a negative supernatural experience is the story of Job (Job 1–2), who is beset by satanic attacks on his wealth (1:13–17), his family (1:18–19), and himself (2:7–8). To carry out these attacks, Satan uses people (1:15, 17), nature (1:16, 19), and disease (2:7). Ultimately God vindicates Job, but not without unimaginable trial.

As with positive supernatural experiences, the most concentrated time frame of negative supernatural experiences found in the Bible comes during the life of Christ. Among other things, demons (including Satan) tempt (Matt. 4:1–11), cause illness (Mark 9:17–20), torture (Mark 5:1–5), bind and enslave (Luke 13:10–16), afflict children (Mark 9:17), and demonize people (Matt. 4:24).

Negative supernatural experiences continue through Acts and the Epistles. Actual instances of demonic attacks are found only in Acts, though demons are mentioned numerous times through the Epistles. In Acts we find only five separate instances of demonic encounter over more than thirty years (Acts 5:5–16; 8:6–7; 16:16–18; 19:11–12, 13–17). In addition to direct demonic attacks, we find instances of persons experiencing God's judgment (Acts 5:1–11), false prophecy (13:6–12), and attempts of pagan audiences to deify the apostles (14:8–13). In the rest of the New Testament, we read of temptations (1 Cor. 7:5; 1 Thess. 3:5), people being led astray (1 Cor. 12:2), satanic schemes to outwit us (2 Cor. 2:11) or take us captive (2 Tim. 2:26), believers being buffeted and tormented (2 Cor. 12:7), enslavement (Gal. 4:3, 9), performance of false signs and wonders (2 Thess. 2:9; Rev. 13:13–14; 16:14; 19:20), devouring (1 Pet. 5:8), deception (Rev. 12:9), and accusations (Rev. 12:10). Clearly the Bible is rich with both positive and negative supernatural experiences!

Contextualizing Supernatural Experience

Christians in majority-world settings are often characterized as connected to the supernatural in ways their secular Western counterparts are not (Hwa 2010; Stafford 2012). Latin American urbanites (Masci 2014) and indigenous groups (Ritchie 2000), African urbanites (Ireland 2012) and their rural counterparts (A. Anderson 2001), and Asian urbanites (Johnson 2015) and their rural counterparts (Cole 2003)—all have become the subjects of intense study over the past twenty years, with one significant commonality: supernatural experiences.

Given this reality, it is not at all surprising that globally Pentecostal churches grow most rapidly. Charismatic and Pentecostal types of churches more readily identify with naming, experiencing, and utilizing God's power as a replacement of traditional powers. Pentecostals do not simply tell adherents to avoid supernatural experiences: they invite them into new, godly experiences through the power of the Holy Spirit. They do not replace animistic systems with secular ones, but with systems in which God offers supernatural experiences that meet the felt needs of adherents even more deeply than their prior belief systems did. The first example of contextualization of supernatural experience, from the Philippines, clearly illustrates this reality.

Cordillera Rehabilitation Center (Cole 2003; Moreau 2012b, 297–300)

Harold Cole, an Assemblies of God missionary to the Philippines, wrote about the ministry of Rev. Antonio Caput Sr. (Tito) and the Cordillera Rehabilitation Center (CRC) after eighteen years of operation (1985 to 2003). At the time Cole wrote, every one of the eighty-three people who had been delivered from demons by Tito continued to faithfully walk with Christ. As you read the following account, bear in mind that Caput did not start the CRC with identity theory or contextualization in mind; he simply developed a means to deal with victims of the demonic in a thoroughly Christ-honoring Filipino fashion.

Having been delivered at the age of eighteen from a paralysis of both arms by a cousin who was a deacon in a local church, Tito had personally experienced the ability of Christians to deliver the oppressed through Christ. Observing local healers' unsuccessful attempts to heal the chronically afflicted, and knowing that there were many such afflicted in the villages around him, Tito knew that through Christ he could demonstrate God's power and bring people to Christ through a healing ministry. As a result he and his wife started the CRC in their home to deliver demonized people. The CRC deliverance process has five stages: (1) predeliverance, (2) preparation for deliverance, (3) deliverance, (4) immediate postdeliverance recovery, and (5) assimilation back into family and village life.

Predeliverance. Tito meets with the family of a prospective "patient" (a term used by local healers of the demonized) so that they can explain to him the problem and the solutions they have already attempted. Many of the patients are so out of control that the family has been forced to tie them up. Most have been brought to traditional healers, who were unsuccessful in delivering them. Tito requires that the family receive Christ and begin attending a Bible-believing church and that they bring any magical protective items they use to his house so that they can burn the items with him. Most of the patients are Kankana-ey, Tito's own people group.

Tito observed that local healers call the demonized "patients" and bring them to live in their houses during their treatment; they are required to bring guards with them to protect the patient and the healer. He copied this methodology while contextualizing his approach to deliverance and restoration. All patients are brought to live at the CRC for their deliverance, and Tito requires the family to provide a guard (usually a family member) to feed, wash, and care for the patients and keep them from running away. Tito also requires the family to provide the food and other provisions necessary for the patient while in residence at the CRC, but he does not otherwise charge them for his ministry.

Preparation. Five days before the deliverance, Tito starts his personal preparation. He prays and fasts for three days and then rests the final two days.

Deliverance. After the preparation period, the patient is brought to the CRC and moved into one of the bedrooms in Tito's house. The room has a barred, locked door and a bunk bed. This is more humane than tying them up, as the families and local healers do. The family-provided guard lives with the patient and is the only one with access for the first two days. In the meantime, Tito and other prayer partners in the church pray for the out-of-sight patient.

After two days of prayer, on the third day Tito explains to the guard what he will do during the deliverance. After explaining to the guard what he will do, Tito pleads the blood of Christ over the patient, looking them in the eyes but never touching them during the deliverance (that is the job of the guard). He commands the demons to leave, refusing to negotiate despite their pleas. As the demons depart, Tito reports that a bad smell of rotten fish is coming from the patient.

Immediate postdeliverance. Once the deliverance is complete, the patient bathes and eats and is given time out of the room but still in the larger compound. Patients also typically express interest in being productive and want to do something to help, such as sweeping around the house. After roughly one week, the patient is ready to move out of the room. The family-assigned guard remains with the patient until the end of this phase.

Assimilation. The patient now moves to a room on the second floor of the education wing of the church (on the same compound as Tito's house) to live with other patients who have also been delivered. There are as many as five patients at a time there, with recovery ranging from three to six months. The women's auxiliary of the church comes to the church every morning around 4:00 a.m. to pray, and they are also available to help with discipleship. On occasion additional deliverance and prayer sessions are needed for the patient.

The patient is required to attend all church meetings and Bible studies that happen on the compound and is also assigned practical duties around the compound, ranging from cooking to landscaping. During this phase, the patient's family is required to come twice per month for reconciliation and discipleship. Once it has been determined that the patient is fully recovered, the church has a celebration service and prays for the patient, who then returns home, restored to normal life at their home, and ready to continue the process of discipleship with the family in their village.

Discussion. In this discussion I follow the outline of identity theory and focus on issues of collective, social, and core identity seen in the depiction of Tito's ministry in the CRC.

Throughout, the case patients' *collective identity* remains intact. They start as Filipino, are engaged in a Filipino practice that parallels that of traditional healers, and resume a normal Filipino village life after assimilation. Those who are not Kankana-ey (Tito's people group) are not challenged to change their familial or tribal affiliation: those are immaterial in the deliverance process. Thus the patient's collective identity, whether framed in tribal or national affiliation, is not disturbed or challenged in the deliverance process.

In terms of the patient's *social identity*, it is significant that Tito will not deliver a person without the entire family coming to Christ. This provides the foundation of a new social identity, one centered on Christ. Second, in the postdeliverance process, the person is given meaningful tasks, which serve to socialize them into a position of handling the normal sets of responsibilities that people are expected to take in their society. Often the demonized are not able to engage in responsible actions, and this provides an opportunity to normalize them into appropriate social roles. Third, together with other patients, they participate in the entire life of the church. Again, this shapes and solidifies their social identity. The final celebration, when the entire church prays for them and sends them off, provides a ritual "seal" on the changes that have taken place. Fourth and finally, the family and the patient are together being socialized through the postdeliverance reconciliation and ongoing Bible study sessions with Tito.

At the *core identity* level, the patient is trapped by the demonic and unable to make a personal identity commitment to Christ until the demons are banished. Once they are banished, the patient enters into a caring, disciplined community that engenders the patient's personal commitment. The jobs the patient takes on in the assimilation phase serve as rituals intensifying their commitment to live a normal life, with normal responsibilities. The twice-monthly meetings with their now-Christian families in reconciliation anchor them into the framework of being part of a Christian family, working through challenging issues in the context of a supportive environment.

Understanding Dreams from God

For the second example of contextualization of supernatural experiences, we turn to the widely reported phenomenon of Muslims having personal encounters (such as dreams) that play a significant role in their coming to faith in Christ (e.g., Garrison 2014, 96). The *More Than Dreams* video series offers five vivid and compelling examples from Egypt, Indonesia, Iran, Nigeria, and Turkey (http://morethandreams.org).

Practitioners have explained the phenomena (Musk 1988; Doyle and Webster 2012; Kronk 2013) and developed evangelistic methodologies framed around the questions that Muslims who have had such dreams ask (Breslin and Jones 2004; Scott 2008; Kronk 2010). To contextualize this, Rick Kronk correctly reports the Muslim belief that the Qur'an was revealed to Muhammad through dreams and visions and that, for Muslims, this mythic element undergirds the idea that truth can be revealed through dreams and visions (Kronk 2013, 360).

In perhaps the seminal article on the topic, Bill Musk (1988, 164) posits, "Dreams are central to the cosmological outlook of ordinary Muslims. From founder to followers, dreams form part of the total paradigm within which Muslims live and move, touch and are touched, meet and are met. They are not optional; they are a meaningful component of life." In Kronk's (2013, 362) analysis of the stories of Muslims who experience dreams of Christ, he concludes:

1. God uses previously acquired information about himself, despite the fact that sometimes that information is woefully incomplete.
2. Dream and vision encounters apparently come unannounced and unprovoked, leaving the "dreamer" with a sense of urgency to respond, but uncertain how to do so.
3. The role of a Christian friend is crucial as a link to assisting the "dreamer" in understanding and responding appropriately to the message received.

Kronk's third point is the link for contextual thinking and application. Scott Breslin and Mike Jones, engaged among Muslims for several decades, had Muslims coming to them on a regular basis with stories of their dreams in which Jesus appeared. These Muslims sought out Christians to try to unravel the spiritual significance of their dreams. Eventually Breslin and Jones (2004) wrote *Understanding Dreams from God* as an evangelistic tool to facilitate conversation with Muslims who experienced a dream from God. That book is the basis for this example of contextualizing the supernatural dimension.

In the book they refer to Jesus as "Isa," a reminder to English readers that the book was originally written in another language for a Muslim audience; I will use that term in this synopsis. Through the book, they introduce readers to key dreams and visions in the Bible and offer guidelines for understanding and testing dreams as well as how to respond to dreams from God. They provide questions at the end of each chapter to facilitate small-group meetings with discussion.

Biblical Discussion (Job 33:14–18)

Breslin and Jones purposefully choose to introduce their readers to dreams in the Bible through Elihu's statement to Job about God's purpose in speaking to people through dreams from Job 33:14–18:

> For God does speak—now one way, now another—
> though no one perceives it.
> In a dream, in a vision of the night,
> when deep sleep falls on people
> as they slumber in their beds,
> he may speak in their ears
> and terrify them with warnings,
> to turn them from wrongdoing
> and keep them from pride,
> to preserve them from the pit,
> their lives from perishing by the sword.

They chose this passage in part because Muslims do not dispute its legitimacy as they do other portions of the Old Testament. Based on Elihu's statement, Breslin and Jones identify four purposes God has in mind when he gives people dreams: (1) to turn people from wrongdoing, (2) to keep us from pride, (3) to preserve our soul from the pit, and (4) to protect our lives. Through the first four chapters of the book, they examine each purpose in turn, explaining and illustrating each with additional stories from the Bible.

Proposed Guidelines

Next, Breslin and Jones turn to application through guidelines for Muslims who have experienced dreams and would like to discover what their dreams may mean. First, they need to understand that not all dreams are from God. Other sources include anxiety, chemical imbalance, and evil spirits. With that in mind, Breslin and Jones state that the person with the dream should confirm that the dream doesn't conflict with the Scriptures. Next, the dreamer should consult with followers of Isa about the dream (Kronk's point 3 above): together with this follower of Isa, they may be able to discern the purpose and character of their dream(s). Additionally, they are encouraged to nurture a willingness to obey God. The concluding chapter of the book encourages readers to respond to God's revelation of himself, offers a brief apologetic of Isa (his claims, his miracles, and his character), and closes by asking them to respond to Isa's invitation to follow him.

Analysis

How might we analyze Breslin and Jones's attempt to contextualize their evangelistic approach to Muslims who have experienced a dream or vision?

First, Breslin and Jones rightly choose to focus their approach through the worldview lens of ordinary Muslims and utilize their dream experiences as possible doors for meaningful evangelistic encounters.

Second, they wisely choose uncontested texts as the basis of their interpretation and discussion (none of the biblical stories of dreams they offer in the book are contested by their Muslim audience). Thus they avoid unnecessary battles over the texts, which could detract from the message.

Third, they strongly encourage readers to connect with followers of Isa (Christians) for help with understanding the dream. Further, they also encourage them to be willing to change in response to God's prompting.

Fourth, they neither seek to generate supernatural experiences nor ignore or discount them. Rather, they take advantage of what they see God is already doing in their setting.

Fifth and finally, I need to address a point related to interpreting Elihu's statement, which is in the form of a poem, as you can see by the layout of the text (a new line for each line in the poem). English poetry generally relies on rhyme. Hebrew poetry, by contrast, relies on parallel ideas and phrases. There are numerous types of poetic parallelism found in the Bible. In these verses, Elihu uses synonymous poetry, in which the second line of each couplet *repeats* or *restates* or *extends* the first line. The two lines in Elihu's poem "to turn them from wrongdoing and keep them from pride" should be interpreted as synonymous thoughts. The same applies to the lines "to preserve them from the pit" and "their lives from perishing by the sword." By treating these as four separate ideas, Breslin and Jones do not demonstrate an understanding of the parallel structure of Hebrew poetry. By missing the existence of synonymous parallelism in Elihu's poem, they miss connective nuances that could enrich their interpretation.

Conclusion

In this chapter I have outlined contextual issues in the supernatural experience dimension. Missiological anthropologist Charles Kraft poses three types of encounters as a framework for engaging in contextual ministry: (1) allegiance (or commitment) encounters, (2) truth encounters, and (3) power encounters (C. Kraft 1991, 2005; see also Moreau 2012b, 300–301). *Allegiance* or *commitment encounters* ask, To whom do we offer allegiance? Kraft reminds us that our faith in Christ is a personal allegiance to Jesus rather than a religious system (C. Kraft 2016, 73–87). *Truth encounters* bring the living truth of the Bible to bear on the circumstance we face and replace the false things we believe with God's truths. *Power encounters* face down the supernatural enemies of God and release us by bringing God's power to bear in our lives. Power encounters span a spectrum from "deep healing" (Kraft, Kearney, and White 1993) to demonic expulsion. Contextualizing supernatural experiences involves all three encounters, as is evident from both the biblical data and the two examples presented in this chapter.

I conclude this chapter with a case study blending several situations I have experienced over the years. As you read the case study, examine your own response to Apostle Mukendi's testimony and the implications of that response in relation to sharing the platform with him at the conference; reflect on how this might impact Andy's message. In what ways do your allegiances, understanding of truth, and experience with power encounters shape your response? Identify the main issues involved in your role as a partner in the long-term postconference growth of the Divine Deliverance Church of Malawi in developing a theological response to the spirit realm in Africa.

CASE STUDY

THE CONFERENCE SPEAKER

Andy was intrigued at the email that had arrived two weeks before, inviting him to be one of the main speakers at a weeklong conference that the Divine Deliverance Church of Malawi was having on spiritual warfare. In the invitation, they mentioned that the conference was one of the ways the church was choosing to respond to the continuing practices of witchcraft and spiritism seen all around the city. A relatively new missionary to the country, Andy was delighted to accept the invitation and, at least initially, was excited to be able to participate with this well-known church and its ministry.

After accepting the invitation, he decided that he needed to find out more about the church itself. He already knew that the Deliverance Church was one of the so-called African Initiated Churches, the fastest-growing segment of the church in Africa. They were highly visible in the city and known for their Pentecostal emphasis. Though Andy himself was not Pentecostal, he and his mission felt comfortable with his involvement. His Google-based research into the church uncovered other information he had not previously known. The church was relatively new, having been founded only fifteen years earlier. It had a certain notoriety because of its huge miracle rallies held in city parks, focusing on healing and deliverance. Andy heard many reports from fellow missionaries of the multiple tens of thousands who attended. He also read up on their regular prayer marches around the city, organized to pray against traditional African spirits, which they believed kept the city in spiritual bondage. As far as Andy could discern, the marches had not had a significant impact on the city.

Throughout its existence, the denomination had actively sought out contact with Western mission agencies. Largely because of the church's reputation, however, those agencies had avoided official public relationships, feeling that the church was too shaky in its doctrine. Andy himself began to feel uncomfortable when he read interviews with church leaders in the local newspapers in which they discussed the visions of angels that guided the church on the timing and locations of their miracle rallies. He also wondered about some of their doctrines, especially polygamy for members and even leadership, trust in dreams and visions, and heavy reliance on the Old Testament rather than the New.

Andy decided to consult with his mission leadership and was informed that despite his reservations, they felt that the time was right to begin to partner with the church informally and that this invitation was just the type of opportunity they had hoped to find. When he pondered with local colleagues why he had been invited, they opined that this was simply another effort on the part of the church to develop contacts with Western mission organizations. They offered prayer for wisdom in Andy's planning and preparation, but since none of them had previous contacts with the church, they could not offer any additional advice.

One week before the conference, Andy received an email with the schedule from the church, in which he learned that Apostle Mukendi of Zaire would be the other main speaker. Pastor Zilikazi, with whom Andy had been developing a relationship, told him that a member of the Conference Committee read of Apostle Mukendi through some articles in *Advance Magazine*, a local monthly periodical eagerly read by many in the church.

Andy found the magazine online and read the articles. As he did so, his anxiety began to grow. Part of Apostle Mukendi's testimony was that he had been a former Satanist and claimed to have met Lucifer face-to-face before coming to Christ. He claimed that magical circumstances surrounded his birth and early childhood, including being breastfed by a mermaid, and that before coming to Christ he had the power to change into a cockroach, change other people into animals, and change fetuses in the womb into eggs.

Of course, Apostle Mukendi declared, since coming to Christ he was not engaged in this type of activity. None of this fit into Andy's picture of a biblical approach to spiritual warfare. Since this was the person with whom he would share the platform during the conference, he knew it was time for some serious prayer on how he should approach his talk.

How would you advise Andy?

11

THE DOCTRINAL
DIMENSION

The final dimension is the doctrinal, or truth, dimension. It is not that the other dimensions do not deal with truth: it is just that in this dimension the focus is centered on expressions of truth, whether ideas or lifestyles. This dimension is by far the most frequently discussed (and argued over). From what I've seen over the past thirty years, I believe it fair to say that more books are published on contextual theology than the rest of the dimensions combined. Some explore how to engage theology in context, while others are examples of contextual theologies. In this chapter I explain contextual approaches to developing (or "doing") theology before turning to a short synopsis of the contextual realities that help us better understand global expressions of theology and theological development.

In a prior book I examined 249 examples of evangelical contextualization and categorized them in multiple ways. One of those was whether the example included the doctrinal (or theological) dimension. Of the 249 examples, 93 did so, making it the second most commonly addressed dimension (after the social dimension) in the database.

What Is Theology?

In relation to contextualization, just what is theology? The underlying Greek terms mean "words about God," and for much of history that has defined the scope of theology. More recently, however, new options have emerged.

Orientations to Theology

Frames of Reference

The Western agenda for the past several centuries has framed theology in legal, philosophical, historical, and/or scientific orientations. Most theologians assumed that their systems or approaches were universal rather than local. Calvin brought the training of a lawyer to his theological works, Jonathan Edwards constructed his theology from a philosopher's vantage point, historical theologians trace (for example) a particular doctrine or teaching through the history of the church, and intelligent-design theologians frame theology from a scientific approach.

Western evangelical systematic theologians offer a spectrum of approaches, but until the last several decades all seemed to assume that their own systematic theology was universal. For the purposes of this discussion, and recognizing the reductionist nature of my definition, I aggregate these approaches into a category I call "cognitive theology." By "cognitive theology" I refer to human expressions of the truths that God has revealed in the Bible and theologians have arranged to make sense to an intended audience. At root the legal, philosophical, historical, and scientific approaches (each systematic in its own way) are all cognitive approaches to constructing theology.

Through the centuries cognitive theologies have been biblical (the view of God in the Pentateuch), propositional (God is love), systematic (the attributes of God), historical (the development of trinitarian thinking), and creedal (the Apostles' Creed). Cognitive theologians declare things about God, the universe, the world, and the beings and things that inhabit the world. They also include the relationships of the created order, such as people in relation to their Creator, spiritual beings in relation to people, and people in relation to the rest of the beings God has created. Cognitive doctrines are not necessarily directly related to "real life." They may be organized as stand-alone ideas or scattered within stories, ethical values, and rituals. The ultimate source of cognitive doctrine for Christians, the Bible, was not written as a pure theological treatise. In terms of sheer text, it is much more story and history (e.g., the Gospels and Acts) than doctrine or theology (e.g., Romans). However, embedded within the story arc of the Bible are the stories of God's interaction with people, of our interaction with one another and the rest of the created order, and of the truths about who we are and what everything else is.

A second orientation to theology is one in which people live out their convictions rather than craft them into cognitive proposals. I refer to this as "lifestyle theology": it involves living in a fashion that is connected to and actively pursuing God's intentions for the created order. One approach is what may be called contextually driven or praxis-oriented theologies (here the plural noun is important). *Praxis*, the Greek word for "action/acting," has become a common term in missiological circles. While in the most general sense it refers to action, it can be used for everything from political actions to moral living, often depending on the theological convictions of the person using the term. For example, in liberation theology circles, praxis commonly refers to political action on behalf of the marginalized or oppressed. An alternative to the praxis approach can be called the experiential approach, seen most clearly in Pentecostal, charismatic, and power-encounter theologies, which lean more toward the spiritual experiences of the believer than the theoretical understanding of those experiences. Being baptized in the Spirit, being slain in the Spirit, being touched by the Spirit, experiencing dreams and visions, casting out demons—these are best experienced rather than discussed.

A third category of theologizing is oral theology, which lies between cognitive and lifestyle theology. Orality, as I noted in chapter 4, takes place in informal or nonformal settings. It can be called a "theology of the street" and is seen in such things as the choruses we sing, what we say to each other in small-group Bible studies, our testimonies, and our prayers. In the context of Africa, Charles Nyamiti calls these "African Nonsystematic Theologies" (1994, 67), and Henry Okullu (1974, 54) argues that if we want to discover African theology, "we should go first to the fields, to the village church, to Christian homes to listen to those spontaneously uttered prayers before people go to bed. . . . We must listen to the throbbing drumbeats and the clapping of hands accompanying the impromptu singing in the independent churches. We must look at the way in which Christianity is being planted in Africa through music, drama, songs, dances, art, paintings. . . . This then is African theology."

We do not systematize oral theologies: we speak, hear, sing, and sometimes dance them instead. This is where the vast bulk of the average Christ-follower's theological experience happens, whether they are Western or majority-world believers. Theology happens in our worship services, in discussions with Christian friends, in small-group Bible studies or discipleship groups, in social media, in our family devotional times, and so on.

"Doing Theology"

I remember my wife's reaction the first time I used the expression "doing theology." "What in the world is that?" she laughingly asked. By "doing theology" I refer to the crafting of theology, whether that is cognitive or lifestyle. Cognitively, it refers to the methods and procedures used to develop theological expressions of God's truths (as ideas). In terms of praxis, I mean living the type of life that reflects God's truths in our actions. These methods vary from person to person, group to group, denomination to denomination, and society to society. They are inevitably defined, developed, and utilized according to the presuppositions (both cognitive and lifestyle) that theologians bring to the task. They are not limited to facts or abstract data: they connect to life and lifestyle commitments. Doing theology includes activities that range from writing this chapter to participating in a recycling program, voting in an election, and protesting an immigration policy—if my framing for doing so is connected to biblical convictions, such as creation care and proper stewardship of God's creation and standing on behalf of the marginalized.

Another question asked by evangelical missiologists over the past few decades has been, What is the starting point—the Bible or culture? (see Moreau 2012b, 59–61). Ultimately, however, the starting point matters less than the "grounding" or normative point (Ezigbo 2008, 57). What is the source of truth no matter where we start? What provides the grounding norms? As theologian Kevin Vanhoozer (2006, 110) declares, "Doctrinal directions are normed by Scripture but realized in contemporary contexts."

Functions of Theology

Theology provides for followers of Christ in several ways. *Cognitive* theology enables us to explain and organize our experiences in life. How do we handle the questions that arise when "bad things happen to good people"? While visiting a Hindu temple with a group of students, I asked the guide what parents might do when their child is afflicted with a deadly disease. According to him, the first thing the parents and the child must understand is that above all karma is at work. In other words, before providing practical advice on which ritual(s) to perform or which deity to placate, the doctrinal foundation needed to be intact. As I reported in chapter 6, sociologist Peter Berger refers to this as the "sacred canopy" (1969), which either protects us from the harshness of life or provides answers when that harshness hits home. Karma, in the sense I discussed in chapter 6, is a mythic doctrine that supplies the reasons behind a Hindu child's illness. Beyond explaining life experiences, cognitive theology also guides our behavior. Ideally, for followers of Christ, it leads us to obedience to the One we follow. It also provides the undergirding for ethical framing by which we are expected to shape our lives (e.g., the Ten Commandments; "the greatest commandment," Matt. 22:36–38).

As noted earlier, theology is not just cognitive: it is also lifestyle. Living a theological life reflects kingdom priorities to the watching world. We live as God would have us live: a "What would Jesus do?" life. This is clearly linked to the cognitive function, but it goes beyond ideals or theory into actual living. Reflecting kingdom priorities champions causes dear to the heart of God, including mercy for the downtrodden, justice for the oppressed and the oppressors, proper stewardship of the created order, and so on. Finally, when we exemplify a kingdom-of-God life, God can use us to woo people to a living relationship with Christ. As happened with Christ himself, however, exemplifying a kingdom-of-God life can also cause people to turn away from Christ when they choose rebellion against God's order.

Contextualizing Doctrine

Contextualizing doctrine can be thought of as a dialogue or dance with multiple partners, with the Bible as the norming partner, the local setting as the primary location for contextualization, and the people who play roles: cross-cultural theologians (when appropriate) and local theologians. Based on the work of Robert Schreiter (1985), William Dyrness (1990) offers a helpful diagram of the overall flow (fig. 11.1). As you can see from figure 11.1, both Scripture and culture need to be opened through analysis. Before there are local believers to contextualize doctrine, there will be communication of the gospel by evangelists and/or missionaries in the setting (who, ideally, have done their homework on the local setting!).

Once the gospel has taken root and a fellowship is formed, the process of the local church taking the primary role of contextualizing may begin. As the embryonic group begins to obey Scripture, themes emerge. They may be areas in which the local culture and Scripture are in agreement, or areas in which they are in conflict or in which questions arise. The local theologizers explore the Scriptures for parallel stories, situations, or teaching. They respond to what they find by trying to embody the scriptural truths they find in their local setting, with a dialogue between Scripture and culture established (in which Scripture continues to play the normative role). Their new theological perspectives impact how they live and (depending on the nature of the culture) may begin to impact the local society with scriptural framing of their lives, and they cycle to reopening the culture in light of the impact of their scripturally framed lifestyles. At the same time, their contextual theology begins to impact how they go to the Scriptures, to which they turn and start that side of the cycle anew.

Well-known African theologian John Mbiti (1976, 16–17) poignantly states: "We have eaten theology with you; we have drunk theology with you; we have dreamed theology with you. We know you theologically. The

Figure 11.1: Interactional model of contextualizing doctrine

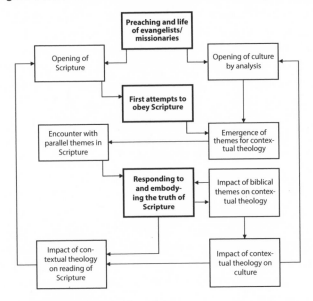

Source: Dyrness 1990, 30. Used with permission.

question is, Do you know us theologically? Would you like to know us theologically?" His question might haunt you the way it does me. How well do I want to know my global sisters and brothers theologically? With this question in mind, for the rest of the chapter I will focus on two components. First, I offer a short list of commonalities theologians in majority-world settings experience, the circumstances in which they are contextualizing theology for themselves and their people. Second, I will offer a more focused case study on contextualizing Christology in African settings. My intention is to offer a methodology rather than a final product; the same approach I use in this chapter could be repeated for a different geographical area as well as for a different theological topic.

Commonalities Faced by Majority-World Theologians

Before we turn to focus on Africa, it will help to zoom out and identify several common factors faced by theologians who wrestle with issues in majority-world settings. I offer this in two categories: socioreligious commonalities and theological commonalities. I combine societal and religious simply because, in many majority-world settings, treating these as separate categories ignores local sensibilities.

Societal and Religious Commonalities

One of the common features that theologians in majority-world settings face is the reality of oppression as a common experience. Christians in many majority-world settings are among the most marginalized, especially in parts of the world with other dominant religions. Often they have little to no security that their basic physical and social needs will be met. It is fair to say that theology written on an empty stomach or when under observation by security forces will have an entirely different orientation from theology written in a climate-controlled office in which the most important pressure is the need to get a manuscript to the publisher by the deadline.

A second common reality of majority-world theological development is the experience of having lived under colonialism and continuing to be dominated by the economic power of the West. This is not true for all majority-world countries, but it is true for most of them. In many cases this includes domination by Western political entities for centuries and independence for only a few decades. The lasting economic structures of colonialism have been morphed rather than dismantled, and the African lament *Not Yet Uhuru* ("not yet free") (Odinga 1967) continues to generate empathy in Asia and Latin America. Referred to as "neocolonialism," the economic and political dependence initiated under colonialism continues today (see Easterly 2006 for a scathing critique of the "White Man's Burden" approach to development): "Neocolonialism mostly walks under the guise of economic assistance and the mask of cooperation. It forges bonds of economic dependence, the heaviest of which is the debt system imposed on the Third World. In short, neocolonialism develops and puts in place a complete dependence machinery for the effective control of all areas of political, economic, and cultural life" ("African Report" 1990, 29).

A third common reality is that the political environments are dramatically different from those of their Western counterparts. Politics in majority-world settings ranges from oppressive dictatorships (North Korea) to strong anti-Christian political systems (Saudi Arabia) and political instability (Sudan, Somalia); theologians living in those settings cannot theologize as though their political circumstances do not exist.

A fourth common reality is that many in the majority world are victims of the ideological struggles that take place in their political landscapes, struggles often having very little to do with theological issues beyond the struggle to define justice and defend one's position. While the Cold War has played out in significant ways, the world's major political and economic powers continue to contend over ideology, and all too often majority-world countries serve as proxies in the struggle.

A fifth significant factor that directly affects theology and the development of theology in majority-world settings is that many majority-world countries are home to other religions. Majority-world theologians (and other church leaders) cannot overlook or otherwise ignore the questions related to their religious neighbors. In some cases this requires on-the-ground apologetic discourse; in other cases it requires addressing the issues that other religions raise or reframing expressions of theology into a Buddhist, Muslim, Hindu, Jewish, Jain, or other audience's worldview. Dialogue and confrontation are neither theoretical nor optional; they stem from living among a non-Christian majority.

Finally, because majority-world theologians often live among people of other faiths, they are more consciously aware that theology has a deeply missional nature. Arguing over debates that have been internal to the Christian church often makes less sense than addressing the needs of their neighbors.

Theological Commonalities

In addition to socioreligious commonalities, majority-world theologians share theological commonalities. First and perhaps the most significant is that majority-world theologians are under no illusion that their theological formulations are timeless and universal. Rather, they are intentionally occasional and recognize the limits of time and place in theology. Additionally, they are intentionally contextual, with a deep appreciation of cultural, social, and historical dimensions of theology.

Second, majority-world theologies are "from the underside": they are perceived and evaluated in relation to dominant streams of established Western theologies. The most visible evidence of this is how frequently they are produced in a trade or international language (English, French, German) rather than the local vernacular. In one sense, they are trapped. If they want to be taken seriously as theologians, they have to publish their approach. In order to publish, there need to be enough readers to justify the costs involved in publication. However, that often necessitates that the publication be in a trade language or an international language (and the latter carries more weight in international theological circles). While this opens the door for global theologians to learn from each other, at the same time it can close the door on those with whom they share a "language of birth" (see, e.g., Njoroge 1992, 133–34).

A third commonality for majority-world theologians is that *who* interprets is just as important as *how* interpretation takes place. Having heard from outsiders long enough, they want to learn from those who have life experiences in common with themselves. Those who remain deeply affected by colonialism (and neocolonialism) express frustration that too much theology intended *for* them comes *from* outsiders.

The fourth commonality is that many in majority-world settings consider social-science tools to be indispensable for theological reflection. To understand the local setting, those tools are more useful than biblical-exegetical or systematic theology tools. Contextual theology should be a dialogue between text and context. For evangelicals, the scriptural text is the normative partner in the dialogue. Ezigbo (2008, 62) explains, "The Scripture is a circumference or the boundary of a contextual Christology. This circumference is not closed-ended but open-ended: it should be broad and elastic enough to allow African Christians to develop some concepts and images that synchronize with their history, culture and experience of Jesus." Yet a genuine dialogue still requires the ability to exegete the context, and the best tools for that task happen to be the social sciences (anthropology, sociology, communication, psychology, and the like).

The final commonality is that majority-world theologians are typically accustomed to seeing God at work today through the types of religious experiences (positive and negative) I discussed in chapter 10. Their theological formulations are not developed as a result of academic theorizing but are wrought in the crucibles of faith lived with the expectation that God will show up today as he did in the times of the Bible. Overall, Douglas Jacobsen (2015, 60–61) captures for Africa what can be said for many majority-world settings: "Many African Christians would say it is better to view the continent as a kind of spiritual laboratory where Christianity is slowly being stripped of its Western biases and renewed as a non-Western religion. This theological experiment is still under way, and it is premature to make predictions about how it will end."

An Example: Contextualizing Christology in Sub-Saharan Africa

I offer the following synopsis with three important limitations. First, given limitations of both space and expertise, it is impossible to present a rich, nuanced, and deep overview of African theologies without glossing over significant differences and overlooking significant nuances that arise within and across the regions. Second, I frame the discussion under two core categories: (1) *selected* societal and religious contours and (2) *selected* christological contours. *Selected* simply refers to the fact that I have consciously selected what to discuss from a vast array of possibilities based on what I, from my limited vantage point, consider to be significant elements. My choices are admittedly biased and not intended to imply that I adequately cover African thought and culture. The word "selected" simply reminds us all that I have purposefully chosen what I cover.

Third, I limit the discussion on theological contours to Christology. I chose Christology rather than theology proper, pneumatology, or soteriology (and so on) as the focus because the most important question of the gospel that every theologian must seek to answer is, Who is Jesus Christ? Yet, given the limitations of the human describing the divine, none of us can ever mine the depths of that question! However, it is the singular question with which every theologian—African, Asian, Latin American, Middle Eastern, and Pacific—must wrestle.

Fourth, following the lead of African theologians such as Charles Nyamiti (1994) and Victor Ezigbo (2014), I limit my synopsis in this section to sub-Saharan Africa. The christological questions and issues of (largely) Christian sub-Saharan Africa differ significantly from those of (largely) Muslim North Africa. For example, sub-Saharan African Christians do not question Christ's deity or sonship, nor the biblical account of the crucifixion. Further, they do not consider Christ as subordinate to Muhammad in any way, and generally they do not face questions on these topics on a day-to-day basis. While any Christology that incorporates North Africa into the picture needs to address these issues, one focusing on sub-Saharan Africa does not. With these four caveats and limitations in place, I turn to the survey.

Selected Societal and Religious Contours

Despite the fact that sub-Saharan Africa is composed of far more than one thousand languages and ethnic groups, Africans themselves have long noted numerous common societal features found across the continent (see, e.g., Je'adayibe 2012). In the following I treat these features as though all Africans agree with what I say; this is clearly an oversimplification for the sake of attempting to squeeze a viable picture of this vast continent into a very limited space.

Perhaps the most significant common feature is that *life is experienced in community* (Chike 2008, 224–25). South African theologian and church leader Desmond Tutu explains, "We say, 'A person is a person through other persons.' I would not know how to be a human being at all except [that] I learned this from other human beings. We are made for a delicate network of relationships, of interdependence" (D. Tutu and N. Tutu 1989, 71). According to Tutu, the Zulu word *ubuntu* best captures the sense that "a person is a person through another person." He posits ubuntu as a core cultural and theological orientation for Africans, which has been picked up by other

African theologians (see, e.g., Gathogo 2008; Battle 2009; Jacobsen 2015, 62–72).

Connected to ubuntu is the understanding that the *departed ancestors continue to live in community* with the living and continue to have influence over them. The living dead are sources of wisdom, knowledge, and guidance, not to be easily ignored. An extremely helpful resource for contemporary African beliefs and practices is the Pew survey "Tolerance and Tension: Islam and Christianity in Sub-Saharan Africa" (Pew Research Center 2010), for which researchers conducted 25,000 face-to-face interviews in 19 sub-Saharan countries. In this study two questions focused on ancestral beliefs and practices (see table 11.1). Of those surveyed, 32 percent believe that sacrifices to the ancestors can protect, and 25 percent indicated they had participated in a ceremony related to their ancestors. In South Africa, Cameroon, Tanzania, Botswana, Liberia, and Ghana, over one-quarter of the Christians interviewed had participated in such a ceremony, a clear indication that in these countries the ancestors continue to play a role in the lives of many Christ-followers.

Ubuntu has multiple positive and negative consequences (Gathogo 2008). On the plus side, people are intimately connected to one another and share a unified worldview. On the minus side, "my people" in terms of ubuntu is linked to "my tribe." Tribalism, "the Commander in Chief of anti-African forces" (49), has since independence trumped any other consideration. A significant amount of the violence in Africa is tribal related. Even Christians are not immune, as seen in Rwanda and DR Congo (Jacobsen 2015, 57–60).

The second common feature is *holism*. For Africans, this means that all of life is intimately interconnected (Titre 2009, 186). Many of the boundary separations seen in the West—family life from job life, religion from culture, faith from science—do not make sense philosophically or practically to Africans. An African proverb captures the sentiment: if you hit a drum on one part, the entire skin vibrates. Neat separation into abstract categories (as I am doing here!) does not fit the worldview of many Africans.

A third common feature is the cultural value of *hospitality*, which is a pervasive feature of African societies. Gathogo (2008, 40) affirms, "For in

Table 11.1

Ancestral Beliefs and Practices of Sub-Saharan Africans

Sacrifices to spirits or ancestors can protect you from bad things happening.	32%
Do you ever participate in traditional African ceremonies or perform special acts to honor or celebrate your ancestors?	25%

Source: Pew Research Center 2010

Africa, an ideal person is primarily hospitable. This hospitality is ideally extended to all people: friends, foes and/or strangers. It is also extended to all departments of life." He connects hospitality to ubuntu: to be African is to be connected and hospitable.

The fourth common feature is the *shared traumatic experiences of slavery intertwined with colonialism*. No one today advances positive outcomes stemming from the brutality of the slave trade, which overlapped with the first four centuries of colonialism. The legacy of the colonial era, especially the final century, is more complex. Hand in hand with Protestant mission work across Africa, colonialism played a significant role in negating and destroying African traditions and worldviews even as it paved the road for the dynamically growing contemporary African church.

In addition to the African church, the effects of colonialism continue today through several negative legacies. First is *ongoing political turmoil* across the continent. After five centuries of colonialism, most sub-Saharan African countries have been politically independent for just over five decades. Since the winds of change swept the continent from the 1950s onward, Africa has seen more attempted coups and revolutions than any other continent. With few exceptions (such as Julius Nyerere of Tanzania and Nelson Mandela of South Africa), too many African presidents have chosen to serve for life (Robert Mugabe of Zimbabwe). An all-too-common story of elections is that they are rigged, delayed, overturned, nullified, or falsified. They appear to offer hope of change but fail to deliver.

A second lasting legacy of colonialism is a *search for identity*. Africans politically define themselves in light of the five centuries of colonial experience, including the slave trade. Many are now seeking to reconstruct themselves from within their own worldviews and reference points rather than continue to rely on colonial thinking and framing. Theological formulations around the concept of identity have played a significant role in African theological discourse (see, e.g., Bediako 1994b).

A third legacy of colonialism is *corruption*, though some recognize that the African nations have been independent long enough that they can no longer lay the blame exclusively at the feet of the colonizers. Corruption from bottom to top in petty and systemic fashion has driven the downfall of governments across the continent like a "train dashing into the night without a driver" (Okullu 1974, 34). Civil servants have been anything but servants on behalf of the citizens, especially those with significant political and economic power. I well remember an Asian-descended businessman recounting to me the most valuable lesson he learned doing business in Kenya: don't be too successful. He recounted from his own experiences that it was important to be able to stay under the radar of government officials lest they take over his business, threatening to shut it down if he refused.

Africa is characterized by *poverty* (Pobee 1992b, 16), which is a fourth negative legacy of colonialism, this stemming from the political turmoil and corruption previously noted. According to the International Monetary Fund, 28 of the 30 worst economies in the world in terms of purchasing power for the average citizen are in Africa (IMF 2017). With roughly 12 percent of the world's population, Africa has roughly 3 percent of the GDP. That means that African countries produce goods and services at only *one-quarter the rate* of the rest of the world. It is difficult to imagine this turning around in the next decade.

The final common feature I record is that of *a religious orientation to life*. What does that include? Table 11.2 offers the overall average results to a selected subset of the Pew survey questions.

When asked whether religion plays an important role in their lives, 96 percent of the people surveyed confirmed that it was either very important or somewhat important (see also Chike 2008, 222–24). Fully 97 percent believe that God exists. Belief in miracles is pervasive (73 percent); not as common yet high were personally witnessing a divine healing miracle (47 percent), belief in evil spirits (48 percent), personally witnessing the expulsion of a demon (41 percent), belief in witchcraft (43 percent), and belief in people having supernatural power such as the evil eye (42 percent). Of significant interest is that more than half (54 percent) believe that God grants health and wealth to those who have enough faith. Clearly a purported theology for Africans that overlooks the supernatural element will be missing significant framing of existing religious belief and practice (see Ezigbo 2010, 217–49).

Table 11.2
Affirmative Responses of Sub-Saharan Africans to the Pew Survey

How important is religion in your life? (very or somewhat important)	96%
Do you believe in God?	97%
Do you believe in miracles?	73%
Have you ever experienced or witnessed a divine healing of an illness or injury?	47%
Do you believe in evil spirits?	48%
Have you ever experienced or witnessed the devil or evil spirits being driven out of a person?	41%
Do you believe in witchcraft?	43%
Do you believe in "evil eye" or that certain people can cast curses or spells?	42%
God will grant wealth and good health to all believers who have enough faith.	54%

Source: Pew Research Center 2010

Though religion was deeply integrated into African life, there was never a single, unified "African Religion." Rather, each ethnolinguistic group believed and practiced what their community believed and practiced. Until the advent of urbanization, ethnolinguistic groups by and large did not intermingle residentially. Their belief systems and practices did not compete with one another, nor did the various communities try to gain converts from other communities. With religions so typically connected to the ancestors and their ancestral territory, there was no perceived need to convert others to one's own ancestral cult. The primary exception took place in cross-group marriage, when the new wife joined a new clan or family and that clan's ancestors effectively became her ancestors. She married the group, not just her husband.

General Theological Contours

Given the African socioreligious commonalities, it is not surprising that "theology in Africa is practical. It is undertaken for the purpose of helping Christians to reflect on who they are called to be as followers of Jesus in the unique cultural context where God has placed them" (Jacobsen 2015, 61). With this in mind, how do Africans approach theology?

During the first thirty or so years of the postcolonial era, African theologians tended to orient themselves in two directions: identity through (1) inculturation or (2) liberation (Moloney 1987). While these two orientations are not mutually exclusive (Levison and Pope-Levison 1994, 40; Stinton 2004, 67–69; 2007, 30–31), most African theologians gravitated in one direction or the other.

The inculturation approach has roots in the idea of "negritude," developed in the 1930s by Francophone African intellectuals living in Paris. Like their intellectual predecessors, African inculturation theologians use African culture and thought categories as indigenous worldview resources, which can be harnessed to enable Africans to better grasp Christian theological framing (see Nyamiti 1994, 64–65; Ezigbo 2008). Westerners also do this, for example, when we refer to Christ as our "Captain." While the term "captain" is in the Bible, it is not used as a metaphor for Christ. African identity or inculturation theologies use anthropological and historical tools to find and utilize African thought processes and thereby communicate Christ by using African sensibilities and idioms.

African theologians using liberation approaches, on the other hand, present Christ as the liberator who on behalf of the oppressed fights to overcome all forms of oppression. As with liberation theologians elsewhere, the exodus event is a hermeneutical key that orients them toward liberative acts of justice by which they struggle on behalf of the marginalized, facing down the evils of colonialism and neocolonialism.

African liberation theologians were most visible in South Africa in the days of apartheid. Today the liberation of women across the continent has become a primary focal point. Liberation theologians utilize political and economic analytic tools to expose injustices, discern ways to combat them, and where possible overthrow those who use political or economic power to oppress others.

Since the early 1990s, Kenyan J. N. Kanyua Mugambi (1991, 1995), South African Charles Villa-Vicencio (1992), and others have articulated a need for "reconstructionist" theology, which "highlights the need for a biblical paradigm of reconstituting society" (Mbuvi 2017, 164). Decades had passed since most African nations had gained political independence, and the exodus model of attaining liberation had been realized politically across the continent. Therefore, reconstructionists argued, African liberation theologians needed to move beyond the exodus event to a social reconstruction paradigm such as that seen in Ezra and Nehemiah (Mbuvi 2017). Reconstruction, it was posited, would come at three levels (personal, cultural, and ecclesial) in the spheres of politics, economics, aesthetics, morality, and theology. In the process, "just as the Renaissance and the Reformation helped European peoples to wake up from their cultural and religious slumbers, so should Africa's cultural and religious re-awakening help the people of this continent to reassert themselves amongst humankind" (Mugambi 1991, 33). Proponents posited that the "theology of reconstruction is a new theological metaphor which should be adopted in Africa to curtail the new challenges which were emerging" (Murage 2007, 154).

From the late 1990s onward, a postcolonial approach has been developed "whose premise is to expose the colonial project in all its forms" (Mbuvi 2017, 164) and provide intellectual space in which new identities can be forged from the ground up (see, e.g., West 2000; Dube Shomanah, Mbuvi, and Mbuwayesango 2012). Building from the frame of postmodernism but recognizing the continuing impact of the colonial era, postcolonial framing takes colonialism, the Enlightenment, and modernity all to task by using the tools of the sociology of knowledge. Postcolonial theologizing is a more radical approach than liberation theology; it even critiques liberation theology as a way of knowing framed in modernist terms and built on Enlightenment presuppositions. Further, proponents argue, because knowledge is socially constructed, sociopolitical liberation is ultimately futile unless grounded in epistemological liberation, in which those who have been acted on or known ("objects") themselves become the actors or knowers ("subjects") (see, e.g., Grant 1992).

In doing so, they move from the epistemic periphery to the epistemic center: *they* determine what is knowledge rather than having it determined for them. "The postcolony is an open space in that its indetermination liberates Africans from the shackles of traditionalism and nativism, on the one hand, and the tyranny of Enlightenment reason, on the other" (Kenzo 2002, 339). Thus free, they go to the Bible as the interpreters without being confined by traditional (Enlightenment-based) theological tools (see, e.g., West 2000).

Selected Christological Contours

Given the four streams of African theology identified just above (inculturation, liberation, reconstruction, postcolonial), to do full justice to the topic would require not just a single book but a multivolume series. Unfortunately, space limits the exploration to only one of the streams. Because the inculturation stream focuses on African cultural constructs (including metaphors, images, symbols, and idioms) as vehicles for understanding Jesus, I will use that approach to lay out several cultural constructs proposed by African theologians as potential vehicles for deepening African understandings of Jesus. In choosing this path, I am following the lead of Victor Ezigbo (2008, 63):

> Africans' images of Jesus Christ do not have to be exactly the same as the ones that are contained in the Bible. The mosaic of images of Jesus in the Bible should function as the circumference that defines the "theological space" within which African Christology can take place. But the biblical representations of Jesus Christ must not suppress the possibility and legitimacy of new Christological expressions. Thus, the task of African theologians transcends merely translating the Christological images in the Bible into African expressions. It involves discovering the African concepts, pictures and images that can effectively communicate the meaning and significance of the person and work of Jesus Christ in Africa.

To put the African constructs in a larger context, in table 11.3 I show three categories of cultural constructs about Christ: African, biblical, and Western (each listed alphabetically). I place the biblical construct list in the center to symbolize its normative role (see also Stinton 2007, 30). The table illustrates our need to use such constructs for better understanding Jesus, and why African (not to mention Asian, Latin American, Middle Eastern, Oceanic, and so on) perspectives deserve a place at the global theological table equal to that of Western perspectives. It also helps illustrate why I believe theology is best done in intercultural partnerships rather than in cultural isolation.

Table 11.3
Constructs and Metaphors for Christ in Three Settings

African constructs	Biblical constructs	Western constructs
Ancestor	Author of Life (Acts 3:15)	Anchor in the Storm
Guest	Bread of Life (John 6:35)	Best Friend
Healer	Bridegroom (Mark 2:19)	Captain of My Ship
Kin, Elder Brother	Gate for the Sheep (John 10:7–9)	Great Physician
Leader	Good Shepherd (John 10:11)	Hero
Liberator	Lamb of God (John 1:29)	Pilot
Life Giver	The Life (John 14:6)	Real Thing
Mediator	Light of the World (John 8:12)	Rock of Ages
Provider	Lion of Judah (Rev. 5:5)	
Revealer	Son of Man (Matt. 9:6)	
Sufferer	The Truth (John 14:6)	
Victor	The Vine (John 15:1)	
	The Way (John 14:6)	
	The Word (John 1:1)	

I limit my discussion to four of the African constructs listed in table 11.3 (cf. Stinton 2004, 71):

1. Christ as Healer
2. Christ as Ancestor
3. Christ as Kin
4. Christ as Victor

As I walk through each construct, I invite you to keep in mind that no single construct, not even a biblical one, captures all that Christ is and does. Further, the list of Western constructs reminds us that we borrow from our own cultural imagery to better communicate Christ to ourselves, even when we end up needing to co-opt terms from their original sense to better fit biblical framing. For example, Jesus as my "best friend" is not a biblical metaphor for Christ, and my American ideals of a "best friend" don't even begin to capture my relationship with Christ. Just as I create "cultural space" for myself by using my own images and metaphors, so do African theologians.

Finally, following Paul Hiebert's (1987) widely used critical contextualization model, for each construct there are three options. First, African theologians might reject it altogether as hopelessly inappropriate or completely incongruent with biblical norms. Second, they might adopt the construct wholesale and incorporate it into the African theological lexicon, in essence "christianizing" it (Olsen 1997, 255). Third and finally, they may choose to adapt, modify, or otherwise transform the construct. However, as Tienou

(1985, 179–80) warns, when done uncritically, this is a potential path of "mnemic" hermeneutics, "which takes elements from Scripture without understanding them in their total context and applies them in another context as if the first context . . . was of little relevance and importance in the task of interpretation." As Tienou (180–84) argues, when African theologians use a mnemic hermeneutic, they run the risk of relying on their own personal or cultural context to determine the interpretation of Scripture, effectively untethering it from its original setting, author, and audience.

Christ the Healer

Numerous authors explore the construct of Christ as healer (including Chike 2008, 228–29; Kolié 1991; Mugabe 1991, 345–46; Schoffeleers 1994; Stinton 2004, 72–129; Titre 2009, 191–92). When the construct is confined to the English term, few have problems. However, contextual theology must utilize local vocabulary rather than import expatriate terms. For many southern Africans, the word *nganga* (or equivalent) refers to a traditional healer who discerns both the cause(s) of an illness and its remedy by directly accessing the spirit realm. At a conference in 1966, Buana Kibongi (1969, 52–53) reported that the Congolese Catholics used *nganga* as a term for priests, noting that the Congolese *nganga* provided a set of religious and moral conceptual tools available for Bible translation and Christian teaching. Over two decades later, Matthew Schoffeleers, who served as a Catholic priest for twenty years in Malawi, observed that African scholars expressed frustration that there were no African indigenous categories for understanding Jesus. Yet, he pointed out, Kibongi's paper on an indigenous construct of potential utility went almost completely unnoticed in the discourse. With Kibongi's observations as a starting point, Schoffeleers (1989, 1994) and Daneel (1988) document ordinary Christians in independent churches across southern Africa who likewise use *nganga* (or its equivalent) for Jesus as a folk theological term. As an example, see the use of *nganga* (*sing'anga*) in the following Christian hymn from Malawi (Schoffeleers 1994, 79):

Yesu sing'anga;	Jesus, the medicine man;
Halleluya, bwerani!	Hallelujah, come!
Yesu sing'anga	Jesus, the medicine man
Amachiza matenda.	Cures diseases.
Yesu sing'anga	Jesus, the medicine man
Amachotsa ziwanda	Drives out evil spirits
Halleluya, bwerani!	Hallelujah, come!

Schoffeleers rightly argues that this merited much more consideration than it had received. Clearly there are parallels between Christ and the *nganga*: both access spiritual power, both effect healing for individuals and communities, and both bring authoritative messages from the spirit realm (see, e.g., Pobee 1979). Mugabe (1991, 345) notes that some African theologians portray the *nganga* as an African pre-Christian construct perfected in Christ: "In Africa the *n'anga* is Christ's predecessor, and it is Christ as the new *n'anga* who fulfills the traditional age."

At the same time, however, there are insurmountable differences, primary among them that the traditional *nganga*, with no connection to Christ, is not accessing Christ's power to heal, nor is traditional healing as efficacious as healing from Jesus. In identifying Christ as healer, African Christians take a holistic approach: Christ heals physical illnesses, but also social brokenness, community brokenness, and "deeply wounded souls" (Titre 2009, 191).

While Schoffeleers (1994, 86) agrees that transformation of the term into biblical categories is a critical concern, he also argues that the popular Christian use of *nganga* for pastor/priest—and for Christ—opens a conceptual door that the theologian should explore. He argues that African theologians have avoided using *nganga* as a title for Jesus largely because they perceived it would lead to syncretism (86). Though the term is widely used by Christians in independent churches, those in the missionary-founded and mainline types of churches avoided it. From his vantage point, this is largely because of concerns that their founding churches and organizations would raise (86).

Several additional terms fit into this construct of Christ as Healer: Life Giver (Mugabe 1991, 345–46; Stinton 2004, 72–129), Provider (Chike 2008, 229), and Sufferer (Mugabe 1991, 347–48; Pobee 1992a, 148–49; Setiloane 1976, 130–31; Waliggo 1991). Methodist church leader and poet Gabriel Setiloane (1976, 130–31) portrays Christ as Sufferer in this moving poem loaded with African imagery (UVELINGQAKI = "The First One" and UNKULUNKULU = "The Great, Great One" are African names for God):

> And yet for us it is when He is on the cross,
> This Jesus of Nazareth, with holed hands
> and open side, like a beast at a sacrifice:
> When He is stripped naked like us,
> Browned and sweating water and blood in the heat of the sun,
> Yet silent,
> That we cannot resist Him.
> How like us He is, this Jesus of Nazareth,
> Beaten, tortured, imprisoned, spat upon, truncheoned,
> Denied by His own, and chased like a thief in the night.
> Despised, and rejected like a dog that has fleas,
> for NO REASON.

No reason, but that He was Son of his Father,
OR . . . Was there a reason?
There was indeed . . .
As in that sheep or goat we offer in sacrifice,
Quiet and uncomplaining.
Its blood falling to the ground to cleanse it, as us:
And making peace between us and our fathers long passed away
He is that LAMB!
His blood cleanses,
not only us,
not only the clan,
not only the tribe,
But all, all MANKIND:
Black and White and Brown and Red,
All Mankind!
HO! . . . Jesus, Lord, Son of Man and Son of God,
Make peace with your blood and sweat and suffering,
With God, *UVELINGQAKI, UNKULUNKULU,*
For the sins of Mankind, our fathers and us,
That standing in the same Sonship with all mankind and you,
Together with you, we can pray to Him above:
FATHER FORGIVE.

Christ the Ancestor

Christ as Ancestor is another widely used construct (e.g., Akrong 1992; Bediako 1994a, 96–99; Kabasélé 1991; Mugabe 1991, 346–47; Nyende 2007, 370–78; Reed and Mtukwa 2010; Stinton 2004, 130–65), even though theologians disagree on how that construct should play out. Despite its use by theologians, and unlike *nganga*, it remains largely in theological discourse and is not widely used by lay Christians (Olsen 1997, 251).

As noted previously, the living dead continue with the community: guiding, cajoling, disciplining, and rewarding. Tanzanian Charles Nyamiti (1984) was the first African theologian to extensively and systematically explore the idea of Christ as Ancestor. Among the Akan of Ghana, ancestors embody the moral ideals of the community, serve as channels of wisdom from the spirit realm, and are the subjects of reverence (Akrong 1992, 121). It is not too much of a stretch to see them as the vine from which the descendant branches sprout and bear fruit (Kabasélé 1991). They mediate between the living and the spirit realm, protecting as well as guiding the living along the best paths. To become an ancestor, a person needs to live long enough to have children (especially sons) and grandchildren (especially grandsons), who will carry on their memory once the progenitor has died. The ancestors need to be perceived as valued members of their community.

Many of these elements apply to Christ; he, too, guides, disciplines, directs, and rewards. Christ mediates between us and God, and he protects us. He founds a new family of God for us and serves as a type of "proto-Ancestor." Christ is part of our lives; we should commune with him regularly, at times seeking his advice and at times simply enjoying his presence. He protects and sustains us as members of his family. He is no *mere* ancestor, however: he is the "greatest ancestor" (Nyende 2007, 378).

As with any analogy, there are areas in which it breaks down. For example, traditionally, certain aspects disqualify him from becoming an ancestor: Christ was never married, he did not father any biological children, and he died at a relatively young age, under the social shame of his crucifixion. Further, bringing the Christ as Ancestor construct into the church without some important distancing from traditional ancestral beliefs and practices clearly poses a danger of syncretism. To date the discussion among academics has yet to resolve several significant questions in connecting Jesus with African ancestors:

> (1) the theological interpretation of the ancestors' identity, including the long-standing debate over whether African ancestors are actually worshipped or merely venerated; (2) the possible place of African ancestors within the Christian faith, especially with respect to certain doctrines regarding Christian saints; and (3) the role of African ancestors as mediators in relation to Christian claims of the sole mediation of Jesus Christ. The intricate issues involved account for the controversy surrounding the image of Jesus as ancestor. (Stinton 2007, 34)

More recently the idea of Christ as Ancestor has gained popularity outside academic circles, though surfacing more among Catholics than Protestants. Ghanaian Presbyterian theologian Kwame Bediako (2004, 26) proposes a transformation of the ancestor construct, positing Christ as our Elder Brother (see below), who "displaces the mediatorial function of our 'spirit-fathers.' For they themselves need saving." Jesus is superior to them in every way related to protection, guidance, mediation, and—ultimately—salvation. Indeed, "while not denying that spiritual forces do operate in the traditional realm, we can maintain that ancestral spirits, as human spirits that have not demonstrated any power over death, the final enemy, cannot be presumed to act in the way tradition ascribed to them" (31). As the one with power over death, Christ alone serves all the positive ancestral roles ascribed traditionally to the ancestors, and as such he is both the ultimate Ancestor and Source of Life for all people (31). In this sense, Bediako's argument is that African Christians will jettison their traditional sacred practices and beliefs in the ancestors once they better believe and experience Christ's superior ability to fulfill the sacred ancestral functions. Their departed ancestors are still biologically connected, but Jesus does what our ancestors can never do: in every sense of the word, he saves us and is the final mediator between us and God. Shall we continue to engage in practices such as offering them libations? Not according to a hymn from Ghana:

> Praise the Lord, hallelujah!
> Praise the Lord, hallelujah!
> He's the only God to worship:
> Why serve other gods instead?
> Rings and amulets are useless
> If by Jesus Christ you're led.
> Shall we worship lifeless idols,
> *Pour libation to our fathers who are dead?*
> No! We have a Saviour who is Christ the Lord.
>   (Stinton 2007, 23, emphasis added)

Christ as Kin

The idea of Christ as kin has multiple manifestations promoted by theologians and expressed in numerous ways by lay Christians (see Stinton 2004, 166–98): as the Eldest Brother, as a loved one, as a husband (especially for single women or widows), as a parent (father *and* mother). Note the images in this short Twi chorus:

> Jesus, He is my all in all.
> Jesus, He is my all in all.
> He's my Mother, my Father, my strong Brother.
> He is my all in all. (Stinton 2004, 169)

Christ the Ancestor also fits this category when the emphasis is on family and clan relationships rather than ancestral continuation and power (as previously described).

The image of Christ as our Elder Brother was developed in a short essay by Sierra Leonean theologian Harry Sawyerr (1978, 66), built on the foundation of Christ's incarnation: "The Incarnation should be so presented as to emphasize that Jesus Christ was the manifestation of God's love for man." Christ was incarnated, lived a completely human life, was crucified, and was raised from the dead. Jesus's affinity for humankind is the basis for seeing the church as "the Great Family" (66), of which Jesus is the head. This will give Christians "a unifying influence that transcends tribe and clan," and "the tribal affiliations of Christians give way to the totality of the community of the Church, with Jesus as its first member" (66; see also Bediako 2004). As first member, Christ is "the firstborn among many brothers" (Rom. 8:29), the Elder Brother (Sawyerr 1978, 167).

As previously mentioned, a common societal reality for Africans is that people belong to communities and that kinship groups are at the heart of communities. John Pobee (1979, 88), Ghanaian theologian, recommends, "Since belonging to a kinship group is a mark of a man, our attempt at constructing an African Christology would emphasize the kinship of Jesus." He points out that in Jesus we see numerous characteristics of being human that the Akan would connect with: he was circumcised, grew up with siblings in a family, was baptized, depended on God, dreaded his impending death, and died—all common kinship experiences (88–90).

Congolese Catholic priest and theologian Francois Kabasélé (1991, 121) indicates that as the Eldest Brother, Jesus is closest to the beginning of the family and to the source of its life, and he is the one who makes the offerings to the ancestors. Mbiti (1972, 56–57) anticipates that when Africans recognize Christ as Eldest Brother, they are able to transition their kin and clan loyalty to solidarity in Christ.

The ideas of Jesus as kin, brother, father (and mother), and "loved one" have been developed by theologians but also are found in common lay choruses and prayers. They are found in both formal and street theologies. Diane Stinton (2004, 199) has it right when she declares, "Insofar as Jesus is appropriated as loved one, these African Christologies help to recover the communal dimensions of the gospel that are often neglected in the more individualistic expressions of Western Christianity."

Christ the Victor

In the New Testament, Christ provides food (Luke 9:10–17), heals diseases (Matt. 4:23), casts out demons (Mark 5:1–20), has power over nature (Mark 4:39), and conquers death through dying (Rom. 6:9; 2 Tim. 1:10). His authority and power are more than just attractive to those who recognize that the powers of this world are arrayed against them: Christ brings life-changing power and authority.

"Christ as Victor" serves as an overarching idea that incorporates Christ as Victor (e.g., Chike 2008, 227–28), Leader/Chief/King (e.g., Pobee 1979, 94–98; Stinton 2004, 201–13; Waruta 1989), and Liberator (e.g., Maimela 1992). That he is the Victor also incorporates that Christ is healer, is above all ancestors, and is our Elder Brother. Kwame Bediako (1983, 97) notes, "Jesus is seen, above all else, as the *Christus Victor*. This arises from Africans' keen awareness of forces and powers at work in the world that threaten the interests of life and harmony. The portrait of Jesus as *Christus Victor* answers to the need for a powerful protector against these forces and powers."

Christ is the victorious *leader*, fitting the African leadership role of the "visible expression of the religious life of his people" (Waruta 1989, 50). Traditionally, chiefs and kings played the major leadership roles (including religious leadership). During the colonial times, however, chiefs were often co-opted by the colonial powers. In many cases the office of chief lost traditional authority and respect, which is one of the reasons using this term for Christ has earned mixed reviews (see Stinton 2004, 211–13). Chiefs and other leaders often received praise names and songs. For example, several are applied to Christ in the following song by Ghanaian author Madam Afua Kuma (1981, 7):

> Jesus: you are solid as a rock!
> The green mamba [*a poisonous snake*] dies at the sight of Jesus.
> Iron rod that cannot be coiled into a headpad: the cobra turns on his
>   back, prostrate before you!
> Jesus, you are the Elephant Hunter, Fearless One!
> You have killed the evil spirit, and cut off its head!
> The drums of the king have announced it in the morning.
> All of your attendants lead the way, dancing with joy.

We discussed the stream of liberation approaches to African theology previously, so I offer only a few words on the specific construct of Jesus as Liberator. First, the liberator construct is not as widely seen among lay Christians in Africa as it is among theologians. Further, when it is found, it is more likely to be used to address the personal-spiritual dimension (freedom from sin, disease, hunger) than the sociopolitical one (freedom from dictators) (Stinton 2004, 37), especially in postapartheid Africa.

Common use of Jesus as Liberator is found among women theologians (e.g., Oduyoye 2001, 2004) who apply the motif to gender discrimination and injustice, which in both traditional and contemporary times is seen across the continent (Amoah and Oduyoye 1988). Jesus is the one who suffers with women in Africa (Stinton 2004, 227) and offers them hope and succor in their suffering. For political theologians (female and male), however, liberation requires action on behalf of the oppressed. While that certainly includes suffering alongside them, it also includes identifying the structures of oppression, exposing them for what they are and do, and working to transform or overcome them in order to establish more just structures for all people.

Conclusion: African Christology

This cursory survey of one stream of Christology demonstrates how challenging it can be to develop local theologies in a globalized world. Christian theology everywhere must be anchored in the same source: the Bible. Theologies *to* or *from* everywhere (e.g., exported and imported theologies) must at the very least be tuned for each new setting, if not reconstructed from the ground up. In this section the glimpse of theological ferment in Africa offers the opportunity to better understand what that entails. As for African evangelical theologies, I close with Kenyan theologian James Kombo's (2012, 146) list of things that must be part and parcel of evangelical theological development:

> (1) actively engaging the African primordial narratives in direct theological discourses. From here we get to identify not only the questions Africa is asking but also the logic and manner of presentation; (2) encouraging the use of vernaculars as languages of change and empowerment in worship and reflections; (3) maintaining candid and vibrant conversations between the good news of Jesus Christ and Africa's current multidimensional challenges and opportunities; . . . (4) encouraging and preparing leadership enabled to answer questions emerging from the African grassroots. This we can do with God's help.

Conclusion

In this chapter I traced some of the contours of contextualizing the doctrinal dimension. Theologians now recognize that no human-constructed theology can be timeless and universally applicable. However, that does not leave us adrift, for we still have the Bible as the anchor for contextual theological development. Further, we have over two millennia of theological arguments, discussions, creeds, and confessions to guide local theological development.

The truths of Scripture do not change: what changes are only our insights into what Scripture actually teaches as we engage the Bible with sisters and brothers whose perspectives differ from ours. Tim Tennent (2005, 176) declares, "It takes a whole world to understand a whole Christ." Paralleling that, as I stated earlier, theology is best done in intercultural partnerships rather than in cultural isolation. We need multiple perspectives to best glean what the Scriptures teach, determine how that teaching applies in our local settings, and discern the questions and issues that arise from local settings.

The case study for this chapter is a statement of faith on tribalism, put together by African seminary students. In light of what you learned in this chapter, what might you identify as topics of relevance drawn from your society for which a statement of faith might help your church?

CASE STUDY

STATEMENT OF FAITH ON TRIBALISM PREPARED BY AFRICAN SEMINARY STUDENTS

Read the following statement of faith related to tribalism, developed by graduate students in an African seminary (presented verbatim below). In the statement they attempt to identify issues of tribalism honestly and bring biblical insights to bear on them. As you read the statement, first, consider your reactions. Does this fit in your worldview or cultural background? Why or why not? Second, consider the forms of racism within your society. If you substitute "racism" for "tribalism," how well does it address the issues Christians in your society face? What might strengthen the statement for you? Finally, what questions (e.g., of clarification, justification, or explanation) might you want to ask the students who developed this statement?

1. We believe that tribalism is a conscious disposition of favor toward one's tribal unit at the expense of other tribes and this disposition expresses itself in word and deed.

2. We believe that a tribalist is one who is devoted to his particular tribe against other tribes and ignores the paths of unity and justice in an attempt to please members of his tribe to the exclusion of others.

3. We believe that tribalism ignores the teaching of the Holy Scripture that all mankind are God's creatures, created in his own image, and are equal before Him (Gen. 1:26, 27; 9:6; Acts 17:26; Eph. 3:6; Col. 3:11).

4. We believe that belonging to a tribe is not in itself sinful, for no human being has the slightest choice. We further believe that although God sanctioned ethnic pluralism in our world, its origin at the tower of Babel was a result of God's judgment on man's rebellion against his will (Gen. 10–11; Acts 17:26–27).

5. We believe that tribalism is a hindrance to the spread of the gospel (Acts 6:1–2, 9:32–10:23; cf. Jon. 1:1–3).

6. We believe that the Great Commission encourages cross-cultural ministries outside one's tribal borders (Matt. 28:19, 20; Acts 1:8). We further believe that Christ himself showed an example by breaking tribal barriers in order to present the gospel to the racially discriminated people of his day (John 4).

7. We believe that the church is God's new society: where believers from different tribal groups are united in Christ into God's family and heavenly citizenship (Eph. 2:19–22; 3:6).

8. We believe that Christ has broken down the barriers of hostility between people of different tribal groupings (Eph. 2:14, 16; Gal. 3:28). We further believe that the problem of tribalism in the church can only be resolved when different tribal groups see themselves in light of their relationship in Christ (Gal. 3:28).

9. We believe that the church should encourage leadership mobility and contact with people of different tribal groups in order to build mutual trust, love, and unity in diversity among Christians of different tribal origins (principle: Acts 9:32–10:23).

10. We believe that in the contemporary urban African church setting, the church is called upon to adapt, adopt, and adjust its programs in order to minister to the needs of different tribes for the church composed of people of diverse tribes, languages, and customs (1 Cor. 9:19–21).

THE FUTURE OF CONTEXTUALIZATION

What Have We Learned?

Contextualization has a certain future, simply because we literally cannot avoid contextualization or pretend that it does not exist (e.g., see Tim Keller discuss the need for contextualization at https://www.youtube.com/watch?v=DR-lJ0Y8Rkg). Every church on the planet is situated in a context that is decidedly different from the first-century churches; every twenty-first-century church is a contextual organism. This should not surprise us, for as we read from the New Testament Epistles, each of the churches of the first century was likewise situated in an environment in which it had to be contextual (see Flemming 2005; Prince 2017). Buttressing that reality is the additional fact that, over the course of the church's history, multiple paradigms of contextualizing the church (and mission) have been developed and used (Bosch 1991; Bevans and Schroeder 2004), even though the term was not adopted for use in mission and church contexts until 1972.

While overwhelmingly accepted as a fact of life by those in the academy, contextualization remains a controversial topic among evangelical pastors, church members, and even some missionaries. From Bible translation (e.g., the heated controversy over changing the terms "Son of God" and/or "God the Father" in Muslim settings: see Brown 2007; Dixon 2007) to church planting movements, from insider movements to contextual scales, there have been plenty of controversies over the past several decades (see also Moreau 2012b). Some outspoken opponents of contextualization lump any ministry practices they don't like under the banner "contextualization" and naively condemn it altogether. Others focus on the more extreme models or approaches and misidentify them as the norm. Still others view any contextualization efforts as compromising the gospel and urge us to drop contextualization altogether because the gospel is universally understandable.

The gospel is indeed universally relevant and understandable, but if I do not contextualize how I communicate it, recipients will not understand it or its relevance to them and their people. Additionally, as I have demonstrated throughout the book, we contextualize not only how we communicate the gospel but also the churches we plant (or join), the ministry practices we engage in, the ethical stances we take, the art we produce, the theology we develop, the systems of exchange, learning, and organization we use, and so on. If we don't contextualize, our churches and Christian organizations will look not only generically foreign, but also foreign in a particular way—whether that be too American, too Korean, or too Brazilian.

Recap

As the world changes, as local societies change, as Christians increasingly go from everywhere to everywhere, they will contextualize (whether accidentally or purposefully). The question is not *whether* they will contextualize, but *how well* they will contextualize. One of my primary intentions is to provide you with a path to think and act contextually in all areas of church and ministry life.

In the social dimension, I have presented five systems that are found in every society: association, kinship, exchange, learning, and organization. Each of these plays significant roles in church and ministry life. Who we gather with, who we do not gather with, who we consider kin, the types of capital we build and exchange and the rules governing those exchanges, how we learn and teach, and how we organize ourselves—all these take place in cultural settings and follow culturally framed rules. Societies in the Bible also followed culturally framed rules, but God enabled the authors to frame some elements as culturally situated (casting lots to determine Judas's replacement) and some as universal (spiritual gifts are for the entire church, not just the gifted individual). Contextualization helps us tease out the differences and ask, based on the text, how we are to identify and *apply* the universal elements, and how we are to identify the cultural elements and *whether* and *how* we are to apply them.

In the mythic dimension, I noted that the stories circulating among us form mythic structures that guide us in life. We tell stories of heroism, sacrifice, adventure, coming of age, redemption, and love (romantic and friendship). We admire and try to emulate those we see as heroes; we try to avoid the mistakes of those who fall short. We rely on a repertoire of stories that we learned while growing up, stories from family, friends, religious leaders, teachers, and so on. The underlying ideals grow deep roots in our hearts and enable us to define the themes that in many ways drive us. Helping new Christ-followers become embedded in the story arc of the Bible in contextual ways is a critical component of cross-cultural ministry.

In the ethical dimension, we explored the implications of the truths we believe about God and the created universe, and the ethical obligations we share as creatures made in God's image and placed on earth with a purpose—to glorify our Creator in all that we think, say, and do.

In the artistic and technological dimension, we overviewed artistic expressions of faith as products of contextually artistic expression, the material components of faith as human-made religious expression, and the technological components of faith as the things we make and use, which in turn reshape us.

In the ritual dimension, we saw ritual as a "symbolic expression of belief through which the participants gain satisfaction," a choreographed performance that physically expresses faith and embeds elements of belief in the participants. Rituals intensify our identification as believers belonging to a community of believers, help us reestablish order after things fall apart (or alternatively, keep them from falling apart in the first place), and enable us to transition from one state to another, to meet the demands of society and the individuals undergoing transition. Our lives are filled with ritual: understanding the roles that rituals play and utilizing them in cross-cultural ministry helps people connect with one another, with the story arc of the Bible, and with proper ways of living.

In the experience dimension, we saw how important supernatural experience is across the world and gained appreciation for contextual framing of our responses. I noted that my intention is not to help you find ways to "generate" supernatural experiences. Rather, my intention is to enable you to understand them, to address them in sensitive, biblical ways, and to welcome the experiences people have that deepen their faith in our living God.

Finally, in the doctrinal dimension, I explained that doctrine is not just about knowing truth: it is also about living truthfully. We explored how culture causes us to go to the Bible in certain ways, and how contextual thinking about what we read in the Bible is critical for appropriately understanding what it teaches.

Together these seven dimensions offer a whole and healthy approach to contextualization. Using them will not guarantee that you will avoid controversy, as we have seen in several chapters throughout the book. However, using the framework offered in this dimensional approach does help ensure that all facets of ministry and church are considered and addressed by following the contextualization role(s) and paradigm(s) that you adopt (for numerous examples, see Moreau 2012b).

Conclusion

As I stated and demonstrated throughout the book, contextualization includes everything a local church or ministry is and does. This ranges across seven dimensions, each playing a role and dynamically interlocking with the other dimensions.

Contextualization is not just about knowing: it is also about putting what one knows into action or practice. Understanding the seven dimensions of contextualization is only a first step. Applying those dimensions in real life is where contextualization comes alive, and I anticipate that as a result of working through this book, you have found discussion and examples that will enable—and possibly empower—you to think, act, and live contextually in ways that honor God and serve local followers of Christ.

WORKS CITED

Abernethy, Bob. 2002. "Exploring Religious America, Part One." *Religion and Ethics NewsWeekly*. April 26, 2002. http://www.pbs.org/wnet/religionand ethics/2002/04/26/april-26-2002-explor ing-religious-america-part-one/11569.

Adeney, Bernard T. 1995. *Strange Virtues: Ethics in a Multicultural World*. Downers Grove, IL: InterVarsity.

"African Report." 1990. In *Third World Theologies: Commonalities and Divergences*, edited by K. C. Abraham, 28–56. Maryknoll, NY: Orbis Books.

Akrong, Abraham. 1992. "Christology from an African Perspective." In *Exploring Afro-Christology*, edited by John Pobee, 119–30. Frankfurt: Peter Lang.

Allaire, Yvan, and Mihaela E. Firsirotu. 1984. "Theories of Organizational Culture." *Organization Studies* 5 (3): 193–226.

Amoah, Elizabeth, and Mercy Amba Oduyoye. 1988. "The Christ for African Women." In *With Passion and Compassion: Third World Women Doing Theology; Reflections from the Women's Commission of the Ecumenical Association of Third World Theologians*, edited by Virginia Fabella and Mercy Amba Oduyoye, 35–46. Maryknoll, NY: Orbis Books.

Anderson, Allan H. 2001. *African Reformation: African Initiated Christianity in the 20th Century*. Trenton, NJ: Africa World Press.

Anderson, Herbert. 2010. "How Rituals Heal." *Word & World* 30 (1): 41–50.

Anderson, Justice C. 2000. "Theological Education by Extension." In *Evangelical Dictionary of World Missions*, edited by A. Scott Moreau, 944. Grand Rapids: Baker Books.

Ang, Choulean. 1988. "The Place of Animism within Popular Buddhism in Cambodia: The Example of the Monastery." *Asian Folklore Studies* 47 (1): 35–41.

Arnold, Clinton E. 1992. *Powers of Darkness: Principalities and Powers in Paul's Letters*. Downers Grove, IL: InterVarsity.

Backues, Lindy. 2015. "Symbols of the Weak, Symbols of the Gospel: The Upside-Down Gospel in Relation to Patronage Systems in West Java, Indonesia." In *Christian Mission and Economic Systems: A Critical Survey of* the Cultural and Religious Dimensions of Economics, edited by John Cheong and Eloise Meneses, 113–47. Pasadena, CA: William Carey.

Bailey, Kenneth E. 2008. *Jesus through Middle Eastern Eyes: Cultural Studies in the Gospels.* Downers Grove, IL: IVP Academic.

Barbour, Ian G. 1974. *Myths, Models and Paradigms: A Comparative Study in Science and Religion.* New York: Harper & Row.

Baskaran, S. Theodore. 1989. "Christian Folk Songs of Tamil Nadu." *Religion and Society* (Bangalore) 33, no. 2 (June): 83–92.

Battle, Michael. 2009. *Ubuntu: I in You and You in Me.* New York: Seabury.

Beaver, R. Pierce. 1965. "Christian Ashrams in India." *Christian Century* 82, no. 28 (July 14, 1965): 887–89.

Bediako, Kwame. 1983. "Biblical Christologies in the Context of African Traditional Religions." In *Sharing Jesus in the Two Thirds World*, edited by Vinay Samuel and Chris Sugden, 81–113. Grand Rapids: Eerdmans.

———. 1994a. "Jesus in African Culture: A Ghanaian Perspective." In *Emerging Voices in Global Christian Theology*, edited by William A. Dyrness, 93–121. Grand Rapids: Eerdmans.

———. 1994b. "Understanding African Theology in the 20th century." *Themelios* 20 (1): 14–20.

———. 2004. *Jesus and the Gospel in Africa: History and Experience.* Maryknoll, NY: Orbis Books.

Beit-Hallahmi, Benjamin. 1989. *Prolegomena to the Psychological Study of Religion.* Lewisburg, PA: Bucknell University Press.

Bell, Catherine M. 1992. *Ritual Theory, Ritual Practice.* New York: Oxford University Press.

Bendle, Lawrence J., Choong-Ki Lee, Jeong-Ja Choi, Tai-Yang Seo, and Bang-Sik Lee. 2014. "A Buddhist Temple and Its Users: The Case of Bulguksa in South Korea." *Contemporary Buddhism* 15 (2): 199–215.

Berger, Peter L. 1969. *The Sacred Canopy: Elements of a Sociological Theory of Religion.* Garden City, NY: Doubleday.

Bessenecker, Scott. 2006. *The New Friars: The Emerging Movement Serving the World's Poor.* Downers Grove, IL: IVP Books.

Bevans, Stephen B., and Roger Schroeder. 2004. *Constants in Context: A Theology of Mission for Today.* American Society of Missiology Series 30. Maryknoll, NY: Orbis Books.

Bonk, Jonathan. 2007. *Missions and Money: Affluence as a Missionary Problem—Revisited.* Rev. ed. Maryknoll, NY: Orbis Books.

Bonk, Jonathan, Geoffrey Hahn, Sang-Cheol Moon, Scott Moreau, Yong Kyu Park, and Nam Yong Sung, eds. 2011. *Accountability in Missions: Korean and Western Case Studies.* Eugene, OR: Wipf & Stock.

Bosch, David J. 1991. *Transforming Mission: Paradigm Shifts in Theology of Mission.* American Society of Missiology Series 16. Maryknoll, NY: Orbis Books.

Brandon, John. 2009. "Crazy Passion." *Christianity Today*, October 16, 2009, 42–45.

Brawer, Naftali. n.d. "What Is Spiritual Capital?" Accessed May 8, 2017. http://www .spiritual-capital.org.

Breslin, Scott, and Mike Jones. 2004. *Understanding Dreams from God.* Pasadena, CA: William Carey.

Brown, Rick. 2007. "Why Muslims Are Repelled by the Term 'Son of God.'"

Evangelical Missions Quarterly 43, no. 4 (October): 422–29.

Bruce, F. F. 1988. *The Book of the Acts.* Rev. ed. Grand Rapids: Eerdmans.

Campbell, Joseph, and Bill D. Moyers. 1988. *The Power of Myth.* New York: Doubleday.

Carr, Karen. 2006. "Healing the Wounds of Trauma: How the Church Can Help." *Evangelical Missions Quarterly* 42, no. 3 (July): 318–23.

Carroll, Beverlee Jill. n.d. "Jen & Li—Confucian Virtues." Accessed June 22, 2017. http://www.world-religions-professor.com/jen.html.

Cheong, John. 2015. "Islamic Banking and Economics: A Mirror for Christian Practices and Mission in Muslim Contexts." In *Christian Mission and Economic Systems: A Critical Survey of the Cultural and Religious Dimensions of Economics*, edited by John Cheong and Eloise Meneses, 43–85. Pasadena, CA: William Carey.

Cheong, John, and Eloise Meneses, eds. 2015. *Christian Mission and Economic Systems: A Critical Survey of the Cultural and Religious Dimensions of Economics.* Pasadena, CA: William Carey.

Chhokar, Jagdeep Singh, Felix C. Brodbeck, and Robert J. House, eds. 2007. *Culture and Leadership across the World: The GLOBE Book of In-Depth Studies of 25 Societies.* Hillsdale, NJ: Lawrence Erlbaum Associates.

Chike, Chigor. 2008. "Proudly African, Proudly Christian: The Roots of Christologies in the African Worldview." *Black Theology* 6 (2): 221–40.

Cho, Yong Joong, and David Greenlee. 1995. "Avoiding Pitfalls on Multi-Cultural Mission Teams." *International Journal of Frontier Missions* 12 (4): 179–84.

Coe, Shoki. 1972. "Contextualizing Theology." In *Mission Trends No. 3: Third World Theologies—Asian, African and Latin American Contributions to a Radical, Theological Realignment in the Church*, edited by Gerald H. Anderson and Thomas F. Stransky, CSP, 19–24. Grand Rapids: Eerdmans.

Cole, Harold L. 2003. "A Model of Contextualized Deliverance Ministry: A Case Study; The Cordillera Rehabilitation Center." *Journal of Asian Mission* 5 (2): 259–73.

Conn, Harvie M. 1984. *Eternal Word and Changing Worlds: Theology, Anthropology, and Mission in Trialogue.* Grand Rapids: Zondervan.

Courson, Jim. 1998. "Deepening the Bonds of Christian Community: Applying Rite of Passage Structure to the Discipling Process in Taiwan." *Missiology* 26, no. 3 (July): 301–13.

Cox, Harvey. 1995. *Fire from Heaven: The Rise of Pentecostal Spirituality and the Reshaping of Religion in the Twenty-First Century.* Reading, MA: Addison-Wesley.

Cru. n.d. "Four Spiritual Laws English." Accessed October 13, 2017. http://crustore.org/fourlawseng.htm.

Daneel, M. L. 1988. *Old and New in Southern Shona Independent Churches.* Vol. 3, *Leadership and Fission Dynamics.* Gweru, Zimbabwe: Mambo.

DeNeui, Paul, ed. 2015. *Becoming the People of God.* SEANET 11. Pasadena, CA: William Carey.

DeSilva, David Arthur. 1995. *Despising Shame: Honor Discourse and Community Maintenance in the Epistle to the Hebrews.* Atlanta: Scholars Press.

———. 2000. *Honor, Patronage, Kinship and Purity: Unlocking New*

Testament Culture. Downers Grove, IL: InterVarsity.

DeVries, Grant. 2007. "Explaining the Atonement to the Arabic Muslim in Terms of Honour and Shame." *St. Francis Magazine* 2, no. 4 (March): 1–68.

Dixon, Roger. 2007. "Identity Theft: Retheologizing the Son of God." *Evangelical Missions Quarterly* 43, no. 2 (April): 220–26.

Doty, William G. 1986. *Mythography: The Study of Myths and Rituals.* Birmingham: University of Alabama Press.

———. 2000. *Mythography: The Study of Myths and Rituals.* 2nd ed. Birmingham: University of Alabama Press.

Doyle, Tom, and Greg Webster. 2012. *Dreams and Visions: Is Jesus Awakening the Muslim World?* Nashville: Thomas Nelson.

Dube Shomanah, Musa W., Andrew Mūtūa Mbuvi, and Dora R. Mbuwayesango. 2012. *Postcolonial Perspectives in African Biblical Interpretations.* Global Perspectives on Biblical Scholarship 13. Atlanta: Society of Biblical Literature.

Dyrness, William. 1990. *Learning about Theology from the Third World.* Grand Rapids: Zondervan.

Easterly, William. 2006. *The White Man's Burden: Why the West's Efforts to Aid the Rest Have Done So Much Ill and So Little Good.* New York: Penguin.

Eliade, Mircea. 1963. *Myth and Reality.* New York: Harper & Row.

Endō, Shūsaku. 1966. *Silence: A Novel.* London: Peter Owen.

Euba, Femi. 2014. "Ritual." *Ecumenica* 7 (1–2): 97–102.

Evans, A. Steven. 2010. "Matters of the Heart: Orality, Story and Cultural Transformation—The Critical Role of Storytelling in Affecting Worldview." *Missiology* 38 (2): 185–99.

Ezigbo, Victor I. 2008. "Rethinking the Sources of African Contextual Christology." *Journal of Theology for Southern Africa* 132:53–70.

———. 2010. *Re-Imagining African Christologies: Conversing with the Interpretations and Appropriations of Jesus Christ in African Christianity.* Princeton Theological Monograph Series 132. Eugene, OR: Pickwick.

———. 2014. "Jesus as God's Communicative and Hermeneutical Act: African Christians on the Person and Significance of Jesus Christ." In *Jesus without Borders: Christology in the Majority World*, edited by Gene L. Green, Stephen T. Pardue, and K. K. Yeo, 37–58. Grand Rapids: Eerdmans.

Feinberg, Paul D. 1982. "An Evangelical Approach to Contextualization of Theology." *Trinity World Forum* 7, no. 3 (Spring): 7.

Ferris, Robert W. 2000. "Theological Education in Non-Western Contexts." *Evangelical Dictionary of World Missions*, edited by A. Scott Moreau, 945–46. Grand Rapids: Baker Books.

Flemming, Dean E. 2005. *Contextualization in the New Testament: Patterns for Theology and Mission.* Downers Grove, IL: InterVarsity.

Francis, Glen R. 1992. "The Gospel for a Sin/Shame–Based Society." *Taiwan Mission Quarterly* 2, no. 2 (October): 5–16.

Garrison, V. David. 2004. *Church Planting Movements: How God Is Redeeming a Lost World.* Bangalore, India: WIGTake Resources.

———. 2014. *A Wind in the House of Islam: How God Is Drawing Muslims around the World to Faith in Jesus Christ.* Monument, CO: WIGTake Resources.

Gathogo, Julius Mutugi. 2008. "African Philosophy as Expressed in the Concepts of Hospitality and Ubuntu." *Journal of Theology for Southern Africa* 130:39–53.

———. 2012. "Reconciliation Paradigm in the Post-Colonial Africa: A Critical Analysis." *Religion & Theology* 19 (1–2): 74–91.

Gehman, Richard J. 1987. *Doing African Christian Theology: An Evangelical Perspective*. Nairobi, Kenya: Evangel Publishing House.

Georges, Jayson. 2010. "From Shame to Honor: A Theological Reading of Romans for Honor-Shame Contexts." *Missiology* 38 (3): 295–307.

Georges, Jayson, and Mark D. Baker. 2016. *Ministering in Honor-Shame Cultures: Biblical Foundations and Practical Essentials*. Downers Grove, IL: IVP Academic.

Goble, Phillip E., and Salim Munayer. 1989. *New Creation Book for Muslims*. Pasadena, CA: Mandate Press.

Golf, Paul, and Pastor Lee. 2013. *The Coming Chinese Church: How Rising Faith in China Is Spilling over Its Boundaries*. Oxford: Monarch.

Goodman, Felicitas D. 1988a. *Ecstasy, Ritual and Alternative Reality: Religion in a Pluralistic World*. Bloomington: Indiana University Press.

———. 1988b. *How about Demons? Possession and Exorcism in the Modern World*. Bloomington: Indiana University Press.

Gosnell, Peter W. 2006. "Honor and Shame Rhetoric as a Unifying Motif in Ephesians." *Bulletin for Biblical Research* 16 (1): 105–28.

Grant, Jacqueline. 1992. "Becoming Subjects in the Christological Debate." In *Exploring Afro-Christology*, edited by John Pobee, 65–83. Frankfurt: Peter Lang.

Green, Tim. 2013a. "Conversion and Identity." In *Longing for Community: Church, Ummah, or Somewhere in Between?*, edited by David Greenlee, 41–51. Pasadena, CA: William Carey.

———. 2013b. "Identity Choices at the Border Zone." In *Longing for Community: Church, Ummah, or Somewhere in Between?*, edited by David Greenlee, 53–66. Pasadena, CA: William Carey.

Greeson, Kevin. 2004. *Camel Training Manual*. Bangalore, India: WIGTake Resources.

Hale, Chris. 2001. "Reclaiming the Bhajan." *Mission Frontiers* 23, no. 2 (June): 16–17.

Hall, Dave. 2000. "Ten Reasons Why Every Church-Planting Team Needs a Worship Leader." *Evangelical Missions Quarterly* 36 (1): 50–53.

Harbinson, Colin, John Franklin, James Tughan, and Phyllis Novak. 2005. "Redeeming the Arts: The Restoration of the Arts to God's Creational Intention." Lausanne Occasional Paper (LOP) No. 46. https://www.lausanne.org/wp-content/uploads/2007/06/LOP46_IG17.pdf.

Hardy, Adam. 2016. "Hindu Temples and the Emanating Cosmos." *Religion and the Arts* 20 (1–2): 112–34.

Harris, G. 1957. "Possession 'Hysteria' in a Kenya Tribe." *American Anthropologist*, n.s., 59, no. 6: 1046–66.

Haynes, Naomi. 2013. "Desirable Dependence, or What We Learn from Pentecostalism." *Journal of the Royal Anthropological Institute* 19 (2): 250–51.

Heller, Natasha. 2014. "Buddha in a Box: The Materiality of Recitation in Contemporary Chinese Buddhism." *Material Religion* 10 (3): 294–315.

Hiebert, Paul G. 1985. *Anthropological Insights for Missionaries*. Grand Rapids: Baker.

———. 1987. "Critical Contextualization." *International Bulletin of Missionary Research* 11 (3): 104–12.

———. 1992. "Spiritual Warfare: Biblical Perspectives." *Mission Focus* 20, no. 3 (September): 41–46.

Hiebert, Paul, and Frances F. Hiebert. 1987. *Case Studies in Missions*. Grand Rapids: Baker.

Hiebert, Paul, and Eloise Hiebert Meneses. 1995. *Incarnational Ministry: Planting Churches in Band, Tribal, Peasant, and Urban Societies*. Grand Rapids: Baker.

Hiebert, Paul, Daniel Shaw, and Tite Tienou. 1999. *Understanding Folk Religion*. Grand Rapids: Baker.

Hill, Harriet, Margaret Hill, Richard Baggé, and Pat Miersma. 2013. *Healing the Wounds of Trauma*. New York: American Bible Society. See http://thi .americanbible.org/products/detail/hwt -books.

Hoefer, Herbert E. 2001. *Churchless Christianity*. Pasadena, CA: William Carey.

———. 2007. "Rooted or Uprooted: The Necessity of Contextualization in Missions." *International Journal of Frontier Missions* 24, no. 2 (April): 131–38.

Hofstede, Geert, and Gert Jan Hofstede. 2005. *Cultures and Organizations: Software of the Mind; Intercultural Cooperation and Its Importance for Survival*. New York: McGraw-Hill.

Hoskins, Edward J. 2011. "What Muslims Really Believe—The Islamic Traditions." *Evangelical Missions Quarterly* 47 (4): 422–28.

House, Robert J., Peter W. Dorfman, Mansour Javidan, Paul J. Hanges, and Mary F. Sully de Luque. 2014. *Strategic Leadership across Cultures: The GLOBE Study of CEO Leadership Behavior and Effectiveness in 24 Countries*. Thousand Oaks, CA: Sage Publications.

House, Robert J., Paul J. Hanges, Mansour Javidan, Peter W. Dorfman, and Vipin Gupta, eds. 2004. *Culture, Leadership, and Organizations: The GLOBE Study of 62 Societies*. Thousand Oaks, CA: Sage Publications.

Howes, John F. 2007. "Christian Prophecy in Japan: Uchimura Kanzō." *Japanese Journal of Religious Studies* 34 (1): 127–50.

Hunter, James Davison. 2010. *To Change the World: The Irony, Tragedy, and Possibility of Christianity in the Late Modern World*. New York: Oxford University Press.

Hwa, Yung. 2010. "A 21st Century Reformation: Recover the Supernatural." *Christianity Today*, September 2, 2010, 32–33. http://www.christianitytoday .com/ct/2010/september/yung.html.

IMF (International Monetary Fund). 2017. "World Economic Outlook Database: April 2017." http://www.imf.org/external/pubs/ft/weo/2017/01/weodata /index.aspx. Also see https://en.wiki pedia.org/wiki/List_of_countries_by_ GDP_(PPP)_per_capita.

Ireland, Jerry M. 2012. "African Traditional Religion and Pentecostal Churches in Lusaka, Zambia: An Assessment." *Journal of Pentecostal Theology* 21 (2): 260–77.

Ishino, Iwao. 1953. "The *Oyabun-Kobun*: A Japanese Ritual Kinship Institution." *American Anthropologist*, n.s., 55 (5): 695–707.

Jacobsen, Douglas G. 2015. *Global Gospel: An Introduction to Christianity on Five Continents*. Grand Rapids: Baker Academic.

Javidan, Mansour, Robert J. House, Peter W. Dorfman, Paul J. Hanges, and Mary F. Sully de Luque. 2006. "Conceptualizing and Measuring Cultures and Their Consequences: A Comparative Review of GLOBE's and Hofstede's Approaches." *Journal of International Business Studies* 37 (6): 897–914.

Je'adayibe, Dogara. 2012. "A Contextual Consideration of the Church, Culture and the Gospel in Africa." *Ogbomoso Journal of Theology* 17 (1): 75–97.

Jenkins, Philip. 2006. *The New Faces of Christianity: Believing the Bible in the Global South.* Oxford: Oxford University Press.

———. 2011. *The Next Christendom: The Coming of Global Christianity.* 3rd ed. Oxford: Oxford University Press.

Johnson, Andrew A. 2015. "A Spirit Map of Bangkok: Spirit Shrines and the City in Thailand." *Journal for the Academic Study of Religion* 28 (3): 293–308.

Jordan, Ivan, and Frank Tucker. 2002. "Using Indigenous Art to Communicate the Christian Message." *Evangelical Missions Quarterly* 38, no. 3 (July): 302–9.

Kabasélé, Francois. 1991. "Christ as Ancestor and Elder Brother." In *Faces of Jesus in Africa Today,* edited by Robert J. Schreiter, 116–27. Maryknoll, NY: Orbis Books.

Keidel, Eudene. 1978. *African Fables That Teach about God.* Scottdale, PA: Herald Press.

Kenzo, Mabiala Justin-Robert. 2002. "Thinking Otherwise about Africa: Postcolonialism, Postmodernism, and the Future of African Theology." *Exchange* 31 (4): 323–41.

Kibongi, R. Buana. 1969. "Priesthood." In *Biblical Revelation and African Beliefs,* edited by Kwesi Dickson and Paul Ellingworth, 47–56. Maryknoll, NY: Orbis Books.

King, Roberta. 2006. "Singing the Lord's Song in a Global World: The Dynamics of Doing Critical Contextualization through Music." *Evangelical Missions Quarterly* 42, no. 1 (January): 68–74.

Klaudt, Kraig. 1997. "The Ashram as a Model for Theological Education." *Theological Education* 34 (1): 25–40.

Knapp, Bettina Liebowitz. 1984. "Indonesian Theatre: A Journal." *Anima* 11 (1): 47–61.

Knippa, Michael. 2016. "Features of Human Anatomy: Marshall McLuhan on Technology in the Global Village." *Lutheran Mission Matters* 24 (3): 371–84.

Kolié, Cécé. 1991. "Jesus as Healer?" In *Faces of Jesus in Africa Today,* edited by Robert J. Schreiter, 128–50. Maryknoll, NY: Orbis Books.

Kombo, James. 2012. "African Theology." In *Global Theology in Evangelical Perspective: Exploring the Contextual Nature of Theology and Mission,* edited by Jeffrey P. Greenman and Gene L. Green, 134–47. Downers Grove, IL: IVP Academic.

Krabill, James R., Frank Fortunato, Robin P. Harris, and Brian Schrag, eds. 2013. *Worship and Mission for the Global Church: An Ethnodoxology Handbook.* (With DVD). Pasadena, CA: William Carey.

Kraft, Charles. 1991. "What Kind of Encounters Do We Need in Our Christian Witness?" *Evangelical Missions Quarterly* 27, no. 3 (July): 258–65.

———. 2005. "Contextualization in Three Crucial Dimensions." In *Appropriate Christianity,* edited by Charles Kraft, 99–115. Pasadena, CA: William Carey.

———. 2016. *Issues in Contextualization*. Pasadena, CA: William Carey.

Kraft, Charles, with Ellen Kearney and Mark H. White. 1993. *Deep Wounds, Deep Healing: Discovering the Vital Link between Spiritual Warfare and Inner Healing*. Ann Arbor, MI: Vine Books/Servant Publications.

Kraft, Kathryn Ann. 2012. *Searching for Heaven in the Real World: A Sociological Discussion of Conversion in the Arab World*. Regnum Studies in Mission. Eugene, OR: Wipf & Stock.

Kronk, Rick. 2010. *Dreams and Visions: Muslims' Miraculous Journey to Jesus*. San Giovanni Teatino, Italy: Destiny Image Europe.

———. 2013. "Dreams and Visions: A Biblical Pattern of Divine Encounter for Muslims." *Evangelical Missions Quarterly* 49 (3): 360–64.

Kuma, Afua. 1981. *Jesus of the Deep Forest*. Accra, Ghana: Asempa.

Lee, Song-Chong. 2011. "Revisiting the Confucian Norms in Korean Church Growth." *International Journal of Humanities and Social Sciences* 1 (13): 87–103.

Levison, John R., and Priscilla Pope-Levison. 1994. "Emergent Christologies in Latin America, Asia, and Africa." *Covenant Quarterly* 52 (2): 29–47.

Lewis, I. M. 1966. "Spirit Possession and Deprivation Cults." *Man*, n.s., 1 (3): 307–29.

Lienhard, Ruth. 2001. "A 'Good Conscience': Differences between Honor and Justice Orientation." *Missiology* 29, no. 2 (April): 131–41.

Lim, David S. 2004. "A Missiological Evaluation of David Yonggi Cho's Church Growth." *Asian Journal of Pentecostal Studies* 7 (1): 125–47.

Little, Don. 2015. *Effective Discipling in Muslim Communities*. Downers Grove, IL: InterVarsity.

Lochhead, David. 1994. "Technology and Interpretation: A Footnote to McLuhan." *Journal of Theology* 98:60–73.

Loewen, Jacob A. 1978. "Myth and Mission: Should a Missionary Study Tribal Myths?" In *Readings in Missionary Anthropology II*, enlarged 1978 ed., edited by William A. Smalley, 287–332. Pasadena, CA: William Carey.

MacKendrick, Kenneth G. 2015. "What Is a Superhero? How Myth Can Be a Metacode." *Bulletin for the Study of Religion* 44 (1): 19–26.

Maimela, Simon S. 1992. "Jesus Christ: The Liberator and Hope of Oppressed Africa." In *Exploring Afro-Christology*, edited by John Pobee, 31–42. Frankfurt: Peter Lang.

Malefijt, Annemarie de Waal. 1968. *Religion and Culture: An Introduction to Anthropology of Religion*. New York: Macmillan.

Malina, Bruce J. 2001. *The New Testament World: Insights from Cultural Anthropology*. Louisville: Westminster John Knox.

Martin, Marie-Louise. 1976. *Kimbangu: An African Prophet and His Church*. Translated by D. M. Moore. Grand Rapids: Eerdmans.

Masci, David. 2014. "Why Has Pentecostalism Grown So Dramatically in Latin America?" Pew Research Center. November 14, 2014. http://www.pew research.org/fact-tank/2014/11/14/why -has-pentecostalism-grown-so-dramati cally-in-latin-america.

Mastra, I. Wayan. 1978. "A Contextualized Church." *Gospel in Context* 1, no. 2 (April): 4–15, 20–21.

Mbiti, John. 1972. "Some African Concepts of Christology." In *Christ and* the *Younger Churches: Theological Contributions from Asia, Africa and Latin America*, edited by Georg F. Vicedom and José Míguez Bonino, 51–62. London: SPCK.

———. 1976. "Theological Impotence and the Universality of the Church." In *Mission Trends No. 3: Third World Theologies*, edited by Gerald Anderson and Thomas Stransky, 6–18. New York: Paulist Press.

———. 1991. *Introduction to African Religion*. Oxford: Heinemann Educational Books.

Mbuvi, Andrew M. 2002. "African Theology from the Perspective of Honor and Shame." In *Urban Face of Mission: Ministering the Gospel in a Diverse and Changing World*, edited by Harvie Conn, Manuel Ortiz, and Susan S. Baker, 279–95. Phillipsburg, NJ: P&R.

———. 2017. "African Biblical Studies: An Introduction to an Emerging Discipline." *Currents in Biblical Research* 15 (2): 149–78.

McCauley, John F. 2013. "Africa's New Big Man Rule? Pentecostalism and Patronage in Ghana." *African Affairs* 112 (446): 1–21.

McGloughlin, William G. 1978. *Revivals, Awakenings and Reform: An Essay on Religion and Social Change in America, 1607–1977*. Chicago: University of Chicago Press.

McLuhan, Marshall. 1964. *Understanding Media: The Extensions of Man*. New York: McGraw-Hill.

———. 1967. *The Medium Is the Message: An Inventory of Effects*. New York: Bantam.

Meneses, Eloise. 2015. "Exchange, Relationships and Reciprocity: Living as a Christian in a Capitalist World." In *Christian Mission and Economic Systems: A Critical Survey of the Cultural and Religious Dimensions of Economics*, edited by John Cheong and Eloise Meneses, 1–26. Pasadena, CA: William Carey.

Mischke, Werner. 2015. *The Global Gospel: Achieving Missional Impact in Our Multicultural World*. Scottsdale, AZ: Mission ONE Resources.

Miura, Hiroshi. 1996. *The Life and Thought of Kanzō Uchimura, 1861–1930*. Grand Rapids: Eerdmans.

Moloney, Raymond. 1987. "African Christology." *Theological Studies* 48 (3): 505–15.

Molyneux, K. Gordon. 1990. "The Place and Function of Hymns in the EJCSK [*Église de Jésus-Christ sur terre par le Prophète Simon Kimbangu*]." *Journal of Religion in Africa* 20, no. 2 (June): 153–87.

———. 1993. *African Christian Theology: The Quest for Selfhood*. San Francisco: Mellen Research University Press.

Moon, Ruth. 2014. "Founder of World's Largest Megachurch Convicted of Embezzling $12 Million." *Christianity Today*, February 24, 2014. http://www .christianitytoday.com/gleanings/2014 /february/founder-of-worlds-largest -megachurch-convicted-cho-yoido .html.

Moon, W. Jay. 2009. *African Proverbs Reveal Christianity in Culture: A Narrative Portrayal of Builsa Proverbs Contextualizing Christianity in Ghana*. Eugene, OR: Pickwick.

———. 2010. "Discipling through the Eyes of Oral Learners." *Missiology* 38 (2): 127–40.

———. 2017. *Intercultural Discipleship: Learning from Global Approaches to Spiritual Formation*. Grand Rapids: Baker Academic.

Moreau, A. Scott. 1994. "The Dangers of an Evangelical Animism." Faith and Learning Paper presented at Wheaton College, Wheaton.

———. 1995. "Religious Borrowing as a Two-Way Street: An Introduction to Animistic Tendencies in the Euro-North American Context." In *Christianity and the Religions: A Biblical Theology of World Religions*, edited by Ed Rommen and Harold Netland, 166–83. Evangelical Missiological Society Series 2. Pasadena, CA: William Carey.

———. 2000a. "Ancestral Beliefs and Practices." In *Evangelical Dictionary of World Missions*, edited by A. Scott Moreau, 58–59. Grand Rapids: Baker Books.

———. 2000b. "Possession Phenomena." In *Evangelical Dictionary of World Missions*, edited by A. Scott Moreau, 771–72. Grand Rapids: Baker Books.

———. 2000c. "Syncretism." In *Evangelical Dictionary of World Missions*, edited by A. Scott Moreau, 924–25. Grand Rapids: Baker Books.

———. 2002a. "Gaining Perspective on Territorial Spirits." In *Deliver Us from Evil: An Uneasy Frontier in Christian Mission*, edited by A. Scott Moreau, Tokunboh Adeyemo, David Burnett, Bryant Myers, and Hwa Yung, 263–78. Monrovia, CA: MARC.

———. 2002b. "A Survey of North American Spiritual Warfare Thinking." In *Deliver Us from Evil: An Uneasy Frontier in Christian Mission*, edited by A. Scott Moreau, Tokunboh Adeyemo, David Burnett, Bryant Myers, and Hwa Yung, 118–27. Monrovia, CA: MARC.

———. 2005. "Contextualization: From an Adapted Message to an Adapted Life." In *The Changing Face of World Missions: Engaging Contemporary Issues and Trends*, by Michael Pocock, Gailyn Van Rheenen, and Douglas McConnell, 321–48. Grand Rapids: Baker Academic.

———. 2006a. "Contextualization, Syncretism and Spiritual Warfare: Identifying the Issues." In *Contextualization and Syncretism: Navigating Cultural Currents*, edited by Gailyn Van Rheenen, 47–69. Pasadena, CA: William Carey.

———. 2006b. "Contextualization That Is Comprehensive." *Missiology* 34, no. 3 (July): 325–35.

———. 2007. "Contextualization That Is Comprehensive." *Lausanne World Pulse*. April 2007. http://www.lausanne worldpulse.com/perspectives/673.

———. 2008. "Holistic Contextualization: Ensuring That Every Facet of Christian Faith Is Localized." In *Mission to the World: Communicating the Gospel in the 21st Century; Essays in Honour of Knud Jørgensen*, edited by Tormod Engelsviken and Thor Strandenaes, 193–204. Oxford: Regnum.

———. 2011. "Insights and Summary through Semantic Analysis." In *Accountability in Missions: Korean and Western Case Studies*, edited by Jonathan Bonk, Scott Moreau, and Jeff Hahn, 299–313. Eugene, OR: Wipf & Stock.

———. 2012a. "Comprehensive Contextualization." In *Discovering the Mission of God*, edited by Michael Barnett, 406–19. Nashville: B&H.

———. 2012b. *Contextualization in World Missions: Mapping and Assessing Evangelical Models*. Grand Rapids: Kregel.

———. 2015. "Discourses on Demonology in North America." In *Witchcraft, Demons and Deliverance: A Global Conversation on an Intercultural*

Challenge, edited by Claudia Währisch-Oblau and Henning Wrogemann, 41–68. Munich: LIT Verlag.

———. 2017. "Cross-Cultural Leadership Challenges and Opportunities in Mission Partnership." Workshop Presentation at European Leadership Forum in Wisla, Poland, May 21.

Moreau, A. Scott, Evvy Hay Campbell, and Susan Greener. 2014. *Effective Intercultural Communication: A Christian Perspective*. Grand Rapids: Baker Academic.

Moxnes, Halvor. 1991. "Patron-Client Relations and the New Community in Luke-Acts." In *The Social World of Luke-Acts*, edited by Jerome H. Neyrey, 241–68. Peabody, MA: Hendrickson.

Mudge, Ronald R. 2014. "Yahweh's Counter-Cultural View of Honor and Shame." *Conversations with the Biblical World* 34:118–35.

Mugabe, Henry Johannes. 1991. "Christology in an African Context." *Review & Expositor* 88 (4): 343–55.

Mugambi, J. N. Kanyua. 1991. "The Future of the Church and the Church of the Future in Africa." In *The Church of Africa: Towards a Theology of Reconstruction*, edited by José B. Chipenda, African Challenge Series 2, 29–50. Nairobi, Kenya: All Africa Conference of Churches.

———. 1995. *From Liberation to Reconstruction: African Christian Theology after the Cold War*. Nairobi, Kenya: East African Educational Publications.

Munsi, Roger Vanzila. 2012. "Japanese Hidden Christians in Contemporary Settings." *Svensk Missionstidskrift* 100 (4): 351–90.

Murage, Josiah Kinyua. 2007. "Development and Reconstruction Theologies of Africa." *Svensk Missionstidskrift* 95 (2): 149–70.

Murray, Henry A. 1960. *Myth and Mythmaking*. New York: G. Braziller.

Musk, Bill. 1988. "Dreams and the Ordinary Muslim." *Missiology* 16 (2): 163–72.

Nabetani, Gyoji. 1983. "An Asian Critique of Church Movements in Japan." *Evangelical Review of Theology* 7, no. 1 (April): 73–78.

Neeley, Paul. 1999. "Noted Ministry." *Evangelical Missions Quarterly* 35, no. 2 (April): 156–60.

Nelson, Reed E. 1989. "Five Principles of Indigenous Church Organization: Lessons from a Brazilian Pentecostal Church." *Missiology* 17, no. 1 (January): 39–51.

Neyrey, Jerome H. 1998. *Honor and Shame in the Gospel of Matthew*. Louisville: Westminster John Knox.

Nieuwkerk, Karin van. 2011. *Muslim Rap, Halal Soaps, and Revolutionary Theater: Artistic Developments in the Muslim World*. Austin: University of Texas Press.

Njoroge, Nyambura J. 1992. "Confessing Christ in Africa Today." In *Exploring Afro-Christology*, edited by John Pobee, 131–36. Frankfurt: Peter Lang.

Nuckolls, Charles W. 1991. "Culture and Causal Thinking: Diagnosis and Prediction in a South Indian Fishing Village." *Ethos* 19:3–51.

Nugent, John C. 2016. *Endangered Gospel: How Fixing the World Is Killing the Church*. Eugene, OR: Cascade Books.

Nyamiti, Charles. 1984. *Christ as Our Ancestor: Christology from an African Perspective*. Mambo Occasional Papers: Missio-Pastoral Series 11. Gweru, Zimbabwe: Mambo Press.

———. 1994. "Contemporary African Christologies: Assessment and Practical Suggestions." In *Paths of African Theology*, edited by Rosino Gibellini, 62–76. Maryknoll, NY: Orbis Books.

Nyende, Peter. 2007. "Hebrews' Christology and Its Contemporary Apprehension in Africa." *Neotestamentica* 41 (2): 361–81.

O'Brien, Peter Thomas. 1982. *Colossians, Philemon*. Word Biblical Commentary 44. Waco: Word.

Odinga, Ajuma Oginga. 1967. *Not Yet Uhuru: The Autobiography of Oginga Odinga*. New York: Hill & Wang.

Oduyoye, Mercy Amba. 2001. *Introducing African Women's Theology*. Cleveland: Pilgrim Press.

———. 2004. *Beads and Strands: Reflections of an African Woman on Christianity in Africa*. Maryknoll, NY: Orbis Books.

O'Flaherty, Wendy Doniger. 1988. *Other Peoples' Myths: The Cave of Echoes*. New York: Macmillan.

Okullu, Henry. 1974. *Church and Politics in East Africa*. Nairobi, Kenya: Uzima.

Olsen, Jørn Henrik. 1997. "Contextualized Christology in Tropical Africa?" *Svensk Missionstidskrift* 85 (3–4): 247–67.

O'Neill, Tom. 2015. "In the Footsteps of Gandhi." *National Geographic* 228 (1): 90–111.

Ozawa, Saburō. 1961. *Uchimura Kanzo fukei jiken* [Uchimura Kanzo's Disrespectful Event]. Tokyo: Shinkyō Shuppansha.

Park, David Moonseok, and Julian C. Müller. 2014. "The Challenge That Confucian Filial Piety Poses for Korean Churches." *Hervormde Teologiese Studies* 70 (2): 1–8.

Parshall, Phil. 1998. "Danger! New Directions in Contextualization; Do Some Approaches to Muslims Cross the Line into Syncretism?" *Evangelical Missions Quarterly* 34, no. 4 (October): 404–6, 409–10.

Paulin, Batairwa K. 2014. "Conversion as Negotiation: Chinese Protestant Responses to Ancestor Related Practices." *Asia Journal of Theology* 28 (1): 119–36.

Perry, Cindy. 1990. "Bhai-Tika and 'Tij Braka': A Case Study in the Contextualization of Two Nepali Festivals." *Missiology* 18, no. 2 (April): 177–83.

Pew Research Center. 2010. "Tolerance and Tension: Islam and Christianity in Sub-Saharan Africa." April 15, 2010. http://www.pewforum.org/2010/04/15/executive-summary-islam-and-christianity-in-sub-saharan-africa.

Pilgrim, Richard B. 1989. "The Japanese *Noh* Drama in Ritual Perspective." *The Eastern Buddhist* 22 (1): 54–70.

Plantinga, Alvin. 2000. *Warranted Christian Belief*. New York: Oxford University Press.

Plueddemann, James. 2009. *Leading across Cultures: Effective Ministry and Mission in the Global Church*. Downers Grove, IL: IVP Academic.

Pobee, John S. 1979. *Toward an African Theology*. Nashville: Abingdon.

———. 1992a. "Confessing Christ a la African Instituted Churches." In *Exploring Afro-Christology*, edited by John Pobee, 145–51. Frankfurt: Peter Lang.

———. 1992b. "In Search of Christology in Africa: Some Considerations for Today." In *Exploring Afro-Christology*, edited by John Pobee, 9–20. Frankfurt: Peter Lang.

Poston, Larry. 2000. "'Cultural Chameleon': Contextualization from a Pauline Perspective." *Evangelical Missions Quarterly* 36, no. 4 (October): 460–69.

Priest, Robert J. 1994. "Missionary Elenctics: Conscience and Culture." *Missiology* 22 (3): 291–315.

Priest, Robert J., and Joseph Paul Priest. 2008. "'They See Everything, and Understand Nothing': Short-Term Mission and Service Learning." *Missiology* 36 (1): 53–73.

Prince, Andrew James. 2017. *Contextualization of the Gospel: Towards an Evangelical Approach in the Light of Scripture and the Church Fathers.* Eugene, OR: Wipf & Stock.

Ralston, Helen. 1987. *Christian Ashrams: A New Religious Movement in Contemporary India.* Lewiston, NY: Edwin Mellen.

Reed, Rod, and Gift Mtukwa. 2010. "Christ Our Ancestor: African Christology and the Danger of Contextualization." *Wesleyan Theological Journal* 45 (1): 144–63.

Reimer, Sam. 2003. *Evangelicals and the Continental Divide: The Conservative Protestant Subculture in Canada and the United States.* Montreal: McGill-Queen's University Press.

Renard, John. 1997. "Comparative Religious Architecture: Islamic and Hindu Ritual Space." *Religion and the Arts* 1 (4): 62–88.

Richard, H. L. 2000. "Singh, (Sadhu) Sundar." In *Evangelical Dictionary of World Missions,* edited by A. Scott Moreau, 879. Grand Rapids: Baker Books.

———. 2004. "New Paradigms for Understanding Hinduism and Contextualization." *Evangelical Missions Quarterly* 40 (3): 308–20.

———. 2015. "New Paradigms for Religion, Multiple Religious Belonging, and Insider Movements." *Missiology* 43 (3): 297–308.

Richards, E. Randolph, and Brandon J. O'Brien. 2012. *Misreading Scripture with Western Eyes: Removing Cultural Blinders to Better Understand the Bible.* Downers Grove, IL: IVP Books.

Richardson, W. W. 1964. "E. Stanley Jones Honored." *Christian Century* 81 (7): 216.

Riedel, Felix. 2015. "Sickening Demons: Some Notes on the Psychosomatics of Ghanaian Films." In *Witchcraft, Demons and Deliverance: A Global Conversation on an Intercultural Challenge,* edited by Claudia Währisch-Oblau and Henning Wrogemann, 93–108. Munich: LIT Verlag.

Ritchie, Mark A. 2000. *Spirit of the Rainforest: A Yanomamö Shaman's Story.* Chicago: Island Lake Press.

Ro, Bong Rin. 1985. *Christian Alternatives to Ancestor Practices.* Taichung, Taiwan, ROC: Asia Theological Association.

Sawyerr, Harry. 1978. "Jesus Christ—Universal Brother." In *African Christian Spirituality,* edited by Aylward Shorter, 65–67. London: Chapman.

Schaeffer, Francis A. 1973. *Art and the Bible: Two Essays.* Downers Grove, IL: IVP Books.

Schilbrack, K. 2010. "Religions: Are There Any?" *Journal of the American Academy of Religion* 78 (4): 1112–38.

Schlorff, Samuel P. 1980. "The Hermeneutical Crisis in Muslim Evangelism." *Evangelical Missions Quarterly* 16 (3): 143–55.

———. 2000. "The Translational Model for Mission in a Resistant Muslim Society: A Critique and an Alternative." *Missiology* 28 (3): 305–28.

Schoffeleers, J. Matthew. 1989. "Folk Christology in Africa: The Dialectics of the Nganga Paradigm." *Journal of Religion in Africa* 19 (2): 157–83.

———. 1994. "Christ in African Folk Theology: The *Nganga* Paradigm." In *Religion in Africa: Experience and Expression*, edited by Thomas D. Blakely, Walter E. A. van Beek, and Dennis L. Thomson, 73–88. London: James Currey.

Schrag, Brian. 2007. "India: Debating Global Missiological Flashpoints: Why Local Arts Are Central to Mission." *International Journal of Frontier Missions* 24 (4): 199–202.

Schreiter, Robert J. 1985. *Constructing Local Theologies*. London: SCM.

Scott, Randal. 2008. "Evangelism and Dreams: Foundational Presuppositions to Interpret God-Given Dreams of the Unreached." *Evangelical Missions Quarterly* 44 (2): 176–84.

Segal, Robert A. 1983. "Victor Turner's Theory of Ritual." *Zygon* 18 (3): 327–35.

———. 2015. "The Modern Study of Myth and Its Relation to Science." *Zygon* 50 (3): 757–71.

Setiloane, Gabriel. 1976. "I Am an African." In *Mission Trends No. 3: Third World Theologies*, edited by Gerald Anderson and Thomas Stransky, 128–31. New York: Paulist Press.

Shenk, David. 1998. "Harris, William Wadé." In *Biographical Dictionary of Christian Missions*, edited by Gerald Anderson, 281. Grand Rapids: Eerdmans.

Shiloah, Amnon, Annemarie Schimmel, Jacob M. Landau, and Oleg Grabar. 2017. "Islamic Arts: Dance and Theatre." *Encyclopedia Britannica*. https://www.britannica.com/topic/Islamic-arts/Dance-and-theatre.

Silko, Leslie Marmon. 1996. *Yellow Woman and a Beauty of the Spirit: Essays on Native American Life Today*. New York: Simon & Schuster.

Singh, Sadhu Sundar. 1922. *At the Master's Feet*. Translated by Arthur and Rebecca J. Parker. New York: Fleming H. Revell.

Smart, Ninian. 1996. *Dimensions of the Sacred: An Anatomy of the World's Beliefs*. Berkeley: University of California Press.

Smith, Jay. 2009. "An Assessment of the Insider's Principle Paradigms." *St. Francis Magazine* 5 (4): 20–51.

Song, Minho. 2006. "Contextualization and Discipleship: Closing the Gap between Theory and Practice." *Evangelical Review of Theology* 30 (3): 249–63.

Spielberg, Faña, and Stuart Dauermann. 1997. "Contextualization: Witness and Reflection; Messianic Jews as a Case." *Missiology* 25, no. 1 (January): 15–35.

Stafford, Tim. 2012. "A New Age of Miracles: Around the World, Wherever Churches Are Growing, Reports of the Miraculous Are Rampant; What Do They Mean?" *Christianity Today*, September 21, 2012, 48–51. http://www.christianitytoday.com/ct/2012/september/a-new-age-of-miracles.html.

Stahl, Janet. 2010. "Telling Our Stories Well: Creating Memorable Images and Shaping Our Identity." *Missiology* 38 (2): 161–71.

Stevens, Ryan. 2007. "India: Debating Global Missiological Flashpoints; Bridging the Gap between Western Workers and India's Hindus." *International Journal of Frontier Missions* 24, no. 4 (October): 179–84.

Stinton, Diane. 2004. *Jesus of Africa: Voices of Contemporary African Christology*. Nairobi, Kenya: Paulines Publications Africa.

———. 2007. "Jesus—Immanuel, Image of the Invisible God: Aspects of Popular Christology in

Sub-Saharan Africa." *Journal of Reformed Theology* 1 (1): 6–40.

Strand, Mark. 2000. "Explaining Sin in a Chinese Context." *Missiology* 28, no. 4 (October): 427–41.

Takenaka, Masao, and Ron O'Grady. 1991. *The Bible through Asian Eyes.* Auckland, NZ: Pace.

Tan, Jason Richard. 2015. "Christian Mission amidst the Cultural and Socioeconomic Dynamics of Bribery and Extortion Practices in the Philippines." In *Christian Mission and Economic Systems: A Critical Survey of the Cultural and Religious Dimensions of Economics*, edited by John Cheong and Eloise Meneses, 87–112. Pasadena, CA: William Carey.

Taylor, John V. 1963. *The Primal Vision—Christian Presence amid African Religions.* London: SCM.

Taylor, Richard W. 1979. "Christian Ashrams as a Style of Mission in India." *International Review of Mission* 68, no. 271 (July): 281–93.

Tennent, Timothy C. 2005. "The Challenge of Churchless Christianity: An Evangelical Assessment." *International Bulletin of Missionary Research* 29, no. 4 (October): 171–77.

———. 2006. "Followers of Jesus (Isa) in Islamic Mosques: A Closer Examination of C–5 'High Spectrum' Contextualization." *International Journal of Frontier Missions* 23 (3): 101–15.

Thornton, W. Philip. 1984. "The Cultural Key to Developing Strong Leaders." *Evangelical Missions Quarterly* 20, no. 3 (July): 234–41.

Tienou, Tite. 1985. "The Problem of Methodology in African Christian Theologies." PhD diss., Fuller Theological Seminary.

Titre, Ande. 2009. "African Christology: Hope for the Anglican Communion."

Journal of Anglican Studies 7 (2): 183–93.

Tran, Van Doan. 2009. "Harmony as a Category of Asian Ethics and Theology." *Sino-Christian Studies* 7:43–65.

TRC (Truth and Reconciliation Commission). n.d. "Amnesty Hearings and Decisions." Accessed October 12, 2017. http://www.justice.gov.za/trc/amntrans /index.htm.

Turner, Harold W. 1977. "The Primal Religions of the World and Their Study." In *Australian Essays in World Religions*, edited by Victor Hayes, 32–37. Bedford Park, Australia: Australian Association for World Religions.

Turner, Terence S. 2012. "The Social Skin." *HAU: Journal of Ethnographic Theory* 2 (2): 486–504.

Turner, Victor. 1977. *The Ritual Process: Structure and Anti-Structure.* Ithaca, NY: Cornell University Press.

Tutu, Desmond, and Naomi Tutu. 1989. *The Words of Desmond Tutu.* New York: HarperCollins.

Valente, Rubia R. 2015. "Institutional Explanations for the Decline of the *Congregação Cristã no Brasil*." *PentecoStudies* 14 (1): 72–96.

Van Bragt, Jan. 2002. "Multiple Religious Belonging of the Japanese People." In *Many Mansions? Multiple Religious Belonging and Christian Identity*, edited by Catherine Cornille, 7–19. Maryknoll, NY: Orbis Books.

Vanhoozer, Kevin J. 2006. "'One Rule to Rule Them All?' Theological Method in an Era of World Christianity." In *Globalizing Theology: Belief and Practice in an Era of World Christianity*, edited by Craig Ott and Harold Netland, 85–126. Grand Rapids: Baker Academic.

Van Rheenen, Gailyn. 1991. *Communicating Christ in Animistic Contexts.* Grand Rapids: Baker.

————. 2006. *Contextualization and Syncretism: Navigating Cultural Currents.* Evangelical Missiological Society Series 13. Pasadena, CA: William Carey.

Villa-Vicencio, Charles. 1992. *A Theology of Reconstruction: Nation-Building and Human Rights.* Cambridge Studies in Ideology and Religion. Cambridge: Cambridge University Press.

Volf, Miroslav. 2003. "Faith Matters: Dancing for God." *Christian Century* 120 (18): 35.

Waliggo, John M. 1991. "African Christology in a Situation of Suffering." In *Faces of Jesus in Africa Today*, edited by Robert J. Schreiter, 164–80. Maryknoll, NY: Orbis Books.

Waruta, Douglas W. 1989. "Who Is Jesus Christ for Africans Today? Prophet, Priest, Potentate." In *Jesus in African Christianity*, edited by J. M. K. Mugambi and Laurenti Magesa, 40–53. Nairobi, Kenya: Initiatives Publishers.

Watson, David F. 2010. *Honor among Christians: The Cultural Key to the Messianic Secret.* Minneapolis: Fortress.

West, Gerald O. 2000. "Mapping African Biblical Interpretation: A Tentative Sketch." In *The Bible in Africa: Transactions, Trajectories, and Trends*, edited by Gerald West and Musa W.

Dube Shomanah, 29–53. Boston: Brill Academic.

Wink, Walter. 1992. *Engaging the Powers: Discernment and Resistance in a World of Domination.* Philadelphia: Fortress.

Woodberry, J. Dudley. 2007. "To the Muslim I Became a Muslim?" *International Journal of Frontier Missions* 24 (1): 23–28.

Wright, Christopher J. H. 2015. "Humility, Integrity, and Simplicity." *International Bulletin of Missionary Research* 39 (4): 214–18.

Wright, Nigel. 1990. *The Satan Syndrome: Putting the Power of Darkness in Its Place.* Grand Rapids: Zondervan.

Wu, Jackson. 2012. *Saving God's Face: A Chinese Contextualization of Salvation through Honor and Shame.* Pasadena, CA: William Carey.

————. 2016. "Ministering in Honor-Shame Cultures: Biblical Foundations and Practical Essentials." *Themelios* 41 (3): 580–81.

————. 2017. "Saving Us from Me: Cultivating Honor and Shame in a Collectivist Church." Paper given at the Honor, Shame and the Gospel Conference. Wheaton. Available at http:// www.patheos.com/blogs/jacksonwu/20 17/07/05/saving-us-cultivating-honor -shame-collectivist-church.

INDEX